Derek Walcott

MANCHESTER
UNIVERSITY PRESS

CONTEMPORARY WORLD WRITERS

SERIES EDITOR   JOHN THIEME

Derek Walcott

JOHN THIEME

811.
09
W14 T

Manchester University Press

Manchester and New York

distributed exclusively in the USA by St. Martin's Press

Copyright © John Thieme 1999

The right of John Thieme to be identified as the author of this work has been asserted by him in accordance with the Copyright, Designs and Patents Act 1988.

Published by Manchester University Press
Oxford Road, Manchester M13 9NR, UK
and Room 400, 175 Fifth Avenue, New York, NY 10010, USA
http://www.man.ac.uk/mup

Distributed exclusively in the USA by
St. Martin's Press, Inc., 175 Fifth Avenue, New York, NY 10010, USA

Distributed exclusively in Canada by
UBC Press, University of British Columbia, 6344 Memorial Road,
Vancouver, BC, Canada V6T 1Z2

British Library Cataloguing-in-Publication Data
A catalogue record for this book is available from the British Library

Library of Congress Cataloging-in-Publication Data applied for

ISBN 0 7190 4205 4 *hardback*
       0 7190 4206 2 *paperback*

First published 1999
06   05   04   03   02   01   00   99   10   9   8   7   6   5   4   3   2   1

Typeset in Aldus
by Koinonia, Manchester
Printed in Great Britain
by Bell & Bain Limited, Glasgow

For Barbara

Contents

Acknowledgements

I first became interested in Derek Walcott's work nearly thirty years ago, when Michael Gilkes sent me a copy of *The Castaway* and shortly afterwards, by which time I was living in Guyana, introduced me to Walcott's play *Franklin*, which he had just directed. My first and greatest debt is therefore to Michael. For many years I read Walcott's successive collections of poetry as they were published, mainly for pleasure, but occasionally venturing a review or an academic comment. Some of this previously published work has been rewritten, and usually expanded, for the present book and I am grateful to the editors and publishers for permission to reprint sections from: 'Community and Exile' (a review of *The Fortunate Traveller* and Earl Lovelace's *Wine of Astonishment*), *Literary Review*, July 1982, 52; 'A Caribbean Don Juan: Derek Walcott's *Joker of Seville*', *World Literature Written in English*, 23:1, 1984, 62–75; chapter on *Ti-Jean and His Brothers* and *Dream on Monkey Mountain*, *A Handbook for Teaching Caribbean Literature*, ed. David Dabydeen, London: Heinemann, 1988, 86–95; 'I decompose, but I composing still': Derek Walcott and "The Spoiler's Return"', *The Yearbook of English Studies*, 25, 1995, 163–72; and 'After Greenwich: Crossing Meridians in Post-Colonial Literatures' from *The Contact and The Culmination: Essays in Honour of Hena Maes-Jelinek*, eds. Marc Delrez and Bénédicte Ledent, Liège: University of Liège, 1997, 353–63.

Numerous people helped me in obtaining material, particularly copies of Walcott's unpublished plays and in this respect I am particularly grateful to Bruce King, Michael Gilkes and Stewart Brown. I am also indebted to Bruce for allowing me to read his *Derek Walcott and West Indian Theatre* in manuscript. My thanks go to the staff of the Inter-Library Loan section of the Brynmor Jones Library at the University of Hull, for their meticulousness and patience; and to library staff at the University of the West Indies and the National Newspaper Library, Colindale.

I have discussed aspects of this layered book with so many people over the years that it is difficult even to remember all the possible debts I may owe. I know that much of my thinking evolved during the course of teaching Walcott to various groups of under-graduates at the University of North London and undergraduates and postgraduates at the University of Hull and among the numerous students who have in some way contributed to this book I would like to single out Linda Price, Sean O'Hagan and Valérie Bada. Academics, other than those mentioned above, who have provided me with insights into aspects of Walcott's writing include Louis James, John Figueroa and Hena Maes-Jelinek. James Booth, Victor Ramraj and Smaro Kamboureli offered valuable advice on particular points. I am also grateful to Diana Fairfax for clarifying a particular point in relation to the RSC and *The Joker of Seville*.

Finally, as always, my thanks to Barbara, without whom it would not have been possible; and to Toffee, despite whom it still was – just.

Series editor's foreword

Contemporary World Writers is an innovative series of authoritative introductions to a range of culturally diverse contemporary writers from outside Britain and the United States, or from 'minority' backgrounds within Britain or the United States. In addition to providing comprehensive general introductions, books in the series also argue stimulating original theses, often but not always related to contemporary debates in post-colonial studies.

The series locates individual writers within their specific cultural contexts, while recognising that such contexts are themselves invariably a complex mixture of hybridised influences. It aims to counter tendencies to appropriate the writers discussed into the canon of English or American literature or to regard them as 'other'.

Each volume includes a chronology of the writer's life, an introductory section on formative contexts and intertexts, discussion of all the writer's major works, a bibliography of primary and secondary works and an index. Issues of racial, national and cultural identity are explored, as are gender and sexuality. Books in the series also examine writers' use of genre, particularly ways in which Western genres are adapted or subverted and 'traditional' local forms are reworked in a contemporary context.

Contemporary World Writers aims to bring together the theoretical impulse which currently dominates post-colonial studies and closely argued readings of particular authors' works, and by so doing to avoid the danger of appropriating the specifics of particular texts into the hegemony of totalising theories.

List of abbreviations

25P	*25 Poems*
AL	*Another Life*
AT	*The Arkansas Testament*
Castaway	*The Castaway and Other Poems*
DC	*Drums and Colours*
DMM	*Dream on Monkey Mountain and Other Plays*
EY	*Epitaph for the Young*
FT	*The Fortunate Traveller*
Gulf	*The Gulf and Other Poems*
HC	*Henri Christophe*
HD	*Harry Dernier*
HE	*The Haytian Earth*
IGN	*In a Green Night*
Joker	*The Joker of Seville and O Babylon!*
'Muse'	*'The Muse of History'*
Poems	*Poems* [1951]
RP	*Remembrance and Pantomime*
SAK	*The Star-Apple Kingdom*
SG	*Sea Grapes*
TDG	*To Die for Grenada*
TP	*Three Plays*
Wine	*The Wine of the Country*

Chronology

1930 Derek Alton Walcott and his twin brother, Roderick Aldon Walcott, born (23 January) in Castries, St. Lucia; sons of Warwick and Alix Walcott.

1931 Father, Warwick Walcott, died.

1941–47 Attended St. Mary's College, Castries.

1944 First published poem, '1944', appeared in *The Voice of St. Lucia*.

1946–47 Wrote plays *Flight and Sanctuary*, *Harry Dernier*, *Another World for the Lost*, *The Matadors* and *A Simple Cornada*.

1947–50 Taught as an Assistant Master at St. Mary's College.

1948 *25 Poems* published in Trinidad; much of Castries destroyed by fire.

1949 *Epitaph for the Young* published in Barbados.

1950 Founded St. Lucia Arts Guild, along with Maurice Mason; Guild launched with production of Walcott's play, *Henri Christophe*; one-act play, *Senza Alcun Sospetto* broadcast on BBC *Caribbean Voices* programme; *Henri Christophe* published in Barbados; left St. Lucia to study at the University College of the West Indies, Mona, Jamaica on Colonial Development and Welfare Scholarship.

1950–54 Student at Mona; took BA General Arts degree, graduating in 1953, followed a postgraduate education course, 1953–54;

president of Mona Dramatic Society; editor of student magazine.

1951   Third volume of verse, *Poems*, published in Jamaica; plays *Paolo and Francesca, Three Assassins* and *The Price of Mercy* performed by St. Lucia Arts Guild.

1952   *Harry Dernier* broadcast on BBC Radio, published in Barbados and performed in Jamaica.

1954   Married Faye Moyston (one son from this marriage); premieres of *The Sea at Dauphin* in Trinidad and *The Charlatan* in Jamaica.

1954–57   Taught in Grenada, St. Lucia and Jamaica: at Grenada Boys' School, St. Mary's College and Jamaica College; worked as feature writer for the Jamaica journal *Public Opinion*.

1956   *The Wine of the Country* performed in Jamaica.

1957   Productions of *Ione* in Jamaica and Trinidad; *Ti-Jean and His Brothers* written on a short visit to New York.

1958   Premiere of *Ti-Jean and His Brothers* in Trinidad. Wrote *Drums and Colours* for Trinidad Caribbean Arts Festival to celebrate inauguration of West Indies Federation; outdoor performance in Port of Spain's Royal Botanical Gardens. Received Jamaica Drama Festival Prize.

1959   Divorce from Faye Moyston; returned to Caribbean and settled in Trinidad; first performance of *Malcochon* in Trinidad; founded Trinidad Theatre Workshop.

1960   Marriage to Margaret Maillard (two daughters from this marriage; subsequently dissolved).

1960–67   Arts Correspondent for *Trinidad Guardian*.

1961   Won Guinness Award for Poetry.

1962   *In a Green Night*, his first collection of poems to appear outside the Caribbean, published in UK; first Trinidad Theatre Workshop production of plays at Little Carib Theatre in Port of Spain: double-bill of Beckett's *Krapp's Last Tape*, directed by Walcott and Dennis Scott's *The Caged*, directed by Slade Hopkinson.

1964   *Selected Poems* published in US.

1965   *The Castaway* published in UK; winner of Royal Society of Literature Award; folk musical, *Batai*, performed as part of Trinidad Carnival's Dimanche Gras show.

1966   Suicide of Walcott's early mentor, the artist Harold Simmons.

1967   First tour by Trinidad Theatre Workshop; premiere of *Dream on Monkey Mountain* in Toronto.

1969   Awarded Trinidad and Tobago's Order of the Hummingbird; *The Gulf* published in UK (US, 1970); winner of Cholmon-deley Award; received Eugene O'Neill Foundation Wesleyan Fellowship for Playwrights; *Dream on Monkey Mountain* performed at Eugene O'Neill Memorial Theatre, Waterford, Connecticut; premiere of *Franklin* in Guyana; one-hour film version of *Dream on Monkey Mountain* recorded in Trinidad by NBC (US National Broadcasting Corporation).

1970   Black Power Revolution in Trinidad; *In a Fine Castle* written in response to this, premiered by Theatre Workshop in Jamaica; performed in Trinidad later in the year; *Dream on Monkey Mountain and Other Plays* published in US (UK, 1972); radio version of *Ti-Jean* recorded in Trinidad by CBC (Canadian Broadcasting Company).

1971   Negro Ensemble production of *Dream on Monkey Mountain* in Los Angeles; won Obie Award for most distinguished foreign off-Broadway production.

1972   Negro Ensemble production of *Dream on Monkey Mountain* taken to Munich Olympics; Hon. D. Litt., University of the West Indies conferred on Walcott.

1973   *Another Life*, poetic autobiography, published in US and UK (winner of Jock Campbell New Statesman Award, 1974); radio version of *In a Fine Castle* recorded in Trinidad by CBC; wrote *Heavenly Peace*, unpublished and unperformed musical about Vietnam War.

1974   *The Joker of Seville*, musical collaboration with Galt Mac-
        Dermot, commissioned by Royal Shakespeare Company;
        premiered by Theatre Workshop in Trinidad.

1975   Record of music from Theatre Workshop production of *The
        Joker of Seville* issued.

1976   *O Babylon!*, another musical with score by Galt MacDermot,
        staged in Trinidad and in Jamaica (as part of Carifesta Arts
        Festival) by Theatre Workshop; television play, *The Snow
        Queen*, written for Trinidad and Tobago television, but
        never screened; resigned from Trinidad Theatre Workshop;
        Sea Grapes published in US and UK.

1977   *Remembrance* premiered by Courtyard Players, St. Croix,
        US Virgin Islands.

1978   *Pantomime* premiered in Trinidad; *The Joker of Seville* and
        O Babylon! published in US (UK, 1979).

1979   *The Star-Apple Kingdom* published in US (UK, 1980);
        Remembrance produced at the New York Shakespeare
        Public Festival; BBC Radio production of *Pantomime*; won
        Welsh Arts Council's Literary Prize; premiere of musical
        Marie Laveau, with score by Galt MacDermot, in St. Thomas,
        US Virgin Islands.

1980   *Remembrance* and *Pantomime* published in US.

1981   Appointed as Professor of Creative Writing at Boston
        University; *The Fortunate Traveller* published in US (UK,
        1982); awarded John D. and Catherine MacArthur Prize;
        first performance of *Beef, No Chicken* in Trinidad.

1982   Married Norline Metivier; *The Last Carnival* (a fully re-
        worked version of *In a Fine Castle*) first performed in Trinidad;
        The Isle is Full of Noises premiered in Hartford, Connec-
        ticut; television play, *The Rig*, filmed in Trinidad (first
        screening, 1984); received Royal Society of Literature's
        Heinemann Award for *The Fortunate Traveller*.

1983   *A Branch of the Blue Nile* premiered in Barbados.

1984   *Midsummer* published in US and UK; premiere of *The Haytian*

Earth in St. Lucia to celebrate the 150th anniversary of Emancipation.

1986   *Collected Poems, 1948–84* published in US and UK; *Three Plays* (*The Last Carnival, Beef, No Chicken* and *A Branch of the Blue Nile*) published in US; *To Die for Grenada* premiered in Cleveland.

1987   *The Arkansas Testament* published in US and UK.

1988   *O Babylon!* staged in London; awarded the Queen's Gold Medal for Poetry.

1989   *The Ghost Dance* premiered in Oneonta.

1990   *Omeros* published in US and UK.

1991   Recipient of the Order of the Caribbean Community; won W. H. Smith Award for *Omeros; Steel,* musical with score by Galt MacDermot, premiered in Boston.

1992   Awarded Nobel Prize for Literature (in year of Columbus quincentennial); productions of three Walcott plays in UK: *The Last Carnival* (Birmingham), *The Odyssey* (Stratford) and *Viva Detroit* (London); Stockholm production of *The Last Carnival* directed by Walcott.

1993   Resumed association with the Trinidad Theatre Workshop; *The Odyssey: A Stage Version* published in US and UK.

1997   *The Bounty* published in US and UK.

1998   *The Capeman,* musical collaboration with Paul Simon, produced on Broadway.

They loved the valley,
rooted in it with a differentiated love,
races as varied as the cocoa pods in complexion,
the snow-speckled trunks enduring the affliction
of envy and hatred that time would remove,
like the sorrow in the rich soil, until eventually
their history dimmed and vanished into fiction.

('A Santa Cruz Quartet', i, *The Bounty*)

Contexts and intertexts

THIS study offers an overview of the whole of Derek Walcott's literary output to date, while also including detailed discussion of a selection of his works. Like all the books in this series, it begins with an account of some of the most important contexts and intertexts which have informed its subject's writing. The aim is to locate Walcott's work in relation to the social and cultural milieux from which it has emerged, to give a sense of the discursive specifics which have gone into its making. In recent decades literary and cultural theorists have increasingly stressed the hybridized quality of post-colonial discourse[1] in an endeavour to escape from the essentialism of Eurocentric constructions of 'other' places, which have for example represented Africa as the 'Dark Continent' and Asia and North Africa as the mysterious and exotic 'Orient'[2] and in so doing have, needless to say, obscured the plural nature of non-Western societies. From the beginning of his writing career Walcott's practice as poet, dramatist and essayist anticipated this theoretical shift. From the outset he promoted a cross-cultural – as opposed to an Afrocentric or Eurocentric – reading of Caribbean, and other, social formations and all his work to date is predicated upon an aesthetic which emphasizes the cultural cross-pollination that he sees as characteristic of the Caribbean region.

As a young writer growing up in St. Lucia in the late colonial period, Walcott found himself, like most of his contemporaries, subjected to a process of 'benign' brainwashing,[3] which involved the inculcation of European cultural standards at the expense of local values; in subsequent years, after the various Caribbean territories achieved their independences in the 1960s and 1970s,[4] he saw the pendulum swing the other way, with African retentions in the region now being privileged over European influences and Creole language forms over Standard English. Nevertheless his writing of six decades – from the 1940s to the 1990s – has shown remarkable consistency of purpose and, although some commentators detect a shift towards folk forms part-way though his career,[5] an attempt to create his own Caribbean tradition, drawing on an eclectic assortment of elements from inside and outside the region, informs his writing from very early on.

The question of what constitutes an appropriate tradition for an author from his background is prominent in all Walcott's writing, from his first collection of verse, *25 Poems* (1948), to his major works of the 1990s, *Omeros* (1990) and *The Odyssey* (1992).[6] Consequently, while a consideration of shaping contexts and intertexts is useful with regard to any post-colonial writer – or indeed any writer – such an approach is particularly valuable in Walcott's case. Much of his work is metaliterary, a self-conscious discussion of the problematics of Caribbean writing and an attempt to evolve suitable forms for the rendition of his own Caribbean experience. Paradoxically perhaps, his quest for a personal, local tradition has found favour with international audiences, particularly in North America, and the numerous awards and accolades which Walcott has received culminated in his winning the 1992 Nobel Prize for literature. This international success raises questions about the extent to which he is a spokesperson for the community and region from which he originated. Although St. Lucia now celebrates an annual Nobel Laureate week,[7] in so doing it is partly honouring a writer whose work is inaccessible to most of its population, not only because of its hermeticism – a problem for 'difficult' poets everywhere – but also because of its use of English as its main language: most St. Lucians speak a francophone Creole. A Caribbean joke neatly points up the distance between the native son and his supposed community:

Man in bookstore.   Do you have *Omeros?*
Young clerk.   Me? Nah, man, is just this bench too
   blasted hard make I shifting about so. Is only old people
   does have omeroids![8]

Writing the kind of poetry he does,[9] Walcott can, then, only
be a 'minority' writer in the Caribbean since his potential
audience is limited. Again this may sound like a statement of the
problems faced by most poets in most societies and periods, but
Caribbean and Caribbean-diaspora poetry of the post-
independence period has been increasingly demotic and poets
such as Louise Bennett, Mikey Smith and Jean 'Binta' Breeze
(Jamaica), Linton Kwesi Johnson and Valerie Bloom (Jamaica/
UK), John Agard (Guyana/UK), Bruce St. John (Barbados) and
Mutabaruka (Trinidad) have all privileged the oral over the
scribal and performance over book publication. In such a climate,
Walcott's 'literary' verse has not always been seen as socially
relevant. One commonplace criticism of his work has involved
an oppositional pairing,[10] in which he is contrasted with the
other major poet of the anglophone Caribbean region, Edward
Kamau Brathwaite, a writer whose work Walcott has criticised
on more than one occasion.[11] Such a contrast does a disservice to
both writers, since it obscures the discursive subtleties of their
poetry: Brathwaite is represented as an Afrocentric, oral, folk
poet; Walcott as a Eurocentric, elitist, literary poet. Both constructions are extremely reductive. Brathwaite is a professional
historian whose doctoral thesis argued the case that slavery led
to the emergence of a 'creole' or hybridized society in Jamaica
and traced its development between 1770 and 1820;[12] and
although there are important differences between the two writers,
this thesis is in some ways remarkably similar to Walcott's
aesthetic position, which also emphasises creolization and the
transformations that Old World ancestral elements undergo in
the Caribbean. The most significant difference in this respect is
that most of Brathwaite's work has been concerned with the
retrieval of submerged African forms in the Caribbean, a crucial
process of recovery since the plantation system systematically
eradicated traces of 'Africa', while Walcott has tended to focus

on the metamorphosis of European discourses in the region. Yet even this is a half-truth: Walcott *has* explored the African psychic legacy in many of his works, among them his early poem 'A Far Cry from Africa',[13] his theatrical masterpiece *Dream on Monkey Mountain* (1967) and, more recently, *Omeros*; and, far from being a poet who has turned his back on the West, Brathwaite took Eliot's *The Waste Land* as a model for his major trilogy *The Arrivants* (1967–69),[14] drawing as extensively on the Anglo-American poet's mini-epic, as Walcott had in his first long poem, *Epitaph for the Young* (1949). In short, while it would be mistaken to argue that significant differences between Walcott and Brathwaite do not exist, the lines dividing them are far more blurred than many critics suggest and in so far as such a binary representation of the relationship between the two writers has the effect of suggesting that Walcott is an elitist, Eurocentric writer, it is extremely misleading. One of the arguments of this study will be that Walcott has tried throughout his career to dismantle such Manichean binarism.

The remainder of this chapter attempts to counter such stereotyping, first by offering a chronological account of key formative influences on Walcott's career, with particular emphasis on his early years in St. Lucia, to which he has returned again and again in his writing, and second by discussing 'The Spoiler's Return', a poem from his 1981 collection *The Fortunate Traveller*, which illustrates how his work incorporates and synthesizes disparate cultural intertexts. It does so recognizing that the formative influences outlined are themselves hybridized, shifting and unstable, that prior to undergoing transformations in Walcott's hands, they already exist in a discursive continuum which is particularly fluid because of the cross-cultural nature of the post-colonial situation. Walcott implicitly suggests that culture exists in a constant state of transition and reinvention and another of the main arguments of this study will be that a *poetics* of migration informs his work (see particularly Chapter 6). The act of travelling recurs throughout his writing and has far more than literal connotations: it functions as a metonym for the journeying between cultures and the erosion of discursive boundaries which is central to his artistic practice.

Derek Alton Walcott was born in Castries, St. Lucia in 1930. Both his grandfathers were white, both his grandmothers were predominately black. In his early poetry he makes much of his mixed racial background, initially presenting it as a problematic legacy – in an oft-quoted passage from 'A Far Cry from Africa' he speaks of being 'poisoned by the blood of both' sides of his ancestry[15] – but quickly coming to see the potential it offers for a creative fusion of traditions. While St. Lucia is a primarily francophone Catholic island, Walcott was born into an English-speaking Methodist family and thus belonged to a 'minority' community for reasons other than his racial origins. In a 1965 article, 'Leaving School', he conveys a sense of what it felt like to be a Methodist growing up in colonial St. Lucia: 'I learnt early to accept early that Methodists went to purgatory or hell, a Catholic hell, only after some strenuous dispensation. I was thus, in boyhood, estranged not only from another God, but from the common life of the island.'[16]

Walcott's mother, Alix, was the respected head teacher of a Methodist infant school; his father, Warwick, who died when he was just a year old, was a civil servant and amateur painter, and during Derek's formative years he was initiated into the arts, particularly literature and painting, by his late father's circle of friends, members of an amateur dramatic group in which Warwick Walcott had been the 'moving spirit'.[17] Walcott presents this group as rather beleaguered: 'Their existence, since most of them came from a religious minority, Anglican, Methodist or lapsed Catholic, had a defensive, doomed frailty in that steamy, narrow-minded climate';[18] and they also belonged to a 'minority' because of their artistic inclinations. Walcott sees himself as having been extremely 'lucky' with regard to the 'older intelligences that help[ed] to shape [his] mind',[19] both his teachers at St. Mary's College, the school he attended in Castries, and his late father's friends. Among the latter, his most important mentor was the professional painter, Harold Simmons, to whom he pays tribute in his poetic autobiography, *Another Life* (1973). Along with his own friend Dunstan St. Omer,[20] who was to become the most important St. Lucian painter of his generation, Walcott was taught painting by Simmons. He was particularly influenced by Cézanne, whose compositional style could, he felt, be transferred to the local landscape,[21] and by Gauguin and Van Gogh, with whom he came to identify on a more personal level.[22] Early on Walcott nurtured ambitions of becoming a painter as well as a poet, but as the years went by he came to realize that, despite his love of painting, his real métier lay in 'metaphor'[23] and he turned his main attention to writing. Nevertheless he has continued to paint water-colours throughout his life and his training in painting shows itself in virtually all his work, not only in the vividly pictorial imagery of his poetry, but also in the attention to visual setting and stagecraft which informs his practice as a dramatist and director of his own plays, for which he usually prepares detailed sketches of set designs.[24] Later Walcott was deeply affected by the suicide of Harold Simmons, in 1966, and in *Another Life* he views this as an index of the difficulty of the artistic life in the Caribbean.[25]

Other family influences were his sister, Pamela, two years older than himself, and his twin brother, Roderick, who shared many of his early artistic aspirations and has become a significant dramatist in his own right. Growing up in his mixed St. Lucian world, exposed to both colonial and folk cultures, Walcott was aware from an early age of the plurality of Caribbean society and the relativism of cultural 'norms'. Arguably, being a twin also gave him a sense of alternative and parallel possibilities for the self and to some extent Roderick and Derek can be seen as mirror-images of one another, reflections which contain reversals. Thus, while both brothers' St. Lucian plays demonstrate a commitment to putting the island's popular culture on stage, Derek's transformation of a folk legend in a play such as *Ti-Jean and His Brothers* (1957) contains a degree of abstract allegorizing that is not to be found in the more immediately accessible celebration of the St. Lucian Lawoz festivals that lies at the heart of Roderick's musical play, *The Banjo Man* (1971).[26]

The landscape in which Walcott grew up also exercised a powerful influence on his development. He realized early on that it was 'a virginal, unpainted world':[27]

> no one had yet written of this landscape
> that it was possible,
> [. . .]
> whole generations died unchristened,
> growths hidden in green darkness, forests
> of history thickening with amnesia.[28]

and devoted himself to 'Adam's task of giving things their names'.[29] He and Dunstan St. Omer took a vow that they would not leave St. Lucia until they had 'put down' its neglected natural history 'in paint, in words'[30] and, in a 1989 interview,[31] Walcott spoke about his attempt to recapture the particular 'tactile' quality of specific St. Lucian trees and plants on the printed page, a process which one can see at work in poems such as 'Sainte Lucie'[32] and 'Cul de Sac Valley', in which he personifies local trees,

> hissing: *What you wish*
> *from us will never be,*
> *your words is English*
> *is a different tree.*[33]

Bringing what Walcott perceived as the hitherto unwritten St. Lucian world into literature was, of course, a project that had social implications; it represented an attempt to invest trees such as the breadfruit and mango with the same status as the elm and the oak[34] and to reclaim ordinary St. Lucian lives from the legacy of the 'nameless, anonymous, hopeless condition'[35] of slavery.

St. Lucia is a small mountainous island (only 233 square miles in area) with lush and varied vegetation. It is situated to the south-east of Martinique and to the north-east of St. Vincent in the Windward Islands. Its mixture of anglophone and francophone cultures is a product of its colonial history: it changed hands between the British and French more than a dozen times before eventually becoming a British colony in 1802. The island is primarily rural and Castries, the capital, is its only city of any size. The split between the capital and the countryside is one of the most extreme in the Caribbean and a 1963 commentator wrote in the island's newspaper:

> The poor, barefoot, uneducated, unsophisticated, shy people in the out-districts looked up with awe and fawning to the well-dressed, well-spoken and better read city folk. … Castries was St. Lucia in every way. … The out-districts were a Never-Never land.[36]

Such a view was, no doubt, entirely reasonable from the colonial St. Lucian point of view, but within the 'Never-Never land', a subaltern culture, dominated by Afro-Caribbean folk forms, existed in parallel with the Europeanized culture of the capital. Part of Walcott's endeavour throughout his career has been to give voice to this hitherto unarticulated world.

Walcott's early years were divided between the 'well-dressed' world of Castries and his colonial education at St. Mary's College, which gave him a familiarity with European classics that would have been matched by few of his English contemporaries, and forays into the 'out-districts'. In 'Leaving School' he records how, equipped with painting and writing materials, he would make 'pilgrimages'[37] into the country, where he would stay at the roadside hotel of a friend of his late father's and write:

> Above the remaining town, were the thick green hills boiling all day with their broadleaved, volcanic vegetation. That was the nature that I had learned to love in child-hood. The one road inland coiled out of Castries up Morne Fortune … and sinuated through a cane-green valley towards snake country. It climbed again across the Atlantic coast with its dirty breakers, its grey unpainted villages with their squat Norman-style cathedrals, to split on the clean windy plain of Vieuxfort, with its runaways and arrowing highways.[38]

These journeys were, then, excursions into the other side of the St. Lucian experience, into the rural landscape and folk customs of the island.

The first section of *Another Life* is entitled 'The Divided Child'. As a boy Walcott appears to have seen himself as the product of multiple divisions: among them divisions between European and African ancestors, between anglophone and francophone linguistic worlds, between Standard English and Creole, between Methodism and Catholicism, between city and countryside and between the colonial educational curriculum and St. Lucian folk culture. Arguably, however, it was his sense that his artistic inclinations separated him from ordinary St. Lucian life that made him feel most 'divided' and in *Another Life* he presents art as an activity that receives scant respect in the Caribbean and, as indicated above, views Harold Simmons's suicide as a synecdoche for the fate of the artist in the region.[39] This, however, mainly relates to Walcott's view as a young aspiring artist and he later began to see positive potential in his 'divided' existence. In 'What the Twilight Says', the 'Overture' to *Dream on Monkey Mountain and Other Plays* (1970), he speaks of 'the writer's making creative use of his schizophrenia'[40] and in both his plays and poetry he attempted to develop a cross-cultural aesthetic practice, long before hybridization theory became internationally fashionable in the 1980s through the work of post-colonial writers and theorists such as Salman Rushdie and Homi Bhabha.[41] Such thinking has particular relevance in the Caribbean. Although some critics have seen Walcott's 'mulatto' aesthetic as special pleading for his own racial group – and such terminology may itself be unfortunate – his position clearly addresses the creolized plurality of the region's culture, something shared by all Caribbean people irrespective of their particular ethnic origins.

After leaving school, Walcott became an assistant master at St. Mary's College.[42] A major fire which destroyed much of Castries in 1948 had an important effect on his imagination, since he saw it as destroying the old colonial world and opening up new possibilities;[43] and he has frequently used the bonfire as an image of the melting-down of traditions in the crucible of the Caribbean, bringing with it a corollary potential for the opening up new cultural formations.[44] Although only eighteen, Walcott had by this time already been writing poems and plays for several years, works which in some ways are extremely derivative, displaying debts to Eliot, Auden, Yeats, Dylan Thomas, Edward Thomas, Joyce, Dante, Baudelaire, Homer, Villon and numerous other European poets. In imitating these writers he saw himself as serving an apprenticeship in literature, which was similar to his learning the craft of painting from Harold Simmons. Borrowing $200 from his mother, he had his first volume of verse, *25 Poems* (1948), printed in Trinidad and set about successfully recuperating the cost by selling it himself. The long poem *Epitaph for the Young* was published in the following year. Walcott had written his first play, *Flight and Sanctuary*, when he was just sixteen and several other one-act verse dramas followed in the 1940s (see Chapter 3). While this early dramatic work 'owed more to printed texts than performance and he brought to drama the same influences and classical values that helped to shape his early poetry',[45] Walcott was becoming aware of a different set of intertexts for his later theatrical practice in the street theatre of St. Lucian folk forms and everyday life, which he discussed in 'What the Twilight Says'.[46] Meanwhile, his reading also opened up alternative possibilities for a locally grounded poetic practice: his discovery of the work of the Jamaican poet, George Campbell, which celebrated Afro-Caribbean identity, provided an impetus for writing about St. Lucian people without the mediation of European discursive conventions.[47]

In 1950, along with Maurice Mason, Walcott founded the St. Lucia Arts Guild, an organization dedicated to promoting the arts in the island. Its opening event was an exhibition of the paintings of Walcott and Dunstan St. Omer and was followed by a performance of Walcott's first major play, *Henri Christophe* (1950), which, although written in Elizabethan verse, took the Haitian Revolution, a defining moment in the history of the Caribbean, as its subject (see Chapter 3). Later that year, Walcott won a scholarship to the Jamaica campus of the University College of the West Indies (UCWI) at Mona and Roderick took over as President of the Arts Guild, which he led for the next eighteen years. Emancipated from the shadow of the 'Big

Brother' who had been born a few minutes before him, 'Roddy' blossomed as an arts administrator and one of the Caribbean's most successful folk dramatists.

Walcott spent four years in Jamaica, where he took a General Arts degree and a postgraduate education course. UCWI had been founded in 1948 with a Medical School and 1950 must have been a particularly interesting year to go there, since it was the year when the College admitted its first cohort of Arts undergraduates.[48] Walcott immediately immersed himself in the cultural life of the University, among other things starting two student newspapers, playing a leading role in the literary society and a writer's workshop and directing plays, including his own *Harry Dernier* in 1952 and *Henri Christophe* in 1954.[49] A third volume of verse, *Poems*, appeared in 1951. Meanwhile his studies introduced him to other Western writers, among them Marvell and the metaphysicals,[50] who came to be important influences on his own poetry. The Mona years also gave him a broader sense of his own West Indianness and extended his knowledge of hispanophone and francophone Caribbean writing.

After leaving the University in 1954, Walcott had periods working as a teacher in Grenada and Jamaica and for the Jamaican journal *Public Opinion*. However, his main interests during the next few years were centred on the theatre and the most significant landmark in his career thus far came when he was commissioned to write a historical pageant for the arts festival held to mark the inauguration in 1958 of the short-lived West Indian Federation.[51] The play he wrote, *Drums and Colours* (1958), drew, once again, on the Haitian Revolution, but now as part of a much broader sweep of Caribbean history, well suited to the occasion of its performance. Its protagonists – four historical figures, Columbus, Raleigh, Toussaint L'Ouverture and George William Gordon (a leading figure in the events surrounding the 1865 Morant Bay uprising in Jamaica), and a fictional black shoemaker named Pompey – are Caribbean heroes representing different strands of racial ancestry. While Walcott has always taken the view that subservience to what he calls 'the muse of history' leaves Caribbean peoples determined by a negative past legacy in which slavery has been the central event, in *Drums and Colours* he fashioned a view of allegory which enabled him to develop concerns that embodied the cross-cultural political promise offered by the Federation and his own beliefs about the direction West Indian society should be taking. This was achieved as much through a dramatic practice that blended elements derived from intertexts ranging from Shakespearean drama to Trinidad Carnival as through the choice and handling of subject-matter.

Walcott's first play to make extensive use of Caribbean folk forms, *Ti-Jean and His Brothers*, was written on a short visit to New York in 1957 and he subsequently received a Rockefeller fellowship, which took him back to the city for a period of nine months in 1958 and 1959. This second visit was crucial in the development of his theatrical vision. In New York he studied various aspects of production and scene design and, equally importantly, encountered a broad range of world drama which made him increasingly aware of the inadequacy of European and North American dramaturgy for his own purposes, except in so far as he could assimilate, adapt and creolize elements. Among the most important of these new influences were Brecht and the Japanese Noh and Kabuki theatres. He was also attracted to other aspects of Japanese culture:

> In New York, I came to the Chinese and Japanese classic theatres through Brecht. I began to go to the texts themselves and, because I draw, I used to look very carefully at the woodcuts of Hokusai and Hiroshige. There was a very strong popular interest in Japanese cinema – in Kurosawa, and films such as *Ugetsu, Gate of Hell, Rashomon*, etc. I had written one play which was derivative of *Rashomon*, called *Malcauchon*. It was the story of a woodcutter and people gathered together under a hut. This was a deliberate imitation, but it was one of those informing imitations that gave me a direction because I could see in the linear shapes, in the geography, in the sort of myth and superstition of the Japanese, correspondences to our own forests and mythology. I also wanted to use the same type of figure founded in this material, a type essential to our own mythology. A woodcutter or coal burner.[52]

Walcott returned to the Caribbean in 1959 and settled in Trinidad, which was to become his adopted home for nearly two decades. He has described its capital, Port of Spain, as the quintessential tropical city: adapting Dr Johnson's dictum on London, he has said that 'the man who cannot live in Port of Spain can never live in the tropics'.[53] Early on in his career, his main interest in theatre seems to have lain in the opportunities it afforded for the use of dramatic verse. He returned from New York with a much stronger commitment to the performance aspects of drama and a desire to develop a Caribbean version of Brechtian people's theatre which would incorporate elements from sources as diverse as the Noh and Kabuki, the American musical and Shakespeare. He founded a theatre company, the Trinidad Theatre Workshop, in 1959 and in the years that followed directed a broad and varied repertory, including plays by Soyinka, Genet, Beckett, Ionesco and Albee as well as several of his own plays and work by other Caribbean dramatists. He has said that he 'was after ... and am still after ... a theatre where someone could do Shakespeare or sing Calypso with equal conviction'[54] and he drew increasingly on Trinidadian popular culture, familiarizing himself with Carnival discourse and related performance forms. Such elements are central in his musical collaborations with the composer Galt MacDermot, *The Joker of Seville* (1974), a creolized reworking of the original Spanish Don Juan play, and *Steel* (1991), a celebration of steel-band and calypso, and in poems such as 'The Spoiler's Return'. Another collaboration with MacDermot, *O Babylon!* (1976), a play about a Rastafarian beach community in Kingston, was a less successful attempt to incorporate elements from Jamaican popular music. Other plays of the late 1960s and 1970s, such as *Franklin* (1969),[55] *In a Fine Castle* (1970)[56] and *Remembrance* (1977) addressed changing social patterns in the post-independence Caribbean. Most interesting of all in this respect, the comic two-hander *Pantomime* (1978) examined the renegotiations of roles taking place in the region through a series of variations on the Man Friday-Robinson Crusoe relationship.

In the Trinidad Theatre Workshop productions, Walcott worked closely with a small group of actors, achieving the highest standards of performance the Caribbean theatre had yet seen.[57] At the same time he was Arts Correspondent for the *Trinidad Guardian*, the island's leading newspaper, an occupation which proved complementary to his work as playwright and director. In addition to reviewing a very broad range of material, Walcott's *Guardian* articles contain numerous pleas for a Caribbean theatre: sometimes for a national theatre for Trinidad, but more generally for an eclectic, hybrid dramatic practice and modes of production appropriate to the Caribbean situation.[58] Taken as a whole these pieces are as much a manifesto for a West Indian theatre as Errol Hill's book *The Trinidad Carnival*[59] which foregrounds *its* intent in its sub-title, 'mandate for a national theatre'. Meanwhile the activities of the Workshop were coming close to bringing such a theatre into being.

Alongside the public figure of the dramatist, theatre director and arts reviewer, another Walcott persona was also evolving during these years: that of a solitary poet, gradually building up an impressive international reputation. His first metropolitan-published volume of verse, *In a Green Night*, appeared in 1962. It brought together what he considered to be the best of his verse to date, including work from as far back as the 1948 *25 Poems*. It was followed by *The Castaway* (1965) and *The Gulf* (1969), volumes mainly, though not exclusively, concerned with Caribbean situations and relationships, in which the predicament of the artist, seen as an isolated Crusoe-like figure hewing a tradition from local raw materials, looms large, particularly in the earlier collection. For Walcott, Crusoe is 'a twentieth century symbol of artistic isolation and breakdown, of withdrawal, of the hermetic exercise that poetry has become, even in the New World' and also 'the embodiment of the schizophrenic Muse whose children are of all races'.[60] In reconstructing him in this way, Walcott is again creolizing a European intertext while also, having established a Caribbean genealogy, suggesting a more universal significance for the figure. The line of descent here is interesting and typical of Walcott's complication

of ancestries: a European stereotype of the imperialist is meta-
morphosed by virtue of being reinvented as a 'schizophrenic'
Caribbean artist and then, as it were, re-exported back to the
world as a Muse 'for the children of all races'. So what begins as
a Caribbean borrowing from Europe is turned upside down with
a Caribbean Crusoe providing a model for artists in other
societies. Walcott's poetics of migration unsettles received notions
of literary lineage. *The Castaway* and *The Gulf* were followed in
1973 by *Another Life*, a poetic autobiography of the same kind
as Wordsworth's *Prelude*, an obvious intertext for a poem
tracing 'the growth of a poet's mind'.[61]

Walcott parted company with the Trinidad Theatre workshop in 1976, an event which some commentators have seen as
providing the basis for his play *A Branch of the Blue Nile*
(1983), and shortly afterwards took up a teaching appointment
in Boston, where he has subsequently lived for parts of the year.
He has been associated with other theatre companies, particularly in the US Virgin Islands and the United States and has
returned regularly to the Caribbean: to St. Lucia and Trinidad,
where he resumed his relationship with the Workshop in 1993.
His later work has continued to draw on Western archetypes,
most notably Adam in *Sea Grapes* (1976) and Homer's
characters in *Omeros* and *The Odyssey*.[62] Like Crusoe and Don
Juan, these characters are wrested from their Old World origins,
sometimes functioning as cross-cultural figures, sometimes as
New World archetypes.

If there has been a change in Walcott's stance in the last two
decades, it has been a shift towards greater involvement with
American mythologies. His representation of the New World as
a second Eden owes much to some of the earliest European-
derived mythography of the Americas;[63] and his use of the
Adam figure, sometimes unfallen but more usually postlapsarian, puts the emphasis on the 'fortunate fall', an idea
popular among nineteenth-century American Puritan writers.[64]
One way of explaining this might be to suggest that he has
become increasingly absorbed in the cultural agendas of his
adopted second home, the United States – and certainly his

collections *Midsummer* (1984) and *The Arkansas Testament* (1987) make more use of American settings – but 'American' poems are to be found in his collections as far back as *In a Green Night*. The more recent collections engage in a dialogue between 'North' and 'South',[65] but from early on Walcott had seen himself as a poet of the Americas. His most famous essay, 'The Muse of History',[66] identifies some of the key qualities of 'the great poets of the New World', among whom he numbers Walt Whitman, Pablo Neruda, Aimé Césaire and St. John Perse, and the act of Adamic naming is seen as pivotal in their work. Walcott's own writing, with its Adamic commitment to creating a discursive universe from an apparent vacuum, belongs firmly in such a broad-based conception of an American tradition. So when he came to put down roots in the 'North', it was altogether more appropriate that he should do so in the United States rather than Europe.

New influences in the Boston years included major poets with whom he became friends, particularly Robert Lowell and two poets who like himself were outsiders in the American East Coast literary establishment, Joseph Brodsky and Seamus Heaney. Since Brodsky and Heaney were peers rather than precursors, the possibility for dialogue and mutual influence proved to be considerable. The friendship with Heaney is particularly interesting, since from early on Walcott had seen parallels between his colonial St. Lucian situation and that of the great Irish writers of the modern period, particularly Yeats, Synge and Joyce.

Finally, Walcott offers the paradox of a poet committed to Adamic innovation whose work is plagued with the anxiety of influence. Arguably the resolution of this paradox lies in his transforming his apparent sources into what Brathwaite has called 'something torn and new'.[67] Walcott's bonfire of tradition melts his intertexts down and rekindles them, phoenix-like, in the crucible of his own Adamic synthesis; and this radically destabilizes conceptions of literary authority. It is as if tradition has undergone a process of migration, taken ship across the wide sargasso sea of the Atlantic, found itself beached, Odysseus-like, in the Caribbean and then, even as it begins to exert influence in the opposite direction, come to doubt whether it had a point of origin in the first place.

A consideration of 'The Spoiler's Return' provides an oppor-tunity to examine Walcott's destabilization of notions of hegemonic authority in more detail. It is a poem which has obvious departure-points in both oral and literary traditions: a calypso composition of the 1950s and Roman and English Augustan satire. So, initially at least, it seems to validate Walcott's view of himself as a divided writer: 'I am a kind of split writer: I have one tradition inside me going in one way, and another tradition going another. The mimetic, the Narrative, and dance element is strong on one side, and the literary, the classical tradition is strong on the other.'[68] The problem with such a binary model is that it obscures the extent to which the two traditions interpenetrate one another. Walcott's work employs *multiple* modes and registers, ranging along a con-tinuum of discourse loosely analogous to the continua that typify the diverse linguistic and social structures of the Carib-bean region. In *Pantomime*, the Man Friday figure, Jackson, laughs when he remembers a man who went to an audition claiming to 'do all kind of acting, classical acting, *Creole* acting'[69] – he is particularly amused by the latter term. *Pantomime* itself has Jackson acting out several versions of both Friday *and* Crusoe, characters who in an unreconstructed version of the Crusoe story might be seen to represent 'classical' and 'Creole' poles; and more generally Walcott's work shows classical and Creole, and also scribal and oral, forms overlapping to a degree where it is not really feasible to see them as discrete. Again, this can be seen as analogous to Caribbean linguistic continua, in which it is difficult to separate out discretely available levels. While it is possible to categorize particular utterances in terms of the extent to which they *approximate* towards Standard English or the notion of a 'pure' Creole and, where poetry is concerned, to arrive at a parallel kind of classification which assesses a degree of approximation towards a 'literary' or 'oral' pole, the extent of possible movement along the continua that is available to an individual speaker or poet – code-mixing – makes it impossible to fix anyone immutably within a given category. Discussions of code-mixing or code-switching[70] in Caribbean writing have not been lacking in recent years, but they have mainly concerned themselves with writers such as Brathwaite, Olive Senior and Mikey Smith, whose work incorporates oral elements in obvious ways. Arguably, Walcott's work moves just as easily across illusory linguistic, literary and social fault-lines, encompassing a discursive sweep that is even broader.

Walcott's use of apparently binary structures is in fact a device that enables him to develop a complex pluralist aesthetic that spans Caribbean linguistic continua and their social and cultural correlatives. 'The Spoiler's Return', with its twin departure-points, provides a particularly interesting instance of his apparent use of a binary strategy, since it employs a range of Creole and Standard registers:

> I sit high on this bridge in Laventille
> watching the city where I left no will
> but my own conscience and rum-eaten wit,
> and limers passing see me where I sit,
> ghost in brown gabardine, bones in a sack,
> And bawl: 'Ay, Spoiler, boy! When you come back?'
> And those who bold don't feel they out of place
> to peel my limeskin back, and see a face
> with eyes as cold as a dead macajuel,
> And if they still can talk, I answer 'Hell'.[71]

The transitions here are subtly achieved. The Standard English of the first three lines includes the odd heightened poetic phrase ('my own conscience and rum-eaten wit'); the fourth line includes the Trinidadian colloquialism 'limers' and with it a hint of a Creole register, but such a register does not really appear until the limers' words are quoted in the sixth line ('And bawl: "Ay, Spoiler, boy! When you come back?"'), after which the persona shifts effortlessly into a similar voice, while still employing syntax that suggests the literary rather than the colloquial. Such shifts are, however, hardly likely to be perceived by casual readers of the poem. The smoothness of the transitions implies a continuum of discourse rather than the representation of a pair of opposed linguistic codes.

At the same time, through its use of both Caribbean and European intertexts, the poem also appears to relate itself to two cultures. From the outset it is located within the discursive traditions of Trinidad Carnival and calypso: it is dedicated to Earl Lovelace, who had published his novel *The Dragon Can't Dance*, a text that incorporates aspects of Carnival and calypso discourse into a complex discussion of Carnival values, in 1979;[72] and it adopts the persona of the Mighty Spoiler, a leading calypsonian of the post-war period,[73] for its narrative voice. In the poem Spoiler has been resurrected from Hell to comment on the state of contemporary Port of Spain and by extension social and political life in the Caribbean more generally. The real-life Spoiler is best remembered as a composer and performer of imaginatively audacious fantasies[74] and in Walcott's poem lines from his calypso 'Bed Bug' are juxtaposed with lines from one of the most famous poems of the seventeenth-century satirist John Wilmot, Earl of Rochester, 'A Satyr against Reason and Mankind'.[75] In 'Bed Bug', having heard about people being reincarnated as animals or insects, the persona elects to come back as a bed bug and prey particularly on corpulent women of social standing.[76] Walcott fuses this idea with the Rochester lines which he introduces with the words:

> join Spoiler' chorus, sing the song with me,
> Lord Rochester, who praised the nimble flea ... (*FT*, 54)

and in so doing appears to be conflating Rochester's poem with Donne's 'The Flea', since, although it contains references to animals, 'A Satyr against Reason and Mankind' makes no mention of a flea. Whether this represents a 'mistake' made by a writer who feels he knows the poem in question so well that he does not need to check the text or deliberate obfuscation that has the effect of making different aspects of both seventeenth-century English verse and the tradition of *le libertinage* more or less homogeneous is a matter of opinion.[77] It is, however, important to remember that this passage and the quotation which it contains are, like everything else in the poem, spoken by the persona of the resurrected Spoiler and consequently it seems reasonable to suggest that the fusion of voices is in keeping with the air of surreal fantasy that pervades the whole piece, an atmosphere in which a dream-like erosion of discrete identities seems perfectly fitting. Such a reading is supported by the quotation itself:

> *Were I, who to my cost already am*
> *One of those strange, prodigious creatures, Man,*
> *A spirit free to choose for my own share,*
> *What case of flesh and blood I pleased to wear,*
> *I hope when I die, after burial,*
> *To come back as an insect or animal.* (FT, 54)

The first four lines here are quoted verbatim from Rochester's satire; the last two move unselfconsciously to Spoiler's 'Bed Bug', in which the calypsonian says that he has heard that after death and burial, people have 'to come back as an insect or an animal'.[78] The bringing together of the two texts is seamless; Walcott integrates them in such a way that the uninitiated reader will probably not spot the point at which the joins are being made.

What is happening in this specific instance is typical of the poem's procedure more generally. 'The Spoiler's Return' juxtaposes and blends the irony of the Trinidadian calypsonian and the Augustan satirist, both Roman and English, in such a way that the effect is one of fusion rather than drawing on dual, but polarized, traditions:

> nothing ain't change but colour and attire,
> so back me up, Old Brigade of Satire,
> back me up, Martial, Juvenal, and Pope
> (to hang theirself I giving plenty rope) ... (FT, 54)

The 'Old Brigade' reference here is, on one level at least, to a group of prominent calypsonians of Spoiler's day. As Errol Hill explains:

During the 1940's and the 1950's, the two principal calypso
tents were the Old Brigade and the Young Brigade. Singers
generally teamed up according to their age. The veteran
singers belonged to the former tent, which boasted a traditional style of performance, while the younger and more
experimental calypsonians joined the Young Brigade. Needless to say keen rivalry existed between the two tents.[79]

Applying the term 'Old Brigade' to the satirists who are
mentioned here has the effect of locating them in a Trinidadian
context and, while it could be argued that this operates as a
counter-discursive strategy, as a kind of reverse colonization, in
which canonical European writing is subverted within a Caribbean framework, as with *Omeros* the main effect is to suggest
the interpenetration and not the oppositional nature of the two
discourses. Walcott collapses the distance between Europe and
the Caribbean and between the twentieth century and the earlier
historical periods in passages which suggest the 'overlapping'
and 'intertwined'[80] aspects of the two satiric traditions and the
ironic strategies they employ:

> Catch us in Satan tent, next carnival:
> Lord Rochester, Quevedo, Juvenal,
> Maestro, Martial, Pope, Dryden, Swift, Lord Byron,
> the lords of irony, the Duke of Iron ...   (*FT*, 60)[81]

Similarly, Spoiler's playful assertion in the poem that he will
call himself 'King Bed Bug the First',[82] which relates to the
Trinidadian practice of crowning Carnival Kings and Queens,
generally considered to have its origins in the parody masquerade
coronations staged by Afro-Trinidadians in the late nineteenth
century,[83] suggests a parallel with the mock-heroic coronations
of Dryden's *MacFlecknoe* and Pope's *Dunciad*; and the insect
imagery used by such satirists as Juvenal and Pope also plays a
prominent part in Walcott's poem:

> So, crown and mitre me Bedbug the First –
> the gift of mockery with which I'm cursed
> is just a insect biting Fame behind,
> a vermin swimming in a glass of wine. (*FT*, 55)

Just as the poem moves between different linguistic registers and brings together satirical traditions, it also occupies a complex position where prosody is concerned and Walcott has said that, depending on one's viewpoint, it is either written in heroic couplets or in a popular form of calypso metre.[84] Thus pentameters such as:

> And those who bold don't feel they out of place
> to peel my limeskin back, and see a face (*FT*, 53)

can equally well be seen as products of a European mock-heroic tradition or as issuing from a calypsonian's voice, even if, as Brathwaite has pointed out, dactyllic rhythms are more prominent than iambic in both calypso and Caribbean speech-patterns more generally.[85]

So 'The Spoiler's Return' provides a classic case of the hybridization that is characteristic of post-colonial texts, but to say this is merely to state the obvious if one does not address its discursive constituents more specifically. It is above all a poem which achieves its effect through references which have their origins in particular moments and places. The lines:

> the slime crab's carapace is waterproof
> and those with hearing aids turn off the truth,
> and their dark glasses let you criticise
> your own presumptions behind their eyes.
> Behind dark glasses is just hollow skull,
> and black still poor, though black is beautiful. (*FT*, 55)

are on one level inescapably about the former Prime Minister of Trinidad, Eric Williams, who wore just such dark glasses and who, popular rumour had it, would in his later years turn off his hearing aid on his comparatively infrequent visits to Parliament. Equally, they can be seen to operate on a more general level to suggest the kind of politician who, while engaging in populist rhetoric, fails to listen to the people, a type which in its broad contours arguably transcends particular time and place. Put another way, the use of Augustan analogies could be seen to construct a binary pattern, in which the local and universal are being paired. Yet there is never a sharp definition between such possible opposites, but rather a sense of a continuum in which hierarchical positioning has ceased to be an issue. Although the *social* world about which he writes continues to be hierarchically structured, Walcott's *discursive* practice in the poem erodes distinctions between 'high' and 'low' cultures; his elision of the supposed gap between canonical European texts and popular Caribbean balladry projects an egalitarian aesthetic.

So, while 'The Spoiler's Return', like so much of Walcott's work, may appear to draw on two opposed traditions, its practice is altogether more complex than this. The poem provides a complex mosaic of references, which, far from suggesting antithetical satiric practices – Caribbean and European, present and past, oral and literary – operates to suggest dialectical continuities across cultures and periods *and* within the utterances of a particular speech act or literary text. This is not to suggest that the poem propounds an easy universalism, but rather that it stages a complex enactment of the continuum model of Caribbean culture, in which discursive specifics are foregrounded rather than obscured. Early on in 'The Spoiler's Return' the persona asserts, 'I decompose, but I composing still' (*FT*, 53). It is a statement which could be seen as a self-referential comment on the procedure adopted in the poem itself (and also in Walcott's work more generally). The various traditions on which 'The Spoiler's Return' draws *decompose* in the Caribbean melting-pot and from this crucible a new tradition, of Walcott's own making, is *composed*.

Finding a voice

WALCOTT'S first volume of poems to be published outside
the Caribbean, *In a Green Night*, did not appear until 1962, but
by this time he had already acquired a considerable reputation
within the region and three privately published volumes of his
verse had appeared more than a decade earlier: the first, *25
Poems*, in 1948, when he was only eighteen. In retrospect these
collections now seem little more than curtain raisers to Walcott's
later achievements and he himself has referred to them as constituting an 'apprenticeship' which was a necessary preparation
for his subsequent career, since, through the 'copying and
imitating and learning'[1] in which he engaged at this time, he
was gradually coming to discover a voice of his own. Although it
would be wrong to dismiss this early prentice-work as mere
juvenilia which the mature poet subsequently had to put behind
him – Walcott included seven of these early poems in *In a Green
Night*[2] – much of the verse in the early volumes, *25 Poems,
Epitaph for the Young* (1949) and *Poems* [1951], is derivative
and all three collections are distinctly uneven in achieved poetic
effect. They do, however, show Walcott wrestling with concerns
that are central in his later poetry, most notably his attempt to
come to terms with his mixed cultural and racial ancestry, the
quest for an appropriate poetic voice and the sense of living in a
postlapsarian environment.

At first sight the dominant theme of all three volumes
seems to be well summed up by the title of *Epitaph for the
Young*. They are permeated by a mood of elegy. Particular

poems such as 'In My Eighteenth Year',[3] 'Elegies' and 'Both
Sides of the Question' in 25 Poems and 'Hart Crane' in *Poems*
are formal elegies: for Walcott's father Warwick, for poets such
as Thomas Chatterton who committed suicide while still young
and for those killed in World War II. More generally, though,
the three early volumes are a sustained elegy for the loss of
youth which Walcott sees as a fall from grace analogous to the
loss of Eden in the Christian myth. He repeatedly seems to
suggest that all meaningful existence is in the past and in
passages such as the following demonstrates a morbid, Romantic
fascination with death:

> we, each
> Flapping boast of the crowing sun, turn in our linen
> graves,
> Face stale mornings, old faces, but these dead on the
> beach,
> Are joyed at the dawn's blood skyed on their dearth of
> days.
> We cocky populations fouling the fallow plans of heaven,
> Shall find perfection in a cemetery under a hill.
> For we have suffered so long, that death shall make all
> even ...[4]

and with Time as the destroyer of youthful innocence and an
uncontaminated artistic vision:

> The innocent eye could paint the sky with moons,
> People the lawns with white caresses, brand sands
> With crusoe terrors, or in the mind's dominion frame a
> rage.
> So it may be greater comfort I am in,
> And this regret is time's imagining.
>
> Now all the branches break, the ruins
> Drop tired birds, and there is but my hand's
> Maddening cancer on the page,
> I cannot translate childhood, none can shut in
> That simple grief, Narcissus in his skin.[5]

The mood of narcissistic melancholy is so strong that it is a relief to find Walcott sometimes turning away from dramatizing his inner angst in the third volume, *Poems*, and engaging in satirical treatments of such subjects as Caribbean tourism (in 'Montego Bay – Travelogue II', 'The North Coast at Night' and 'The Sunny Caribbean'), inter-racial relationships ('Margaret Verlieu Dies') and the new breed of mid-century Caribbean politicians ('The Statesman'). *Poems* is also notable for a small group of poems concerned with a more precise realization of the specifics of Jamaican place ('Kingston by Daylight', 'Kingston Nocturne' and 'The North Coast at Night').

However, the morbid obsession with decay, ageing and dying remains uppermost in all three collections and there are numerous poems about early death and suicide. In the most sustained and powerful of the shorter poems, 'The Cracked Playground', Walcott writes of the need to escape from his sense of having lost faith in everything, including the notion of faith itself, and details a number of possible forms which such escape might take, among them a death which would restore the prelapsarian perfection he has associated with the youthful state:

> the mind screams – 'Escape!
> Escape to islands, to the absolute sea,
> To the girl's mouth, the suicide's morphine
> Dig down the bone in its familiar place,
> Unfurl the flesh on a familiar sky.'
> And under reason a sick wind murmurs – 'Die'.
>
> Bounced by a horror of ennui we strike out
> To a place not place, a time not time, a mind
> Deprived of need for love, and insulation,
> The perfect love, the horror of the old,
> The perfect ego, the perfect nation,
> The perfect weather, the perfect common cold,
> The perfect summer where no owls are blind. (*Poems*, 19)

While initially, like the passage from 'The Yellow Cemetery' quoted above, these stanzas may seem to draw on the poetic trope of Death the Great Leveller in a fairly generalized way, there is a hint of a particular Caribbean inflection when Walcott lists 'the perfect nation' (in a line which interestingly pairs it with a similarly idealized conception of subjectivity) among the needs that will become irrelevant in death. So what at first appears to be an expression of existential angst can also be seen as the product of Caribbean specifics; and on several occasions in the early poems the sense of lost perfection, cracked innocence and psychic fragmentation is related to the racial divisions of Caribbean society. Occasionally a more positive note intrudes in poems which envisage love as bridging such binaries. In *25 Poems*, 'Travelogue' makes an appeal for a federation of the heart that will heal the psychic and political wounds inflicted by colonialism:

> Let all on islands of the heart construct the day
> Of the federated archipelago, black
> And white live apart, but dream the same dreams.
>
> (*25P*, 17)

In *Poems*, 'Erotic Pastoral' also creates an Edenic vision, at odds with the prevalent pessimism of the early volumes, though the most striking stanza articulates its ideal of inter-racial harmony through a metaphysical conceit in which hybridization is associated with the decay inherent in flesh:

> Put away thoughts of race,
> First in the idle woods
> Love built the garden before genetics broke.
> There's no pride nor disgrace
> In skins where the worm broods.
> The first miscegenation that time spoke
> Was when the skin wed dust, the bone in the womb's
> groove.   (*Poems*, 25)

In Walcott's later work, the Caribbean is frequently constituted as an ambivalent Paradise – variously an unfallen and a fallen Eden.[6] Here the emphasis is heavily on fallen experience; it is usually more personal, sometimes cryptically so, and for the most part less subtly expressed. Walcott tends to view his mixed racial and cultural heritage as a postlapsarian predicament which can only find resolution in death. Hence the prominence of

artistic suicide in the three volumes. There is as yet little awareness of the positive potential of cultural cross-pollination.
Nevertheless, some poems in the two collections of shorter
pieces show the first glimmerings of Walcott embarking on his
voyage to discover an appropriate artistic practice for his mixed
Caribbean experience. In these the late adolescent existential
angst is tempered by a commitment to building a Caribbean
future from the debris of colonialism:

> Whether you are brown, lonely, golden or black, young
> Man, construct the day of companions, and
> …
> raise the world your fathers did not make.
>
> There are no worlds to conquer, but worlds to recreate.
>   ('Call for Breakers and Builders', 25P, 19)

While such a passage is primarily an exhortation towards community and nation-building, it is also possible to read it as a self-
referential expression of the need to construct a new Caribbean
aesthetic practice. In moments like this Walcott seems to be
delineating the task required of the Caribbean artist. As yet there
is comparatively little stress on the need to create a distinctive
regional poetics, something which is prominent in Walcott's
drama virtually from the outset and in his poetry from the
1960s onwards, but the role of language in the process of recon-
struction is explicit in a passage on bridge-building in *Poems*:

> Perhaps I could build something from the broken language
> Of columns, splintered cups, the death of love
> And understand dead petals in the yard.
>   ('The Pursuit of April – A Letter', *Poems*, 29)

Epitaph for the Young explores the problem of finding an
appropriate poetic voice in a more developed way than the two
collections of shorter poems. Walcott has spoken of this volume
as a work that anticipates issues which he would later engage
with in his poetic autobiography, *Another Life;*[7] and it explicitly
foregrounds the problematic situation of the Caribbean writer
and consequently, although no satisfactory solutions are offered,
represents Walcott's earliest sustained discussion of the quest

for an aesthetic practice appropriate to St. Lucia and the Caribbean region.

The poem makes extensive use of European literary models and has been criticized for its derivativeness. An early reviewer, Keith Alleyne, found Walcott wearing 'the top hat in the tropics'[8] and, in drawing attention to many of the poem's numerous intertexts, particularly took Walcott to task for finding in Eliot 'not merely an influence, but a complete formula',[9] which enabled him to join the ranks of poets of crisis. Later critics such as Robert Hamner, who sees the poem's central voyage motif as a quest for 'a source of authority',[10] and Stewart Brown, who particularly discusses the influence of Eliot and Baudelaire on Walcott's early verse, while also identifying debts to Yeats, Synge, Joyce, Auden and Dylan Thomas,[11] have not demurred from this assessment, although, like Alleyne, both these commentators are sympathetic to the dilemma in which Walcott found himself as a young poet growing up in a 'colonial' culture and Brown is particularly sensitive to the different and opposing interpretations that can be put on such a wholesale use of intertexts from 'another' culture. In a short monograph on Walcott's poetry Ned Thomas also raises this issue, asking 'Where is the line drawn between being a wide assimilator of influences for your own purposes and being yourself assimilated?'[12] and this is a crucial question for the whole of Walcott's work, not simply the early poetry, though the degree of unreconstituted assimilation is at its greatest here. It is crucial, both with regard to the originality of Walcott's poetry and drama and also with regard to its ideological positioning. Simply to absorb European intertexts is to remain a 'colonial' poet. In contrast, creative adaptation and counter-discursive subversion of such influences suggests a 'post-colonial' consciousness, even if Europe still remains a departure-point and the work is being produced in the colonial period. Of course, most literary texts habitually operate in terms of a hybridized admixture of discursive elements rather than a straightforwardly complicitous or adversarial response to what is perceived of as 'tradition' and so the opposition suggested in the previous sentence oversimplifies in its starkness. Thus the watershed between 'colonial' and 'post-colonial' becomes more difficult to define than might initially seem to be the case.

In their classic discussion of post-colonial literary theory and practice, *The Empire Writes Back* (1989), Bill Ashcroft, Gareth Griffiths and Helen Tiffin use the term 'post-colonial' in a manner which has now become widely accepted in literary and cultural studies 'to cover all the culture affected by the imperial process from the moment of colonization to the present day'.[13] If at first this usage seems to be at odds with the way post-colonial has generally been used by historians (that is, to indicate the post-*independence* period), and to collapse the distance between what is *temporally* colonial and what is not, it does at least have the virtue of identifying 'a continuity of pre-occupations throughout the historical process initiated by European imperial aggression'.[14] Cultural production in (post-)colonial situations inevitably exists in a hybrid discursive continuum and individual writers are rarely, if ever, able to immerse themselves fully in either of the opposed roles of enslaved imitator or emancipated originator. So, although it remains important to locate writers precisely in terms of the specifics of their discursive positioning, the 'line' between being an assimilator and being assimilated can be far from clear-cut.

This said, in *Epitaph for the Young* – and for the most part in *25 Poems* and *Poems* – the extent and nature of the numerous literary borrowings suggest a greater degree of unassimilated derivativeness than is to be found in Walcott's later verse. Indeed, when he speaks of serving a poetic apprenticeship, his self-training in the mimicry of earlier poets' styles suggests, as Stewart Brown has noted, an identification with young acolytes in the schools of the masters of European art, required to become expert copyists before developing a distinctive mode of their own.[15] However, careful scrutiny reveals a very complex response to European art.

Epitaph for the Young is a Modernist poem in the tradition of Eliot and Pound and its central controlling metaphor of the journey is strongly indebted to a work by a poet who was an important influence on Eliot: Baudelaire's *Le Voyage*.[16] Eliot's presence is ubiquitous in the poem: there are allusions to the full range of his poetry from the early 'Love Song of J. Alfred Prufrock' to the late *Four Quartets*. Eliotean imagery is particularly prominent: drought and rain imagery derived from *The Waste Land*; rose imagery, associated with the Virgin Mary and Anglo-Catholicism, from Eliot's post-*Ash-Wednesday* verse; and throughout Walcott's stress on the broken and cracked nature of contemporary experience bears the American poet's imprint. Like the early Eliot, Walcott presents his readers with 'a heap of broken images'[17] and, as Alleyne points out,[18] engineers a sense of cultural crisis. It is, however, questionable whether such a mood of Modernist angst, seen by some as Eliot's response to the post-World War I predicament of the West, is suitable for adaptation to the situation of a young poet growing up in the late colonial Caribbean. Is it, as Alleyne suggests, simply 'a formula' or does it have an appropriateness in Walcott's Caribbean context?

Epitaph for the Young is a much more lyrical poem than anything in Eliot. It deals, cryptically, with an adolescent love affair; it once again includes elegiac references to Walcott's father Warwick; and it treats the poet's artistic ambitions in a more personal, and self-indulgent, manner than slavish imitation of Eliot's austere classicism would ever allow. In fact, the poem is not simply imitative; it engages in a dialectical relationship with Eliot. Thus a passage such as the following, redolent with echoes of Eliot is the dramatic utterance of a persona:

> '... I say the Word only to those who hear, and who are
>   not here to hear,
> Not to those who are afraid of distraction
> Of the thrush in the rose garden, not those who fear the
>   desert
> Yet cannot desert, in the desert where there is no water,
> In this timeless city where the crowd of spinning faces
>   evolves in the violent air
> Sand and sandpaper ...

I say this with my mouth, you listen not with these ears,
Because they are mine, but listening with yours ...
I say this not out of time, but in time, not timeless
But rhymeless and out of time.
For the
For the wheel turns and the impatient suffer
And the peasant passes distracted by insinuations
Here and now in Castries and Hampstead, burnt nothing,
A Little Giddying,
But where was I?'   (EY, 23)

The passage contains clear allusions to the rose garden and
'Word' imagery of *Ash-Wednesday*;[19] there are references to
the desert, the wheel and the limbo-like state of modern city-
dwellers, whom Eliot likens to the wandering souls in Dante's
Inferno, of *The Waste Land*;[20] and there are allusions to the
titles of two of the *Four Quartets*, 'Burnt Norton' and 'Little
Gidding'. The whole passage is, however, highly self-conscious
and reads more like parody than pastiche. As a dramatic utterance, a speech by the poet-persona to a spirit-guide who leads
him through an underworld, it can hardly be taken as an
unmediated expression of Walcott's own views: the spirit-guide
in question would seem to be Eliot. So what one is confronted
with is a playful, parodic reworking of Eliot, in which the poet
assumes a similar relationship to Eliot, as that which Eliot
assumes to Dante, *his* spirit-guide, particularly in *The Waste
Land* – and, further back, which Dante assumes to Virgil in *The
Divine Comedy* and Virgil's Aeneas assumes to Anchises in *The
Aeneid*. The intertextual layers are dense and overlapping,
suggesting the debt to Eliot is far from formulaic and implying a
model of literary genealogy which resists the very notion of
texts deriving from other texts in a straightforward linear
succession for a model which has more in common with Michel
Foucault's archaeological account of cultural transmission.
Foucault takes the view that 'a particular discourse cannot be
resolved by a prior system of significations'[21] and argues against
the attempt to locate originary moments. The young Walcott
has almost certainly not thought through his position in relation
to the issue of tradition in this way: the repeated stress on the

loss of the Eden of childhood suggests an elegiac longing for an originary moment, an ultimate source in which perfection *could* be located. Nevertheless there is the recognition that such perfection no longer exists and, as the passage addressing the spirit-guide illustrates, his practice in *Epitaph for the Young* involves a Foucault-like archaeological layering of traces, with each apparent source-text barely concealing further and deeper strata beneath. Clearly such a conception of tradition has universal valency, but it is one which has particular resonance in post-colonial contexts, where the grounds of what constitutes authority are, more or less inevitably, subject to seismological disturbance.

Although this parodic passage could be read as incidental, a digression from the poem's central concerns, it illuminates Walcott's practice throughout *Epitaph for the Young*. And his apparent obsession with Eliot, and his Modernist contemporary Pound, whose ideas on literary and cultural influence have much in common with Eliot's, is especially appropriate when one takes into account the particular situation in which the two earlier writers were working – as American expatriates in Europe committed to constructing a tradition that would salvage something from what they saw as the wreckage of post-World War I Europe and the decline of the West more generally. Both were committed internationalists who attempted to arrive at a cross-cultural aesthetic practice which, while it remained conservative and ethnocentric in crucial respects, did at least desert Anglo-American parochialism in favour of a dialogue with an eclectic selection of past writers from a range of European and Asian cultures. As Walcott matures, his view of what constitutes an appropriate body of influences for a Caribbean writer will prove even more diverse, operating along a discursive continuum which elides the boundaries between high art and popular culture, engaging with Caribbean folk forms at one pole and at an opposite extreme attempting to forge a world-based tradition, in which Asian, African and pan-American elements are fused with European. In *Epitaph for the Young* this is not yet apparent. However, like the two other early volumes, it shows Walcott embarking on the project of evolving an appropriate tradition and in so doing transcending colonial mimesis. Eliot is, then, far more than a 'formula' for the young Walcott. The uneasy discursive relationship which the early volumes establish with their various intertexts under-mines the notion of a straightforward line of influence and in so doing interrogates Western literary hegemonies more generally. So amid Walcott's late adolescent agonizings, one finds the seeds of the complicated tussle with tradition that will inform much of this later poetry.

Although *In a Green Night* includes poems from the earlier collections, it represents a major step forward in Walcott's verse. Several of the same subjects recur, but the cryptically subjective passages and the straining for effect that frequently mar the poetry of the first three volumes are replaced by a style that aims at greater clarity and a more sustained engagement with the external natural and social milieux of the Caribbean, particularly St. Lucia. While some of the poems continue to dramatize the sense of lost innocence that dominates the earlier verse, others show Walcott beginning (albeit for the most part *in absentia*) to fulfil the vow he had taken with Dunstan St. Omer 'that we would never leave the island / until we had put down in paint, in words'[22] the St. Lucian natural world in all its variety. Walcott had committed himself to this endeavour in the know-ledge that 'no one had yet written of this landscape / that it was possible'[23] and now he sought to evolve a style that would realize the 'several postures of this virginal island' (*IGN*, 16) on the printed page. In a self-referential reflection on the process of writing in the penultimate poem in the collection, 'Islands', he describes his goal as follows:

> I seek
> As climate seeks its style, to write
> Verse crisp as sand, clear as sunlight,
> Cold as the curled wave, ordinary
> As a tumbler of island water. (*IGN*, 77)

Typically, this crisp, clear ordinariness is conveyed through the use of similes – similes and metaphors proliferate throughout the volume – but there is a directness here that is rare in the earlier volumes. The quest for an appropriate tradition is still implicit. European literary influences remain strong – there are prominent references to Virgil, Horace, Catullus, Villon, Dante, Chaucer, Shakespeare, Sir Thomas Browne, Traherne, Donne, Marvell, Blake, Wordsworth, Baudelaire and Eliot – while at an opposite extreme the volume includes Walcott's first poems employing Creole registers: 'Tales of the Islands, VI', 'Pocomania' and 'Parang'. However, the anxiety of influence is no longer the pivotal point of the poems in the same way and the crisp, Standard English advocated in 'Islands' predominates. In the opening poem of *In a Green Night*, 'Prelude', which had previously appeared in 25 *Poems*,[24] the poet resolves that his life:

> must not be made public
> Until I have learned to suffer
> In accurate iambics. (*IGN*, 11)

The decision to make this the first poem in the collection seems highly appropriate, since these lines articulate the commitment to a more restrained poetic practice that characterizes most of the verse in the volume.

The vow to chronicle the island world is fulfilled in various ways in *In a Green Night*. In 'As John to Patmos', there is a simple statement that 'This island is heaven – away from the dustblown blood of cities' and a resolve 'To praise lovelong, the living and the brown dead' (*IGN*, 12). In 'A Sea-Chantey' a 'litany of islands' (*IGN*, 66) expressed in onomatopeic verse:

> Anguilla, Adina
> Antigua, Cannelles
> Andreuille, all the l's
> Voyelles of the liquid Antilles,
> The names tremble like needles
> [...]
> The music uncurls with
> The soft vowels of inlets ... (*IGN*, 64–6)

suggests a similarly celebratory and reverential response. Elsewhere the mood can be considerably more complex. In the title poem[25] the Caribbean is a 'green yet ageing orange tree' proclaiming 'perfected fables' but, like the apple tree in Eden, containing a 'cyclic chemistry / That dooms and glories her at once' (*IGN*, 73). In 'Return to D'Ennery, Rain', the poetic persona is an 'imprisoned' onlooker coming back to a crippled village and struggling with a complex of emotions, among them the impossibility of finding a 'home' (*IGN*, 33). However, although the sense of existential loss that had dominated the earlier volumes reappears here, it is contextualized by an admission, in the last line, that the persona is engaging in self-pity and in verse which evokes the village ambience with clarity and precision:

> The hospital is quiet in the rain.
> A naked boy drives pigs into the bush.
> The coast shudders with every surge. The beach
> Admits a beaten heron. Filth and foam. (*IGN*, 33)

The capacity to link topographical contemplation, social commentary and personal reflection does much to broaden the significance of the poetry, especially since poems such as 'Choc Bay' and 'The Banyan Tree, Old Year's Night', which initially seem to be as meditations on landscape, turn out to be pervaded by social and cultural history.

On more than one occasion Walcott's commitment to chronicling the St. Lucian landscape is related to the need for a cultural vision grounded in the politics of decolonization. At the beginning of 'Roots', he is explicit about the vicarious, second-hand status conferred on cultures that are habitually defined through comparison with European 'originals':

> Merely a naturalist's notebook?
> Then till our Homer with truer perception erect it,
> Stripped of all memory of rhetoric,
> As the pealed bark shows white;
> Not, as when the blue mist unravelled Sorcière,
> The mountain, our guests whispered, 'Switzerland.'
> When they conquer you, you have to read their books …
>
> (*IGN*, 60)

and the poem as a whole, like much of Walcott's verse, can be read as an attempt to perform just such a Homeric role for the Caribbean. 'Prelude', too, writes back against the situation of being cast away from the supposed centres of cultural authority and constructed by 'the eye of another':[26]

> Meanwhile the steamers which divide horizons prove
> Us lost;
> Found only
> In tourist booklets, behind ardent binoculars;
> Found in the blue reflection of eyes
> That have known cities and think us here happy. (*IGN*, 11)

The poems in *In a Green Night* frequently offer release from such alterity through an emphasis on a home-grown vision – the 'truer perception' of a local 'Homer' – which will replace the tourist gaze. Thus, 'To a Painter in England', a poem dedicated to Harold Simmons, focuses on pictorial representations of temperate zones and tropical landscapes, demonstrating a clear preference for the latter, while suggesting the possibilities which 'personal islands' have had for European poets such as Gauguin.[27]

When Walcott does return to the theme of lost innocence in *In a Green Night*, the treatment, though still cryptic at times, is generally more probing. 'The Banyan Tree, Old Year's Night' discusses the problem of locating not Eden, but the Fall; finding a moment of originary rupture proves as difficult as finding a moment of originary beginnings. Colonialism may be to blame for the poet's sense of exile, but the sources of his melancholy remain 'Blank as the rain on the deserted mind' (*IGN*, 72). 'Orient and Immortal Wheat' relates the thirteen-year-old Walcott's response to living in what he feels is a 'monstrous' natural world to 'the fever called original sin' (*IGN*, 48), bringing together a complex set of emotions apparently connected with puberty, loss of faith and the attempt to transfer a European landscape vision onto the local world. Disease, decay and disillusion are to the fore, but even here there is the promise of release through a creolized Wordsworthian epiphany:

> He wept again, though why, he was unsure,
> At dazzling visions of reflected tin.
> So heaven is revealed to fevered eyes,
> So is sin born, and innocence made wise,
> By intimations of hot galvanize. (*IGN*, 48)

So *In a Green Night* represents a coming of age for Walcott, the first clear step on his Odyssean journey towards becoming a Caribbean Homer. While many of the poems in the collection belong with his best work,[28] two in particular, 'A Far Cry from Africa' and 'Ruins of a Great House',[29] have found a special place in the Walcott canon. This chapter concludes with a brief discussion of them.

'A Far Cry from Africa' is a classic, if over-quoted, poem in which, taking the Mau Mau freedom struggle in Kenya as his departure-point, the poet discusses the dilemma of being torn between Africa and Europe. Although it may appear to be a dramatization of Walcott's own particular racial angst, it can equally well be read as a more generalized investigation of the Caribbean psyche's divided cultural and ethnic allegiances. The opening stanza employs stereotypical constructions of Africa as savage:

> A wind is ruffling the tawny pelt
> Of Africa. Kikuyu quick as flies
> batten upon the bloodstream of the veldt (*IGN*, 18)

and seems to locate the discussion within the conventions of Western media reporting of Africa, as well as colonial discourse more generally:

> Corpses are scattered through a paradise.
> …
> What is that to the white child hacked in bed?
> To savages, expendable as Jews? (*IGN*, 18)

However, when the poem moves to the opposite side of the savage/civilized binary so often used to construct the relationship between Africa and Europe, it expresses scepticism about such a bifurcation and the boundary between supposed European rationality and African animality is eroded:

The violence of beast on beast is read
As natural law, but upright man
Seeks his divinity with inflicting pain.
Delirious as these worried beasts, his wars
Dance to the tightened carcass of a drum. (*IGN*, 18)

Thus far in the poem the debate has been conducted in the third person, but in the final stanza the poem changes its angle of focalization by introducing a racially mixed 'I' persona, suggestive of Walcott himself:

I who am poisoned with the blood of both,
Where shall I turn, divided to the vein? (*IGN*, 18)

The conclusion posits a choice between Africa and Europe, but the terms in which this is framed are particularly interesting: Europe is seen as 'the English tongue I love?', while Africa becomes life itself as the poem concludes, 'How shall I turn from Africa and live?' (*IGN*, 18). Later Walcott works invariably resist the adversarial divisiveness promulgated by binary classifications, arguing instead for a cross-cultural fusion or a stance which allows identity to slip between the nets of static essentialist categorization. 'A Far Cry from Africa' may seem to fall into the trap of creating what certain post-colonial critics have referred to as 'Manichean'[30] divisions and certainly mixed racial ancestry is hardly being seen as a source of strength ('poisoned by the blood of both'). However, the final stanza, comprised of a series of five unanswered questions, refuses to make a choice and in so doing could be seen to resist such dualism and to anticipate later, more positive, constructions of hybridization.

'Ruins of a Great House' also confronts issues central to Caribbean culture, taking the fate of a former estate house as a metonym for the passing of Empire. This focus on a house follows in the tradition of English texts such as Marvell's 'Upon Appleton House' and Jane Austen's *Mansfield Park*, where the house represents the security of a supposedly stable Old World social order, and such a correspondence is also highly appropriate to the subject-matter since it locates the poem within an

English tradition of meditative and topographical verse, which like the house itself is crumbling in the Caribbean environment. The poem's epigraph, from Sir Thomas Browne's *Urn Burial*, emphasizes the transience of human life and the opening lines also suggest the ephemerality of existence:

> Stones only, the *disjecta membra* of this Great House,
> Whose moth-like girls are mixed with candledust,
> Remain to file the lizard's dragonish claws … (IGN, 19)

While this is a classical commonplace, the passage also comments on the particular fragility of the former plantocracy's way of life and the poem goes on to suggest that the colonial presence has been but a passing phase in a perennial Caribbean natural cycle: 'Deciduous beauty prospered and is gone' (IGN, 19). Its assessment of what the house has represented is decidedly ambivalent and, although the early part of the poem is primarily negative, elegiac passages rub shoulders with outright indictments of the imperial presence:

> The imperious rakes are gone, their bright girls gone,
> The river flows, obliterating hurt. (IGN, 19)
>
> I thought next,
> Of men like Hawkins, Walter Raleigh, Drake,
> Ancestral murderers and poets, more perplexed
> In memory now by every ulcerous crime.
> The world's green age then was a rotting lime
> Whose stench became the charnel's galleon's text.
>
> (IGN, 20)

As 'In a Far Cry from Africa', an 'I' persona is introduced mid-way though the poem and the second half dramatizes this figure's grappling with an equally acute dilemma. The protagonist becomes 'Ablaze with rage' at the thought that 'Some slave is rotting in this manorial lake' (IGN, 20), but immediately balances this anger with compassion, reflecting, like Marlow in Conrad's *Heart of Darkness*,[31] that England too has once been colonized. This lofty cyclic view supersedes a response rooted in 'bitter faction' and the poem ends by asserting the unavoidability of compassion and the consanguinity of peoples in a final line, 'as well as if a manor of thy friend's' (*IGN*, 20), which alludes to John Donne's famous 'No man is an island' sermon. The passage comes from the sentence, 'If a clod be washed away, Europe is the loss, as well as if a manor of thy friend's or thine own were ...'.[32] Again there is ambivalence. It is possible to put the emphasis on *Europe*'s loss and to read the conclusion as straightforwardly anti-colonial. However, a more obvious interpretation is that human fates are indivisible and so the Caribbean protagonist needs to put aside the sense of historical wrong and accept that 'The river flows, obliterating hurt'. Such advocacy of reconciliation is typical of Walcott's response to Caribbean history,[33] and it has not always made him popular in the Caribbean since it has been seen to demonstrate too much sympathy for (ex-)colonizer figures. It is, however, part and parcel of his rejection of oppositional aesthetics rooted in notions of cultural and racial binaries and, as in 'A Far Cry from Africa', demonstrates his unwillingness to accept the essentialism inherent in 'Manichean' classification.

Founding a West Indian theatre

W HEN Walcott first began writing plays in the 1940s, theatre in the Caribbean region was in one sense waiting to be discovered. While the larger islands, particularly Jamaica, had developed theatrical traditions,[1] the middle-class ambience of proscenium arch drama had ensured that it remained the preserve of the colonial classes. At an opposite extreme, the people's theatre of Carnival, masquerade and seasonal festivals had yet to achieve recognition as serious art and there had been comparatively few attempts at a fusion of 'classical' and 'Creole' forms. In Walcott's words, 'If there was nothing, there was everything to be made'.[2] First in St. Lucia, then during his student days in Jamaica, but most importantly during his years with the Trinidad Theatre Workshop, he has, as a writer, director, critic and polemicist, done more than anyone – with the possible exception of the Trinidadian dramatist and theatre historian Errol Hill – to develop a distinctive Caribbean theatre. This chapter deals with his plays from his very earliest work, written in the 1940s, up to his masterpiece, *Dream on Monkey Mountain* (1967), illustrating his gradual evolution of a theatrical practice appropriate to the region's culture.

In 'What the Twilight Says', his 'Overture' to *Dream on Monkey Mountain and Other Plays*, Walcott refers to *Henri Christophe* (1950) as his 'first play'.[3] He had previously written a number of short verse-dramas: *Flight and Sanctuary* and *Harry Dernier*, when he was just sixteen, and three further one-act plays –

Another World for the Lost, The Matadors and *A Simple Cornada* – in the following year. However, apart from *Harry Dernier*, a twenty-minute 'play for radio production',[4] which was broadcast and staged in 1952,[5] none of these early plays was performed and so in one sense *Henri Christophe* really was his first play. It was also much more ambitious in scope than his earlier incursions into drama and shows him grappling at some length with debates about Caribbean history and culture that would be central to his later work.

While most of Walcott's plays have employed Caribbean themes and settings, at first sight neither *Flight and Sanctuary* nor *Harry Dernier* has any obvious regional content. Both appear to focus on anguished solitary protagonists wrestling with more generalized existential dilemmas. Set in a time of plague, *Flight and Sanctuary*[6] is about a hermit who eventually decides to relinquish his solitary existence and return to the city he has deserted to help tend the sick. *Harry Dernier* focuses on the figure of the last man on earth, a tormented defrocked priest[7] who reviews the human condition and questions the value of life. Both characters have to choose between an ideal of personal integrity that can only be achieved through alienation from society and making a commitment to the perpetuation of civilization and notions of community. As Judy Stone sees it, *Flight and Sanctuary* 'presents a harsh analogy of the dilemma of the artist who must isolate himself from the world in order to create, but who must not lose touch with the world which is his source of creative inspiration'.[8] Harry Dernier is tempted, in his post-holocaust world, with the possibility of recreating life at the very moment when the human race faces extinction, but rejects this because of his belief that 'Our sin is flesh' (*HD*, 9). This theme of guilty postlapsarian sexuality has its parallels in Walcott's early poetry, but interestingly also anticipates his later fascination with the figure of Robinson Crusoe as a Caribbean Adam.[9] When a second voice – seemingly no more than an emanation of Dernier's imagination, since he says at the end 'she died too' (*HD*, 10) – comes into the text, it is that of a woman who calls herself Lily the Lady, and Dernier identifies her with Lilith, the first wife of Adam in Rabbinical mythology.

Although neither *Flight and Sanctuary* nor *Harry Dernier* contains an explicit Caribbean dimension, a sound effect direction for *Harry Dernier* insists that 'the sea be heard all of the time' (*HD*, 1) and a 'desert island' simile is introduced at one point (*HD*, 7). It is also possible to see both plays as metaliterary works about the situation of the Caribbean artist facing 'death to the spirit [trying] to survive ... under colonial conditions'[10] and consequently torn between a self-protective impulse towards withdrawal and a contrary pull towards commitment. This dilemma can be seen to embody a conflict between the popular Western post-Romantic image of the artist as a being apart and the Afro-Caribbean view of the artist as the voice of a community, functioning, like the griot in West African societies, as the repository of the tribe's history and culture. The tension between these two views runs right through Walcott's *œuvre*, the main difference between these early works and the bulk of his writing being that the balance here is tipped in favour of the Western artistic inheritance, which proves to be a legacy of despair.

If the themes of the plays and their use of outsider figures confronting existential dilemmas suggests affinities with twentieth-century writers such as Sartre, Camus and Beckett, the mood is rather one of Jacobean gloom and, as would subsequently be the case with *Henri Christophe*, Walcott's dramatic practice is indebted to Elizabethan and Jacobean tragic models: Kyd, Webster and Shakespeare among them. And if the predicament of Harry Dernier initially suggests either a generalized twentieth-century angst or a more specifically late 1940s response to the European holocaust, a passage in 'What the Twilight Says', in which Walcott discusses the moment when he began writing drama, conflates the threat to civilization in Europe with the legacy of slavery and has more to say about the Caribbean problem of constructing a tradition from the wreckage of the Middle Passage than the horrors of concentration camps.[11] Consequently it seems entirely legitimate to see a *Caribbean* post-holocaust context as providing the backdrop to *Harry Dernier*.

Like V. S. Naipaul, Walcott felt that 'he lived in a society which denied itself heroes';[12] unlike Naipaul his response was not emigration and an aesthetics which denied putative Caribbean hero-figures, but rather an attempt to confer heroic status on Caribbean figures as diverse as St. Lucian fishermen and charcoal-burners and the leaders of the Haitian Revolution. While Walcott's plays of the 1950s may seem very varied, moving between heroic tragedies and chronicles written in a style imitative of Elizabethan verse-drama on the one hand and folk-plays employing Creole registers on the other, all of his drama of the period demonstrates a commitment to 'the forging of a language that went beyond mimicry'.[13] He attempts to invest his literary representations of local people and subjects with a dignity which would liberate them from the 'self-contempt' from which he felt their real-life originals suffered:

> It did not matter how rhetorical, how dramatically heightened the language was if its tone were true, whether its subject was the rise and fall of a Haitian king or a small-island fisherman, and the only way to re-create this language was to share in the torture of its articulation. This did not mean the jettisoning of 'culture' but, by the writer's making creative use of his schizophrenia, an electric fusion of the old and the new.[14]

The 'Haitian king' and 'small-island fisherman' mentioned here are specific references to Henri Christophe and Afa, the protagonist of Walcott's one-act play, *The Sea at Dauphin* (1954).

The appearance of *Henri Christophe* was a landmark in West Indian theatre. Its first performance in Castries in 1950 did much to help establish the St. Lucian Arts Guild; and a 1952 production in London was hailed as 'an event of the first importance' in the 'development of an indigenous culture'.[15] It was Walcott's twin brother, Roddy, who first suggested that he should write a play about the Haitian Revolution,[16] and the history of the black Jacobins provided him with a subject not only for *Henri Christophe*, but also for scenes in *Drums and Colours* (1958) and for *The Haytian Earth* (1984). Walcott immediately saw parallels between post-independence Haiti and contemporary St. Lucia, even though Haiti had, in the wake of the French Revolution, thrown off the colonial yoke at the very beginning of the nineteenth century and become the first black republic in the Americas, while St. Lucia remained a colony in the mid-twentieth century. A dramatization of aspects of the history of post-revolutionary Haiti offered possibilities for an allegory exploring problems of 'independence', among them nation-building, leadership and the reconstructions of identity; and in the leading players in this history Walcott found tragic heroes racked by 'Manichean' crises about racial identity which again struck a chord in his own experience:

> Full of precocious rage, I was drawn, like a child's mind to fire, to the Manichean conflicts of Haiti's history. The parallels were there in my own island, but not the heroes.
> …
> [The black Jacobins'] self-disgust foreshadowed ours, that wrestling contradiction of being white in mind and black in body, as if the flesh were coal from which the spirit like tormented smoke writhed to escape.[17]

Henri Christophe, the third of the triumvirate of ex-slave rulers who successively governed Haiti after the Revolution, particularly captured Walcott's imagination as a man whom he perceived as torn between excessive violence and the commissioning of visionary architectural projects; in Christophe he located the raw material for a complex and flawed tragic hero,[18] whom he modelled on those of Elizabethan and Greek drama.

Walcott's decision to make Christophe his hero is particularly interesting. Earlier literary treatments of the events of the Haitian Revolution and its aftermath had centred on the more obviously heroic figure of Toussaint L'Ouverture, widely regarded as the military and diplomatic genius of the first phase of the Revolution and the individual most directly responsible for the ousting of the French. Wordsworth and Lamartine had focused on Toussaint, and in the twentieth-century Caribbean the Martiniquan poet Aimé Césaire, an important precursor for Walcott, and the Trinidadian C. L. R. James had followed suit –

in James's case not only in his classic study of the Haitian Revolution, *The Black Jacobins* (1938),[19] but also in a play, *Toussaint L'Ouverture* (1936).[20] However, in Judy Stone's opinion, 'Walcott chose for his Hamlet the enigma, the lesser man but the more complex mortal',[21] a view which is supported by an early passage in the play, which refers to Christophe as 'a two-sided mirror' and represents him as a fusion of his two predecessors:

> under
> His easy surface, ripples of dark
> Strive with the light, or like a coin's two sides,
> Or like the world half-blind when moons are absent,
> ·And brilliant in the glare of sun.
> Under that certain majesty he hides
> The teaching of Toussaint, the danger of Dessalines. (*HC*, 13)

Henri Christophe abounds in references to Elizabethan and Jacobean drama and Walcott draws on the traditions of such theatre for the kind of 'complex' tragic hero he presents in the play. Bruce King has commented, 'The complexity of behaviour is Shakespearean, the disillusionment Websterian'[22] and Walcott himself has said that his black Jacobins were 'Jacobean … because they flared from a mind drenched in Elizabethan literature out of the same darkness as Webster's Flamineo, from a flickering world of mutilation and heresy'.[23] While the mood is Jacobean, the aspirations of the protagonists are more Elizabethan, more Marlovian than Websterian. The fascination with kingship that motivates both Walcott's Dessalines and Christophe shows a clear debt to Marlowe's Tamburlaine and his Christophe also resembles the Marlovian figure of the overreacher in his megalomania and the hyperbolical language in which he expresses his aspirations. Thus he hopes to achieve immortality through his building projects:

> my primer is blood or honour;
> My pieces, cathedrals that I would build,
> Would have made brick biographies, green ruin,
> Played over by children and girls dressed like butterflies
> in a tropic summer. (*HC*, 36)

Although these projects are associated with a vision of whiteness:

> Let us build white-pointed citadels,
> Crusted with white perfections over
> This epilogue of Eden, a prosperous Hayti ... (*HC*, 40–1)

his 'Manicheism' is not simply a product of the 'wrestling contradiction of being white in mind and black in body'. The play incorporates intertexts from both *Richard III* and *Macbeth*[24] and Christophe has more in common with the protagonists of these plays than with Hamlet. Like both of them, he is a killer-poet who walks to a throne through blood – the word is as much a leitmotif in the play as it is in *Macbeth* – and whose tragedy is compounded with his poetic sensibility.

Another strong parallel with Shakespearean tragedy emerges from *Henri Christophe*'s use of Manichean allegory in a manner reminiscent of *Othello*.[25] Walcott's use of the word 'Manichean' to describe similarities between the Haitian situation and his own St. Lucian society anticipates the recent trend (mentioned in Chapter 2) in analyses of colonial and related discourses to see Manichean allegory as lying at the heart of racial stereotyping. Such allegory, as Abdul JanMohamed sees it, involves the construction of 'interchangeable oppositions between white and black, good and evil, superiority and inferiority, civilization and savagery, intelligence and emotion, rationality and sensuality, self and other, subject and object'.[26] It is a discourse which reached its peak in the pseudo-scientific racial binaries of the late Victorian heyday of Empire and with origins that can be traced back to Plato,[27] although whether it is appropriate to term such binarism 'Manichean' is debatable, since such a usage of the term is at odds with the orthodox Christian view of Manicheism as a heresy with *Eastern* origins. In other words, the post-colonial critique of Manichean allegory constructs Western thought as binary, while the traditional Christian position is monistic: in Augustinian theology Manicheism is seen as a heresy precisely because it posits a dualistic universe, whereas the orthodox position insists that because God is omnipotent, evil is simply an absence, the privation of good. Walcott's use of the term 'Manichean' in his early work – his later writing increasingly rejects this paradigm in favour of a continuum model of cultures – is, however, arguably more schizophrenic than that of the analysts of Manichean allegory. He both constructs and frustrates 'Manichean' dualities, dramatizing the hold such binarism has on the *Caribbean* imagination caught between different cultural codes, rather than specifically seeing it as an attribute of colonial discourse, and suggesting that this is a *psychological* trap, a product of colonial brainwashing, which stifles individual development. A more radical post-colonial reading of the Western construction of alterity might well return to the traditional Christian view of Manicheism as a heresy and address the exclusionist practice of silencing the subaltern subject through denying his or her very existence. If at first this seems far-fetched, it is of course a practice which lies at the heart of a 'Manichean' text such as *Heart of Darkness*, in which the real darkness to which Conrad's Africans are consigned is the darkness of being silenced, rendered as fleeting shadows in the bush, who are unrepresentable in concrete terms. While they may exist as the 'savage' half of an opposition which is designed to cement the Western sense of itself as 'civilized', such savagery is in fact more of an absence than an inferior partner in a two-way power relationship.

Walcott's Christophe does, however, emerge as a psychological victim of binary constructions, whose tragic destiny issues from similar causes to those that bring down Othello. Both protagonists are seduced into accepting a view of their social environment which is based on dualism. Othello's tragedy occurs because he succumbs to the binaries of Iago's rhetoric, in which Desdemona is cast on the negative side of the rational/ sensual, civilization/savagery divide. Even if one disputes the extent to which Othello's sense of his racial identity informs his perceptions, it seems reasonable to conclude that his own descent into animalistic imagery involves a similar acceptance of being on the inferior side of what are supposedly 'Manichean' binaries.

Walcott's Christophe follows a very similar path in the penultimate scene of the play. He is persuaded by his secretary Vastey that the white archbishop Brelle is conspiring against him because of '[h]is obvious love for clear complexions' and seems to accept Vastey's claim that Brelle still regards blacks as 'baboons' (*HC*, 45). Like Dessalines before him, Christophe feels he has achieved stature through his metamorphosis from slave to king, but now he falls victim to Vastey's binary rhetoric and it is not long before he is using it himself:

> I am not a civilized man, father;
> I am at heart very primitive; there is that urge –
> A beast in the jungle among primitive angers
> Clawing down opposition; what is the expression –
> The instinct? (*HC*, 49–50)

The consequence is both a personal and national tragedy, since both protagonist and country fail to achieve the 'federation of complexions' (*HC*, 31), of which one character dreams. The theme is clearly one which has considerable relevance to all periods of Caribbean history; and it had a particular urgency in the late colonial period when the various territories were moving towards independence and the possibility of political federation and debates about dismantling prevalent racial hierarchies, which privileged the white and fair-skinned, were very much in the air.

Christophe's failure to achieve racial harmony is also narrativized through his relationship with Pétion, a mulatto general who rules the southern half of the country while Christophe holds sway in the north, in the latter part of the play. Most significantly of all, however, his architectural visions are not only entangled with whiteness, but are also characterized by a need for 'foreign' validation:

> I shall build chateaux
> That shall obstruct the strongest season
> So high the hawk shall giddy in its gyre
> before it settles on the carved turrets.
> My floors shall reflect the faces that pass over them,
> And foreign trees spread out the shape of government;
> On emerald lawns I will hold councils.
> I'll pave a room with golden coins, so rich,
> The old archbishop will smile indulgently at heaven from
> The authenticity of my chateaux. (*HC*, 41)

It is perhaps the crowning tragic irony of the play that he seeks 'authenticity' through mimicking European codes.[28]

One might say the same of Walcott's play itself. *Henri Christophe* belongs to his 'apprenticeship' period and the weight of 'foreign' references is heavy enough to threaten the whole structure. If one accepts such a view the ultimate Manichean tragic protagonist is not Christophe, but Walcott himself. There is evidence to support such a reading: the play not only shows both Christophe and Dessalines perpetuating the Manichean divisions of the society rather than dismantling them as a consequence of being victims of 'that wrestling contradiction of being white in mind and black in body', it also falls into a similar trap itself as a consequence of its wholesale use of Elizabethan and Jacobean intertexts, which sometimes sit uneasily alongside its subject rather than being seamlessly integrated into the play. In another sense, however, the play breaks down Manichean divisions. While Christophe succumbs to the view that casts him as the inferior partner in a hierarchized binary opposition, seeing himself towards the end in terms of animal imagery and speaking of achieving happiness through purely sensual means, he does so in poetry that clearly belies his self-estimate of himself as simply a savage sensualist. So where this particular binary is concerned, Walcott's poetry, like Shakespeare's in *Othello*, undermines the construction of blackness in terms of the negative sides of such Manichean racial equations as 'good and evil, superiority and inferiority, civilization and savagery, intelligence and emotion [and] rationality and sensuality'. Christophe emerges as a 'mulatto of style',[29] a complex hybridized protagonist, whose tragedy emerges from his failure to accept his complexity.

Hybridization is less obviously to the fore in the style of the play, though the use of Elizabethan modes for the Haitian subject inevitably generates multiple tensions. There are, however, a few 'Creole' stylistic elements, such as French patois in the murderers' scene and invocations to the gods of Haitian *vodun* – which ruffle the 'classic' surface of the play. This said, the play remains closer to the European end of a Caribbean discursive continuum.

When it was first staged in 1954, *The Sea at Dauphin* was Walcott's most fully realized St. Lucian play thus far in his career. It employs local registers throughout, blending franco-phone patois elements with anglophone Creole, and this immersion in everyday St. Lucian speech is complemented by a similar commitment to the local world in the use of a beach setting, which allows the sea to function as a major protagonist in the action. Like much of Walcott's dramatic work from this period, the play went through more than one version: in this case, according to Judy Stone, being developed from an earlier comic play.[30] It is about a St. Lucian fisherman, Afa, who defies the elements by going to sea with his younger brother Augustin on a particularly windy day. At the same time Afa refuses to take Augustin's godfather, the East Indian Hounakin, a septua-genarian who has just been widowed, with them, since he suspects that he is courting death. Afa and Augustin return from their day's fishing to find that Hounakin has 'fallen' from a high cliff and died; and at the end a sense of continuity across the generations is suggested when Afa agrees to let the son of another dead fisherman go with them the next day.

The title suggests the central focus of the play: the *sea* at Dauphin. As in Synge's *Riders to the Sea*, which is an obvious intertext,[31] the sea comes to signify the existential condition and going to sea a primal encounter with death. Afa and Augustin survive on this occasion, but the play ends with Afa saying that their turn will come 'one day' (*DMM*, 80). On one level, then, *The Sea at Dauphin* offers a simple, albeit powerfully articulated statement of an existential truism, but it is not without dramatic tension. This emerges not only from suspense concerning the fate of the characters, but also from a more abstract exploration of the nature of the sea and the mysterious compulsion it has for fishermen, whom the young Walcott saw as a breed apart in St. Lucia.[32] Initially Afa sees the sea as a natural force which is oblivious to human feelings and doubts whether it has any link with 'this new thing, compassion' (*DMM*, 53). However, as the action develops he changes his mind, finding the sea more caring than the harsh, island landscape:

> The land is hard, this Dauphin land have stone
> Where it should have some heart. The sea
> It have compassion in the end. (*DMM*, 61)

This movement parallels that of several of Walcott's best-known early poems, such as 'Ruins of a Great House' in which a meditation on the bitter legacy of the plantocracy is supplanted by compassion.[33] Here, anticipating Walcott's later view that 'the sea is history',[34] the ocean is an element which offers release from the constraints of the social world of the island; and for the fishermen it becomes a religion which is preferable to the Catholicism that controls the lives of the St. Lucian peasantry.

While *Riders to the Sea* provided Walcott with the confidence to attempt a play which engaged with the folk culture and language and took the sea as a central metaphor for the existential situation, ultimately *The Sea at Dauphin*'s powerful imaginative evocation of the distinctive apartness of fishermen's lives leaves Synge to one side. In 'What the Twilight Says' Walcott writes, 'The migratory West Indian feels rootless on his own earth, chafing at its beaches'[35] and throughout his career he has exhibited a fascination for the wandering Odyssean protagonist. Afa and his fellow-fishermen provide an early instance of those who elude social entrapment, existing as they do outside the constraints of colonial society in a daily encounter with death.

Throughout his career Walcott has repeatedly taken the human consequences of the end of Empire as a theme for his drama. *Henri Christophe* (which dealt with a much earlier attainment of a republic) apart, *The Wine of the Country* (1956), a full-length one-act play produced during his time in Jamaica,[36] was his first dramatic treatment of this subject. Judy Stone sees it as the first of five versions of *Franklin*;[37] Bruce King sees it as a forerunner of *In a Fine Castle*,[38] a play which would itself be reworked several times as *The Last Carnival*. Stone's view seems the more apt in this instance, since there are a number of links between *Wine* and *Franklin*, notably a St. Lucian setting and an ageing protagonist who personifies the twilight of Empire and who fails to find renewal through a relationship with a younger woman. In contrast, *In a Fine Castle* is set in Trinidad and its only obvious link with *Wine* is its representation of the effects of social and political change on a privileged French Creole family. French Creoles figure in *Wine*, but are not accorded the same centrality. However, although the parallels between *Wine* and *Franklin* are strong, they are not really the same play: the names and racial identities of both the protagonists and other characters differ; so do the dénouements, although in both plays the central figure's younger lover dies. Moreover, they are stylistically very different in conception.

The Wine of the Country is primarily about the predicament of being racially mixed at the time of the 'last sunset'[39] of Empire, and its protagonist, Bemminger, finds this more of a curse than a blessing. He tells the French Creole Mrs Vertlieu:

> I have been spurned and booted by two peoples,
> Bewildered between two cultures and two tongues,
> Between desire and despair, between death and hope,
> My people mock me as I am not black,
> Your people mock me as I am not white,
> And yet I am divisible to both, what has my skin
> To do with my desires, is my death different,
> Don't I bend when I age, can't I talk English,
> …
> Is it so strange, because I am a mongrel sort of man
> To think that my true purpose is nobility,
> Is every virtue white, every grace golden haired,
> That I'm a mirror for every prejudice. (*Wine*, 15–16)

Other characters refer to Bemminger as 'A man without a country. … A black Englishman. A mongrel of a mulatto' (*Wine*, 5), 'a twilit soul / Caught in a dimness between black and white' (*Wine*, 35), 'a delicate quisling, a spy in either territory' (*Wine*, 46), 'a phenomenon cast up on the beach / By the ebb of monarchy, in a colonial twilight' (*Wine*, 20) and as 'a joke, neither flesh nor fowl, … an embittered phenomenon' (*Wine*, 15). The tone of the play is informed by a similar bitterness and Bemminger himself succumbs to the view of him as a 'phenomenon', to a racially determined definition of character which denies him the 'nobility' that he seeks. Overall the play sites him as a case-study and makes no plea for the positive potential of mixed racial identity, though there are passages such as that quoted above which appeal to the notion of an essential humanity that transcends ethnic categorization. For the most part character is seen as fixed and stereotypes abound: other figures include a stage Irishman, a young colonial administrator whose Jewishness is emphasized and the French Creole Vertlieu family, who complement Bemminger as 'a passing breed' (*Wine*, 32) and are represented as suffering from racial taint brought on by miscegenation: Mrs Vertlieu says 'we have a degeneration in our blood, / From intermarriage, idleness and money' (*Wine*, 12) and Bemminger refers to her daughter Marguerite, who is his lover but who, during the action, tells him she will not be leaving the island with him as she has promised, as 'a festering lily, or rotting alabaster, disfigured marble' (*Wine*, 35). Bemminger sees his mind as 'a colony, an island outpost of the hypocritical white' (*Wine*, 45) and throughout the play there is no sign of Walcott's more positive interpretation of cultural schizophrenia, nor of a hybridized theatrical practice. Much of *The Wine of the Country* is written in a rather stilted blank verse which, notwithstanding passages that celebrate the local language and landscape and Bemminger's relationship with it, such as the opening:

> I remember how we first came to this district,
> We had travelled in the jeep all afternoon
> Climbing the narrow road, across the spine
> Of the island, from Cicerone to Quatre Chemin, a road
> Feathered with green bamboos and the long shadows
> Of those trees across the road, through several villages
> With the dim sea soundless on the horizon,
> A country quiet as an old man's mind … (*Wine*, 1)[40]

is marred by a homiletic strain better suited to classical tragedy:

> A felicity that is really serene can avoid
> The domination of the worm. (*Wine*, 22)

> Life is a blind bet, a tired beggar
> Stumbling into a grave, all else is accident. (*Wine*, 25)

Despite suggestions in the play that Bemminger's predicament could culminate in tragedy – his servant Williams tells him 'I suppose you feel like a king abdicating. / A hero dying in a tragedy' (*Wine*, 5) –, the text never really locates him within such a genre. Bemminger takes the view that 'This is the age of footstool tragedies' (*Wine*, 6), but the play is finally more of a maudlin exercise in 'mulatto' special pleading than a modern-day tragedy of the 'ordinary' man, like, say, Arthur Miller's *Death of a Salesman*. When, at the end, Marguerite is killed in a car crash and Bemminger's departure from his home is undertaken alone, the effect is closer to melodrama than tragedy. Later, more naturalistic, Walcott treatments of characters beached by the end of Empire, such as *Franklin*, *The Last Carnival* and *Remembrance*, are more successful and one cannot help but conclude that this is at least partly due to their use of subtler theatrical modes.

Walcott's next significant play, *Ione* (1957), was his most concerted attempt, thus far in his career, to bridge the divide between classical drama and St. Lucian folk experience. It is a tragedy based on family conflicts, which observes the classical unities of time, place and action and contains numerous other Greek elements, among them: a strong sense of fate, a blind prophetess, off-stage killing, a chorus of women and characters whose names echo those of classical protagonists, most obviously Achille and Helene.[41] However, as in *Omeros*, Walcott's most extended 'Greek' work, the debt to classical literature is at best tangential. *Ione* is not an adaptation of a Greek original, but rather an attempt to create a world of equivalent status to that of classical drama, a play which sets out to invest St. Lucian characters with the heroic dignity of the protagonists of Attic tragedy.

It was not an attempt that found favour with contemporary reviewers, who took the view that the play was unrealistic.[42] Judy Stone counters this opinion by pointing out that Walcott was not working in a realistic mode and emphasizing the archetypal quality of the tragedy and the extent to which it anticipates later Walcott plays which fuse the classical and the Creole.[43] This seems partly valid but, despite the use of a local storytelling frame and modified forms of Creole, the play lacks the immersion in local folk discourses that characterizes many of Walcott's later attempts to creolize classical forms and originals. Here such creolization operates mainly on a thematic level: a quasi-classical tale becomes Caribbean, but a tension remains which again demonstrates Walcott's wrestling-match with the problem of Manichean division.

The action of the play centres around the feud between two 'hill tribes',[44] the clans Victorin and Alexandre whose leaders are half-brothers, and the contrast between the two daughters of Victorin, Ione and Helene. Victorin, whose character is more developed than that of his half-brother, has inherited his father's property but is troubled by his ownership and, when the feud is rekindled, he offers to share the land with Alexandre. He feels cursed and his fatalistic psychology is very much in keeping with the mood of the whole play. Alexandre, who is illegitimate, is primarily motivated by his sense of being a 'little bastard' (*Ione*, 35) and his jealousy of his 'big brother, the rightful son' (*Ione*, 34). Complementing this classically simple dichotomy, which is reminiscent of the Edgar/Edmund opposition in *King Lear*, is the equally archetypal pairing of Ione and Helene. The event which triggers the tragedy is Helene's adultery with Achille, a member of the Alexandre clan. She is seen as a 'jamette',[45] while Ione is considered a 'virgin'.

Clearly these two pairings – of legitimate and illegitimate son and Madonna and whore – parallel one another in that they both represent a Manichean opposition between 'purity' and 'impurity'. So once again one finds Walcott returning to the problem which dominates his early writing. At first *Ione* may seem to accept such binary classification all too readily, but in fact the play dismantles such dualities by interrogating the very notion of purity. Victorin expresses a view of kingship, which echoes similar sentiments in *Henri Christophe*. He has a strong sense of being diminished by his New World location, regarding himself as 'no more a king ... just an old nigger in a dusty country' (*Ione*, 39) and feels that this would not have been the case in Africa. In the dénouement Achille further questions notions of legitimacy *and* Caribbean 'purity', saying that the 'bastard branches' of the 'Victorin tree' invalidate its claim to 'clean' blood and asserts that 'we are all niggers. Since the time we leave the real country, we have no place' (*Ione*, 47). Although this leaves the idea of African cultural authenticity unchallenged, it nevertheless represents a coming to terms with the 'mongrel'[46] aspect of the Caribbean situation; and the tragedy can be seen to be a product of the Manichean moral imagination which resists the inescapable reality of hybridization.

Similarly, Ione is no virgin but a widow who, since her husband's death, has become pregnant by a visiting American anthropologist. She emerges as the main tragic protagonist of the play, because of her Antigone-like refusal to accept the conventional binaries of her social world. She seeks self-definition outside tribal classification, saying, in the most memorable remark of the play, 'I am no Victorin. I am Ione. Moin Ione' (*Ione*, 45). This emphasis on enunciating her name suggests a conception of selfhood which denies originary versions of identity.[47] Later, facing the total collapse of her world at the end of the play, she makes a similar remark, 'They cannot break my name. Ione Victorin', but now contemplates escaping Caribbean space by walking 'the dark road to Guinea' (*Ione*, 53). This seems to move in an opposite direction, since it posits the possibility of fulfilment through a sentimentalized African atavism, which would be surprising in a writer who until recently frequently criticized African revivalism,[48] but Ione's character also holds out another possibility. Earlier she has spoken in terms which suggest future post-colonial possibilities rather than a return to an originary, pre-colonial golden era: 'here in my body I have a promise growing, and a strong mixed seed' (*Ione*, 42). This is a promise which points in a diametrically opposed direction to Africa: towards a Caribbean future which celebrates the hybridization of the region's culture. In *Ione* Walcott is finally equivocal about the 'promise' of fulfilment through cultural cross-pollination and it is only suggested on a *thematic* level. In his next play, *Ti-Jean and His Brothers*, he takes a much more positive view of hybridization and it becomes central to the dramatic *form*.

Ti-Jean and His Brothers, Walcott's finest play of the 1950s, has like much of his drama been through several versions.[49] Originally written during a short stay in New York in 1957, it received its premiere in Trinidad in 1958 and is best known in the version printed in *Dream on Monkey Mountain and Other Plays*. Talking about the play in 1970, Walcott referred to it as his most West Indian play thus far[50] and it is as if writing it at a distance from the region gave him the vision and inspiration to draw on the St. Lucian folk world in a way that he had never managed to do while at 'home'. This typifies the direction in which his quest for a Caribbean theatre would develop during the next two decades, with his growing awareness of international cross-currents enabling him to put the colonial mimesis of his 'apprenticeship' period behind him and engage in a closer encounter with the local.

On the surface *Ti-Jean and His Brothers* is a fairly simple dramatization of a tale from a St. Lucian folk cycle which has counterparts in other parts of the world. it is a tale of three brothers, each of whom must in turn face the Devil. A comment in 'What the Twilight Says' makes it clear that Walcott knew the legend from an early age and was fascinated by its narrative structure:

> They sang of children lost in the middle of a forest, where the leaves' ears pricked at the rustling of devils, and one did not know if to weep for the first two brothers of every legend, one strong, the other foolish. All these sank like a stain. And taught us symmetry. The true folk tale concealed a structure as universal as the skeleton, the one armature from Br'er Anancy to King Lear. It kept the same digital rhythm of three movements, three acts, three moral revelations, whether it was the tale of three sons or of three bears, whether it ended in tragedy or happily ever after.[51]

His own version of the Ti-Jean legend initially seems to have more affinity with the story of Goldilocks and the three bears, or the movement of a Caribbean Anancy story than with *King Lear*. Each of the three brothers has to answer the Devil's challenge to make him feel angry. Success will bring a bowlful of sovereigns and a wish granted; failure will result in his being eaten by the Devil. Gros Jean, the eldest brother who relies on brute force, and Mi-Jean, the middle brother, who is foolishly besotted with rhetoric and philosophy, both fail. Ti-Jean (Petit, or Little Jean), the youngest, succeeds, because he relies on instinct and common sense.

Walcott's play invests the classically simple structure of the original folk tale with multiple and complex layers of allegory.[52] The Devil is identified with a colonial Planter and the struggle against this figure clearly lends itself to interpretation as an allegory of the dispossessed Caribbean peasantry's fight for survival under colonialism and gradual movement towards the independent consciousness represented by Ti-Jean's stance. Thus, while Gros Jean represents an adversarial stance towards colonial subjugation and can be identified both with the leaders of slave revolts and with artists espousing an oppositional attitude towards European aspects of Caribbean culture, and Mi-Jean the acculturation and psychological brainwashing of Eurocentric Caribbean intellectuals, Ti-Jean embodies a set of common-sense folk values which have not been compromised by colonial domination. However, the play does not simply celebrate the folk tradition and the Devil is also identified with Papa Bois (Father Forest), a traditional St. Lucian figure, representative of folk wisdom. If on a general level this implies the relativism of moral judgements and the fact that no culture has a monopoly of virtue, on a more specific level it suggests that an ossified folk tradition exercises a stulti-fying influence on the Caribbean imagination. In the final speech of the play, the Frog who has a choric role in the work, says:

> And so it was that Ti-Jean, a fool like all heroes, passed through the tangled opinions of this life, loosening the rotting faggots of knowledge from old men to bear them safely on his shoulder. (*DMM*, 166)

Like the Guyanese novelist Wilson Harris and Edward Kamau Brathwaite, Walcott suggests the need for myth to be regenerated if it is to have valency in contemporary situations. '[R]otting faggots of knowledge' have to be creatively transformed into something new, which will facilitate the birth of a post-colonial consciousness rather than inhibit personal growth. Ti-Jean is the personification of such a new mentality, but more significantly the whole play enacts a revisionist mythography. Read on another level of allegory, it is again a metatheatrical piece, concerned like so much of Walcott's work with the problem of fashioning a Caribbean dramatic practice, and beyond this a Caribbean cultural tradition more generally.

The Prologue to *Ti-Jean*, which provides a framework for the subsequent action, immediately foregrounds the extent to which the play is a reworking of a pre-existing legend and establishes a cross-cultural ambience. The curtain rises on four forest creatures and the impoverished mother of the three brothers. Two of the creatures begin a dialogue and their words make it clear that they will offer choric commentary on the action:

> *Frog.*   Greek-croak, Greek-croak.
> *Cricket.*   Greek-croak, Greek-croak.
> > [*The others join*]
> *Frog* [Sneezing].   Aeschylus me!
> > And all that rain and no moon tonight.
> *Cricket.*   The moon always there even fighting the rain
> > Creek-crak, it is cold, but the moon always there
> > And Ti-Jean in the moon just like the story.
> > > (*DMM*, 85)

'Greek-croak, suggests the creatures have the same role as the chorus in a classical Greek play (and could be seen to allude more specifically to Aristophanes' *The Frogs*); and the punning rendition of the Frog's sneeze as 'Aeschylus me!' also suggests that classical texts may be uppermost. However, a local tradition is equally present from the outset: in the use of animal fable and in references which suggest a fusion of classical and Creole narrative modes. By the Cricket's second speech, the phrase 'Greek-croak' has given way to 'Creek-crak', a Caribbean storyteller's phrase, normally used in a call-and-response context to establish a dialogue between narrator and audience. So, while the very first utterances of the play establish a relationship with classical theatre, it is equally clear that the story is an outcrop of the folk tradition[53] and this proves to be the dominant influence as the play unravels, using a rich mixture of song, dance and mime and drawing on influences such as Brecht and the Japanese Noh theatre which Walcott had become better acquainted with in New York.

Another fascinating character in *Ti-Jean* is the Devil's associate, the Bolom, an unborn foetus[54] suggestive of multiple allegorical possibilities. When Ti-Jean eventually outwits the Devil and succeeds in getting him to display emotion, the Devil grants his wish that the Bolom be given life. It is a much more affirmative ending than in the majority of Walcott's earlier plays and one attractive reading of this birth is that it is that of a new Caribbean artistic consciousness which grasps the value of the folk heritage. At the same time the Devil himself becomes humanized and, like so many of Walcott's early dramatic prota-gonists, also seems to be escaping from Manichean definition. So, despite its apparent simplicity and its origins in folk fable, *Ti-Jean* proves to be Walcott's most complex play of the 1950s.

In 1957 Walcott's career received a major boost when he was commissioned to write an epic play to be performed at the arts festival held to mark the opening of the Federal West Indian Parliament in April 1958.[55] In his Foreword to the printed text of the play the director, Noel Vaz, describes the dilemma facing those[56] responsible for suggesting that it should be a centrepiece for the Federation celebrations:

> Should the piece be a history lesson told in a series of tableaux with commentary – a pageant, in fact, colourful and shifting …? Or might it be conceived as a dramatic text with a linked sequence, a saga told by a poet with concern and insight?[57]

After scripts by three other writers had been considered and rejected, Walcott was commissioned to write the play and, as a linked poetic saga informed by 'concern and insight', the work he produced, *Drums and Colours*, largely conformed to Vaz's second alternative, although one particular scene, offering a dramatized version of Millais's painting 'The Boyhood of Raleigh' *is* 'a tableau', at least in so far as it has its origins in the pictorial. Elsewhere, as Judy Stone has commented, 'movement took priority over the picture'.[58]

Walcott evolved a structure which shaped historical episodes spanning four centuries into a coherent narrative, made a degree of psychological complexity in some of the characters possible and outlined a position on Caribbean aesthetics and the development of the federal ideal. Nevertheless, the challenge of encapsulating four hundred and fifty years of the region's history into a single play must have been daunting for a writer who, as is clear from 'The Muse of History', has been distrustful both of the partisan tendencies of Caribbean historical narratives and of linear historiography more generally.

Writing some three years after *Drums and Colours*, V. S. Naipaul summarized the problems facing the West Indian historian in a notorious passage in *The Middle Passage* (1962):

> How shall the history of this West Indian futility be written? What tone shall the historian adopt? Shall he be as academic as Sir Alan Burns, protesting from time to time at some brutality, and setting West Indian brutality in the context of European brutality? ... Shall he like the West Indian historians who can only now begin to face their history, be icily detached and tell the story of the slave trade as if it were just another aspect of mercantilism? The history of the islands can never be satisfactorily told. Brutality is not the only problem. History is built around achievement and creation and nothing was created in the West Indies.[59]

In an interview Walcott's retort to the often-quoted final sentence of this passage was 'Perhaps it should read that "Nothing was created *by the British* in the West Indies"?'[60] Yet Naipaul's comments do at least point up some of the particular problems of 'tone' and positioning facing the Caribbean historian

– *and* the creative writer who engages with historiography. Given that there can be no 'pure' history, that *all* accounts of the past are inevitably ideologically constructed and discursively mediated,[61] writing the history of societies that have been colonized still presents particularly acute problems, since their 'official' discourse has traditionally been the prerogative of the colonial ruling class. A 'satisfactory' retelling of colonial history does not, however, simply involve producing narratives which make Caliban and not Prospero the agent of history and, in his most famous statement on the subject, 'The Muse of History', Walcott speaks of the inadequacy of both 'a literature of recrimination and despair, a literature of remorse written by the descendants of slaves [and] a literature of remorse written by the descendants of masters'.[62]

'The Muse of History' also offers a more radical critique of the distortions of imperialist historiography by taking the view that 'history' itself is a discipline which imposes a Western filter on events, because of its stress on linear, causological explanation, antipathetic to the frequently cyclic mythography of non-Western societies. Noting that 'the method by which we are taught the past, the progress from motive to event, is the same by [sic] which we read narrative fiction',[63] Walcott aligns himself with the patrician writers of the New World who 'reject the idea of history as time for its original concept as myth, the partial recall of the race'.[64]

In *Drums and Colours* the need to produce a version of history appropriate to the politics of Federation steered Walcott towards a consensual narrative in which, to borrow another phrase from 'The Muse of History', he endeavoured to 'assimilat[e] the features of every ancestor'.[65] While the chronology of the play appears at first sight to be more or less linear, the use of a contemporary frame and the fusing together of different historical moments involve a degree of refashioning history as myth. The play charts a progressive movement from 'Conquest' to 'Rebellion', but also suggests cyclic recurrences in dramatizing the corrosive force of the materialism and racial divisiveness that are seen to have characterized the evolution of

Caribbean society across the centuries, though here too the present appears to contain the potential for change: for a non-exploitative economics and a multi-racial community.

The events of *Drums and Colours* focus on four main historical experiences: Columbus's 'discovery'; Raleigh's quest for El Dorado; the Haitian Revolution; and Emancipation and its aftermath. In the last case time is foreshortened and Jamaica's 1865 Morant Bay rebellion is relocated in the 1830s, the decade of Emancipation. The 'Sixty-Five' uprising had already been treated by the Jamaican writers V. S. Reid and Roger Mais,[66] both of whom had used it as a focus for commenting on contemporary political developments. In the Prologue to *Drums and Colours* the Chorus speaks of showing 'the lives of four litigious men' (*DC*, 4) and several commentators on the play have been content to see it as dealing with its four obvious historical protagonists – Columbus, Raleigh, Toussaint L'Ouverture and George William Gordon, an advocate of constitutional change who was executed in the aftermath of the Morant Bay rebellion – sometimes adding a fifth 'hero', Pompey, a black shoemaker of Walcott's own creation.[67] However, Walcott's play replaces a view of history centred on the lives of great men with a *people's* history well suited to the nationalist and federalist mood of its period. In a very explicit statement of the play's intent Gordon is made to say:

> The potential of a country is the mass of its people
> That torrent may be poisoned by the discolouring intellect
> Of ambitious conquerors, and the blame is theirs. (*DC*, 83)

Elsewhere the stress on a people's history and future 'potential' is more subtly conveyed. Each of the episodes introduces ordinary Caribbean personages, fictional characters who displace the 'heroes' from centre-stage and in so doing contribute to the formulation of a different kind of historical narrative. The main figure in the Columbus sections is the mestizo (part-Spanish, part-Taino Indian) Paco and Columbus himself becomes a bit-player in his own tragedy, albeit one who expresses his now-tainted vision of the New World in moving poetry. Similarly, in the nineteenth-century Jamaican episodes, Gordon appears in just one short scene and the main character is Pompey whose instatement as protagonist effectively defines notions of what constitutes a hero.

In addition to the four historical episodes, *Drums and Colours* employs a contemporary framing action, a device which Walcott also introduces in *Ti-Jean and His Brothers* and *The Joker of Seville* and through which it becomes clear that he is reworking pre-existing material. The contemporary action of *Drums and Colours* is set in Trinidad at the time of Carnival and from the opening stage direction it is clear that the Carnival frame is intended to create a non-Eurocentric context: 'The stage is set with a centrepiece of regimental and African drums, with the flags of Britain, France, Spain and Holland'. A group of masqueraders, led by a character called Mano, decide to 'change round the Carnival' (*DC*, 3), re-enacting scenes from Caribbean history. The choice of Carnival for the frame is complemented by the incorporation of song and dance elements from what is perhaps the most vibrant form of folk theatre in the anglophone Caribbean and one which Walcott would subsequently return to repeatedly in his quest for an indigenous theatrical practice. Setting the action within the context of Carnival is also highly appropriate in another sense: the festival evolved from the ex-slaves' appropriation of French planters' fêtes to celebrate Emancipation,[68] and so it provides an excellent correlative for an alternative historiography in which creolization replaces Eurocentricity.

Drums and Colours also stresses the multi-racial nature of Carnival and in so doing promotes federalism not only as a union of nations, but also as an ideal of inter-racial harmony. Within the particular historical actions racially-mixed characters are prominent: Paco in the Columbus section, a mulatto named Anton in the Haitian scenes and Gordon rather than the black leader, Paul Bogle, in the Morant Bay episodes. Anton is the most fully developed character in the play, an ironist who sees life as theatre and feels his ethnic make-up extends into all aspects of his existence, obliging him to play a double role: 'I am myself a division, / By the fact that I am half African and French,

I must become both spectator and victim. It is amusing' (DC, 64). Elsewhere in the Haitian sections Henri Christophe complains against the butchering of mulattoes. However, lest this concern with the fortunes of ethnically mixed characters suggests special pleading on Walcott's part for his own racial group, or at least his sense of the dialogic psychic identity of the racially mixed, it should be added that Anton also sees Toussaint, a former coachman for his family, as a split protagonist: 'I have seen his black face tormented with division / Between duty to his people and the love of our family' (DC, 65). So psychic duality or multiplicity is seen as an aspect of Caribbean subjectivity which cuts across racial difference. In the historical episodes it leads to tragedy, but in the 'potential' of the federal future it offers the promise of a transformation of consciousness. When Pompey is apparently killed towards the end, Mano, who has become the Maroon leader of the inter-racial group he has joined in the mountains, prefaces an ecumenical funeral oration with a comment on his religion, saying 'Pompey was an every-thingist, now he is a nowherian' (DC, 98). Such a frustration of categorization opens up the possibility of creative metamorphosis.

The scene takes place in a space beyond the confines of colonial society where Mano and his group are forging a micro-cosm of the kind of inter-racial harmony to be found in the Carnival frame and which the play associates with the ideal of federalism; and this theme is even enacted in their creation of a culinary dish, calaloo, made from the various ancestral strands that they represent. Locating these key scenes in a Maroon encampment, and amid Carnival's suspension of normal hier-archies, effectively moves the play beyond the divisions of the earlier historical episodes. The carnivalization of history and the attempt to produce a play that transcends received generic conventions – at the outset the masqueraders decide to wear the masks of both tragedy and comedy – represent a significant step forward in Walcott's endeavour to achieve a hybridized theatrical practice appropriate to the region. At the very end nineteenth- and twentieth-century actions are collapsed together and the moment of Emancipation becomes that of Federation. Pompey, who has been killed in the nineteenth-century action, is resurrected and with him the possibility of regeneration through the multi-cultural ideal of Carnival.

In the late 1950s Walcott wrote two more one-act plays, the unpublished *Joumard* (1959), a comedy about 'wily destitutes attempting to raise drinking money on Easter Sunday by preaching around a spurious corpse',[69] and the better-known *Malcochon, or Six in the Rain* (1959),[70] a spare moral fable about guilt and responsibility.

The plot of *Malcochon* is once again extremely simple: six fugitives from a storm – a husband and wife, an old man and his 'nephew', a thief and a deaf-mute (or 'Moumou') – shelter together in a disused copra hut in the forest. The husband believes his wife has committed adultery with an overseer; the nephew blames the old man for his father's, the old man's brother's, death, since he has been hanged for murdering his wife after she was unfaithful with the old man. The thief, Chantal, is a figure who has been demonized by society and the nephew recalls, 'In the old days they used to frighten us as children / About Chantal the woodcutter and madman of the forest' (*DMM*, 181).

The action is again introduced by a Conteur (or storyteller) and musicians and, as in *Ti-Jean* and in major later Walcott plays such as *Dream on Monkey Mountain* and *The Joker of Seville*, there is the sense of a well-known tale being retold. Here the received story is that of how 'Chantal the brute / Took the white planter Regis' life' (*DMM*, 171). So there are three separate strands of criminal or 'sinful' behaviour coursing through the play and the six characters' coming together in the forest shed seems to suggest an elemental moral reckoning beyond society's laws. As the old man puts it:

> In the life of man, all his darkness, all his sins
> Can meet in one place, in the middle of a forest. Like a
>   beast. Yes,
> Like to meet a beast with no name in the track of the
>   bamboo.   (*DMM*, 180)

In this environment the pariah Chantal assumes the role of confessor and judge and in a mock trial absolves both the errant wife and the old man of their sins. Meanwhile the body of the planter Regis has been washed down the hillside and the question of where blame for his murder lies remains unanswered. Interestingly, two critics who provide narrative summaries of the play's action differ on what has actually happened. Theodore Colson states that it is Moumou who has killed Regis,[71] while Robert Hamner takes the view that Chantal 'killed Regis in defending Moumou'.[72] In fact the issue is left open and this is central to the play's message. Its Sophoclean epigraph asks 'Who is the slayer, who the victim?' (*DMM*, 167) and this is reiterated by Chantal towards the end when he asks, 'Who is the murderer, who the dead …?' (*DMM*, 203). Finally *Malcochon* has at least as much in common with the ethic of the final part of a Greek trilogy,[73] in which there is a movement beyond a cycle of crime and punishment, as Kurosawa's moral relativism.[74] The play not only dramatizes a movement beyond legalistic definitions of guilt and innocence, but also undermines the stereotyping that places a figure like Chantal beyond the social pale by demonizing him as a 'beast' and 'madman'. Like the sea at Dauphin, the forest of the play is an environment in which Manichean divisions cease to obtain. The old man refuses to leave the dying Chantal, saying 'You are my brother. You are not the beast and the madman' (*DMM*, 204) and this assertion of fraternity is parallelled by a comment on the human condition made by the Conteur:

> Like the staining of clear springs the mind of man,
> In blood he must end as in blood he began
> Like mist that rises from a muddy stream
> Between beasthood and Godhead groping in a dream.
>
> (*DMM*, 205)

While on one level this is a poetic version of classic thinking on humanity's position in the chain of being, in a post-colonial context it has the effect of further eroding the Manichean binaries that have placed Chantal beyond the social pale.

During the 1960s Walcott was heavily engaged in theatre, developing the skills and repertory of the Trinidad Theatre Workshop which he had founded in 1959. He wrote fewer new plays, but the decade saw the premiere of his finest play thus far – and arguably the finest Caribbean play to have been produced to date – *Dream on Monkey Mountain* (1967), a work which follows *Ti-Jean and His Brothers* in exploring the nature of Caribbean cultural identity by fusing together a broad range of cultural intertexts. During the first part of the decade Walcott was also acting as Arts Reviewer for the *Trinidad Guardian* and wrote numerous articles on theatre which, taken together, come to constitute a manifesto for the establishment of a National Theatre in Trinidad and more generally for a West Indian drama rooted in the local experience.[75] *Dream on Monkey Mountain* can be seen as a manifestation of these ideas in practice; like *Ti-Jean* it is a metatheatrical piece enacting Walcott's ideas on what Caribbean theatre should be. At the same time it is far more than this. It is also Walcott's most sustained and probing dramatic investigation of Caribbean origins, specifically the region's relationships with Africa and Europe.

Its dramatic mode is far more complex than that of *Ti-Jean*. Walcott's 'Note on Production' says that 'The play is a dream, one that exists as much in the given minds of its principal characters as in that of its writer' (*DMM*, 208). Initially this psychodrama seems to be located within the consciousness of the play's central character Makak, but, as the note indicates, it is intended to be a product of the collective consciousness of all the characters. Together, as the epigraphs to the two parts (taken from Sartre's Prologue to Fanon's *Wretched of the Earth*) indicate, they represent the dissociated Caribbean psyche, pulled two ways by the cultural schizophrenia instilled by colonialism.

Once again the form leans heavily on ritual and symbolic elements. The play opens with an elaborate mime in which setting, lighting, movement, dance and song are combined to initiate its main themes. This mime gives way to a call-and-response lament sung by a Conteur and chorus, which introduces the audience to the black charcoal-burner Makak, who has been jailed for being drunk and disorderly. Thus, before the narrative action begins, the drama has been located first in a non-verbal and then in an oral folk context. This opening scene is, along with the Epilogue, the most naturalistic in the play, but even here there are strong symbolic elements. Makak's situation in jail can be seen as a metaphor for the mental situation induced by the colonial psychology, and a mock trial conducted by the Corporal who is his jailer and two fellow-prisoners (suggestive of the two thieves crucified with Christ) parodies Jesus's appearance before Pilate and thus establishes Makak as some kind of Messiah figure.

As the action unravels, there are numerous other elements which are dependent on masquerade, music and mime for their effect: among them a *burroquite* or 'donkey dance' (*DMM*, 242),[76] singing and dancing by a religious sisterhood (*DMM*, 243), an impromptu dance which includes the singing of a bongo and a healing mime (*DMM*, 262–4) and a final song about homecoming (*DMM*, 326). And performance, particularly mime, is in one sense the subject of *Dream on Monkey Mountain*, since it is about the powerful effects of colonial brainwashing, which encourages the complicity of European mimesis in one kind of colonial subject and an adversarial rejection of such influence in favour of the equally problematic notion of a return to 'pure' African ancestral roots in another. Both responses are psychologically damaging, because they involve a repression of the hybridized reality of the Caribbean situation. As Sartre puts it, in the passage from his Introduction to Fanon's *Wretched of the Earth* which Walcott quotes as the epigraph to the second part of the play, 'The status of "native" is a nervous condition introduced and maintained by the settler among colonised people with their consent' (*DMM*, 277). Makak is a classic example of such 'nervousness', but he is not the only character in the play to suffer from the syndrome.

The long central section deserts any semblance of naturalism for the expressionist structure of the 'dream'. Initially the dream seems to be Makak's vision of a White Goddess figure who instils in him a belief that he must act as a racial redeemer by leading his people back to Africa. The paradox of being impelled

towards Africa by a European Muse again seems to suggest the
Manichean binaries that Walcott sees as characteristic of the
schizophrenic colonial psyche, and the Fanon epigraph to Part
Two sees the colonial subject as the product of 'two bewitchings'
(DMM, 277), but the play itself both proposes an aesthetic and a
view of Caribbean identity which move beyond this. Makak
descends from Monkey Mountain, performs acts of healing and
acquires a reputation as a messianic deliverer. He is imprisoned,
escapes from jail after wounding the Corporal and returns to the
mountain in the company of his two fellow-prisoners. He now
appears deranged and with the two felons humouring his 'mad-
ness' and Makak deciding he has been a 'king among shadows'
(DMM, 304), this episode seems strongly redolent of the scenes
on the heath in King Lear. It ends with the comic 'Apotheosis' of
Makak as an African chieftain.

In the Apotheosis scene (Part II, Scene 3), the dream reaches
its climax in a riot of parody and pantomime. The scene
functions as a kind of dream-within-the-dream and since it has
been initiated by the Corporal, Lestrade, at the end of the previous scene, it may seem to be primarily the product of his mind.
It is, however, introduced by the Chorus and so, like the whole
of the central section, is best viewed as a collective fantasy. In
this scene the Chorus is called 'the tribes' and seems to take on a
communal African identity. It sings a 'chant of a tribal triumph'
(DMM, 308) and functions like the praise-singers of West
African societies. Some of the detail is drawn from specific
African traditions – thus a reference to a 'golden stool' (DMM,
309) alludes to the central symbol of the Ashanti nation[77] – but
much of it is more generalized parody of African atavism.
Earlier in the play Walcott has mocked Caribbean mimicry of
European standards; here he pokes fun at 'back to Africa' movements. This is particularly apparent in the portrayal of Lestrade
who develops from being a staunch defender of 'Roman law' and
becomes an advocate of 'tribal law' (DMM, 311).

At Lestrade's instigation, prisoners are brought before
Makak in a fantasy of black revenge. They include such disparate
figures as Sir Francis Drake, Mandrake the Magician, Sir Cecil

Rhodes and Al Jolson. Their common crime is said to be their whiteness, but in some cases it is more specific. Drake and Rhodes were archetypal imperialists; the comic-strip hero Mandrake has a black servant, Lothar; Al Jolson performed in black-face. In fact, all the prisoners appear to be people who have in some way contributed to the repression of blacks, either by exploiting them economically, appropriating their culture or excluding them from official versions of history. 'Tribal law' quickly condemns them to be hanged.

Next a comic catalogue of tributes is brought before Makak. These include 'An offer to revise the origins of slavery. A floral tribute of lilies from the Ku Klux Klan. ... An offer from Hollywood' (*DMM*, 313–14), but all these tokens of restitution from the white world are summarily rejected by the tribes. At this point black intransigence will allow only an adversarial response which, like the negritudinist position, is as an expression of the other side of the Manichean binaries constructed by colonialism. The adoption of such a stance leaves the colonized subject still being determined by a colonial discourse of alterity, even though an about-face has occurred. Makak's friend, Moustique, tells him he is in danger of replacing his former love for the white moon with a deep hatred which will require its destruction and this proves prophetic.

Lestrade urges Makak to behead the apparition of the White Goddess in a powerful poetic passage which sums up the injurious effects of European cultural conditioning, while also suggesting that its power is dependent on the colonial subject's own complicity:

> She is lime, snow, marble, moonlight, lilies, cloud, foam and bleaching cream, the mother of civilization and the confounder of blackness. I too have longed for her. She is the colour of the law, religion, paper, art, and if you want peace, if you want to discuss the beautiful depth of your blackness, nigger, chop off her head! When you do this, you will kill Venus, the Virgin, the Sleeping Beauty. She is the white light that paralysed your mind, that led you into confusion. It is you who created her, so kill her! kill her! The law has spoken. (*DMM*, 319)

Makak is finally persuaded and the scene ends with his beheading the apparition. In so doing he clearly exorcises the stranglehold which the European side of his heritage has appeared to have on him. However, since the Goddess has been responsible for initiating his African dream, the beheading also involves a repudiation of Afrocentric cultural essentialism. This is confirmed by the fact that immediately before he takes the action, Makak removes the African robe in which he has been dressed during the Apotheosis scene. Thus the twin 'bewitchings' of Europe and Africa are rejected simultaneously.

In the Epilogue Makak awakens from his dream to find himself still in prison. Hitherto he has been called only Makak ('Monkey'), but now he moves beyond being a colonial mimic, aping European or supposed African modes of behaviour (which are themselves European inventions and correspond to the negative side of the binary oppositions identified by JanMohamed[78]) and is given an individual name, Felix Hobain. The play ends with his realizing:

> Lord, I have been washed from shore to shore, as a tree in the ocean. The branches of my fingers, the roots of my feet, could grip nothing, but now, God, they have found ground
> …
> now this old hermit is going back home, back to the beginning, to the green beginning of this world. (*DMM*, 326)

The image of the uprooted tree washed across the ocean suggests the legacy of the Middle Passage.[79] However, the conclusion clearly argues against a return to Africa. 'Home' for Makak is the Caribbean landscape of his more immediate 'origins' and it is now viewed as a place of Edenic promise offering a fresh start. This notion is in keeping with the belief, central to all Walcott's later work and expressed particularly forcefully in 'The Muse of History', that historical determinism must be rejected in favour of an aesthetic in which the New World artist creates the Americas anew through an Adamic vision. As in *Ti-Jean*, the quest for a Caribbean aesthetic is enacted on the level of form as well as theme. On this level, the beheading of the White Goddess mainly signifies emancipation from a European Muse and the play as a whole is again uncompromisingly committed to the evolution of a distinctive Caribbean theatrical practice.

Although Makak is the central figure in *Dream on Monkey Mountain*, the search for identity is also played out in the minds of other characters. Moustique acts as a Sancho Panza to Makak's Don Quixote and is as much a pragmatist as he is an idealist. When in the central scenes he exploits Makak's messianic appeal by pretending to be him, it suggests an alternative version of the same quest, itself highly ambivalent since he may be regarded as either a cynical opportunist who sells the dream or a more creative trickster-figure – like Ti-Jean or like Anansi, the spiderman hero of many Afro-Caribbean children's stories[80] – who justifiably makes the most of the material possibilities it affords.

Corporal Lestrade, who begins as a vivid study of the negative aspects of cultural schizophrenia, provides another foil to Makak. Named after the bumbling Scotland Yard inspector of the Sherlock Holmes stories,[81] he is a racially mixed character who initially appears as a staunch defender of the colonial order. He separates himself off from the island's blacks, viewing them as existing on a lower evolutionary plane than himself:

> In the beginning was the ape, and the ape had no name, so God call him man. Now there were various tribes of the ape, it had gorilla, baboon, orang-outan, chimpanzee, the blue-arsed monkey and the marmoset, and God looked at his handiwork, and saw that it was good. For some of the apes had straighten their backbone, and start walking upright, but there was one tribe unfortunately that lingered behind, and that was the nigger. Now if you apes will behave like gentlemen, who knows what could happen? The bottle could go round, but first it behoves me, Corporal Lestrade, to perform my duty according to the rules of Her Majesty's Government, so don't interrupt. … (*DMM*, 216–17).

In its equation of blackness, animality and savagery, such language can again be related to the rhetoric of racial Manicheism, but as a mulatto Lestrade himself represents a challenge to such binaries, since he embodies both sides of the supposed ethnic divide. Ultimately his inner struggle is as central to the play as Makak's – as in *Henri Christophe* the central protagonist is black, but the mulatto predicament is also important and expressive of the cultural dilemma enacted by the play as a whole – and in repudiating blackness, Lestrade is rejecting half of himself. However, during the course of the dream he performs a complete about-face and in a moment typical of shifts in Caribbean attitudes around the time of Independence appears to replace his Eurocentric perspective with an Afrocentric one. Finally it is Lestrade who persuades Makak to behead the White Goddess and this act of symbolic emancipation frees both men from their roles as mimics, liberating them into an emergent Caribbean consciousness and enabling them to escape from the strait-jacket of being constructed as 'others'. The beheading of the Goddess is as clear a movement forward into a post-colonial consciousness and a view of identity which acknowledges hybridization as the birth of the Bolom at the end of *Ti-Jean*.

At the end of *Dream on Monkey Mountain* Lestrade re-emerges as the colonial administrator he was at the outset. This could support the view that the dream has been Makak's after all, but in the latter half of Part Two Lestrade is centre-stage, and the action seems to emanate primarily from *his* mind. So ultimately he stands alongside Makak as another powerful study of split consciousness. The suggestion is that the coming to terms with hybrid origins is an issue of relevance for all Caribbean people irrespective of their ethnic make-up, and again it is mirrored in the complex cultural provenance of the play and its 'dream' of a future in which the emphasis is on the Caribbean present, not an impossible attempt to retrieve a supposedly homogeneous ancestral past. Ultimately all the characters exorcise the inhibiting legacy of such cultural essentialism and the play frustrates the possibility of discovering such authenticity. Henceforth in Walcott's drama, even in plays such as *The Joker of Seville* and *The Odyssey* which take their departure-points from Europe, the emphasis is firmly on the creolization of all cultures.

The poet as castaway

WHILE Walcott's plays from *Ti-Jean and His Brothers* onwards demonstrate an increasing engagement with folk forms and community values, his poetry of the 1960s and early 1970s remains very much that of an individual, isolated observer. Such a figure is the central protagonist in his next collection, *The Castaway* (1965), where three poems, 'The Castaway', 'Crusoe's Journal' and 'Crusoe's Island', are focused on the character that gives the volume its title, while others are filtered through a persona who is also cast away in the sense that he seems to see life as an onlooker. Whether in the Caribbean:

> In our treacherous
> seasonless climate's
> dry heat or muggy heat or rain
> I'm measuring winter by this November sun's
> diagonals shafting the window pane ... ('November Sun')[1]

or in North America:

> Through the wide, grey loft window,
> I watched that winter morning, my first snow
> crusting the sill, puzzle the black,
> nuzzling tom. ('A Village Life', *Castaway*, 16)

this figure repeatedly appears as a man alone in a room, looking at the world through a window. The emphasis on perception frequently leads to reflections on themes that had dominated Walcott's earlier work. Shafts of Caribbean sunlight and American snowfalls both bring intimations of mortality; a meditation on

Othello (in 'Goats and Monkeys') rekindles the mood of racial angst and the tussle with Manichean binaries that had been so prominent in the early plays; and, while the verse now sometimes incorporates intertexts from the growing body of Caribbean literature,[2] there is the continued wrestling-match with European discourses, confirming the writer's own assessment of himself as someone who is '[s]chizophrenic, wrenched by two styles' ('Codicil', *Castaway*, 61).

The use of the Crusoe figure foregrounds the struggle to construct a tradition. Along with texts such as *The Tempest* and *Heart of Darkness*, *Robinson Crusoe* is one of a group of canonical English texts which deal with colonialism explicitly and in a Caribbean context the decision to take such texts as departure-points inevitably raises expectations that the resultant 'counter-discourse' will contest the hegemonic authority of the English master-narratives that provide its supposed sources. One might therefore expect a Caribbean reworking of Defoe's archetypal imperialist to adopt an adversarial response, but predictably perhaps Walcott's Crusoe proves to be far more complex. In a talk he gave on 'The Figure of Crusoe' in 1965, Walcott offered a reading of the character in which he is simultaneously Adam, Columbus, God, Ben Gunn, Prospero, a missionary who instructs Friday and a beachcomber from Conrad, Stevenson or Marryat;[3] and ultimately his Crusoe is Proteus, constantly changing his shape to a point where he is as much Caliban as Prospero, as much Friday as Defoe's prototypical colonizer, as much 'the distorted, surrealist Crusoe of Bunuel'[4] as that of Defoe. In the talk, the figure of Crusoe emerges as both a Caribbean Everyman and more specifically as a type of the Caribbean writer, constructing a discursive universe from an apparent vacuum, and the shipwrecked protagonists of *The Castaway*, particularly 'Crusoe's Journal', are very similar in conception. 'Crusoe's Journal' also takes the view that 'All shapes, all objects multiplied from his, / our ocean's Proteus (*Castaway*, 51). So, instead of contrasting or inverting the assumed hierarchies of the colonial text, Walcott creates a multiplicity of Crusoes who collectively dismantle the very idea of hierarchical positioning.

In 'Crusoe's Journal' Walcott begins by stressing the pragmatism of Defoe's text:

> even the bare necessities
> of style are turned to use,
> like those plain tools he salvages
> from shipwreck, hewing a prose
> as odorous as raw wood to the adze. (*Castaway*, 51)

Defoe and Crusoe are, then, seen as giving practical expression to 'Adam's task of giving things their names',[5] the role which Walcott had taken upon himself as an artist committed to making the St. Lucian landscape possible. Walcott also identified with the plain carpentry of Defoe's prose style for another reason. Talking about the influence of his Methodist upbringing in a 1986 interview, he says:

> Decency and understanding are what I've learned from being a Methodist. Always, one was responsible to God for one's inner conduct and not to any immense hierarchy of angels and saints. In a way I think I tried to say that in some earlier poems. There's also a very strong sense of carpentry in Protestantism, in making things simply and in a utilitarian way.[6]

Elsewhere in the same interview, he talks of 'the metaphor of the shipwreck' as '[o]ne of the more positive aspects of the Crusoe idea', saying that because all the races that have come to the region have 'been brought here under situations of servitude or rejection … you look around you and you have to make your own tools',[7] a view which suggests the relevance of Defoe's Protestant ethic in Caribbean contexts.

As 'Crusoe's Journal' continues, irony is directed at the castaway figure when he is seen as a Columbus turning 'savages' into 'good Fridays', 'converted cannibals [who] learn with him to eat the flesh of Christ' (*Castaway*, 51), but this is only temporary and the poem subsequently returns to the trope of the artist as castaway, using the model of Crusoe's journals to create from a vacuum: 'We learn to shape from them, where nothing was / The language of a race' (*Castaway*, 52). So what might seem to be a private solipsistic vision comes to assume a communal significance.

In the other poems in the collection that focus explicitly on the figure of the castaway, the emphasis is more on the marooned predicament of the Caribbean artist. In 'The Castaway' his 'starved eye devours the seascape for the morsel / Of a sail' (*Castaway*, 9). In 'Crusoe's Island' he is a fallen Adam, '[c]razed' by the 'paradisal calm' (*Castaway*, 55) of his solitary situation, who seems to despair as he reflects on his inability to return to the purity of his youth or to produce a transfigurative art which will bless the local world, here personified by black girls on a Tobago beach.

'The Almond Trees' uses the image of women on a Caribbean beach in a more sustained way to provide commentary on the evolution of the region's culture and society. The poem opens with an allusion to Naipaul's *Middle Passage* comment on Caribbean history, 'History is built around achievement and creation and nothing was created in the West Indies',[8] which makes it clear that history is the subject of the poem:

> There's nothing here
> this early;
> cold sand
> cold churning ocean, the Atlantic,
> no visible history,
>
> except this stand
> of twisted, coppery sea-almond trees. (*Castaway*, 36)

The trees, then, are the Caribbean alternative to history. As the poem proceeds, they are likened to 'brown daphnes' sunbathing on 'this further shore of Africa' (*Castaway*, 36), personification which draws on Greek myths of wood-nymphs and more specifically the legend that Daphne, pursued by Apollo, was turned into a tree. If the women initially seem to be tourists 'toasting their flesh' in 'fierce, acetylene air' which will 'sear a pale skin copper' (*Castaway*, 36–7), as the poem progresses it becomes clear that something else is intended. The 'Almond Trees' charts the movement of Caribbean society since colonization, suggesting that a gradual darkening process has taken place. Trees and women endure a furnace which seems to be the crucible of Caribbean history. Divested of identity by the experience of the Middle Passage and slavery, the women have had 'Greek or Roman tags', slave names analogous to the Latin botanical names used for trees conferred on them, but have nevertheless become '[w]elded in one flame' (*Castaway*, 37). The suggestion is that through suffering, and *pace* Naipaul, the traumas of the Middle Passage and slavery have been transformed into a history of endurance and cultural pride. Walcott does not here, as in 'The Muse of History', wipe the cultural slate clean. Instead he suggests a coming to terms with Caribbean history, which once again will obliterate hurt:

> One sunburnt body now acknowledges
> that past and its own metamorphosis
> as, moving from the sun, she kneels to spread
> her wrap within the bent arms of this grove
> that grieves in silence, like parental love. (*Castaway*, 37)

Other poems in *The Castaway* also survey the Caribbean past from a present vantage point. In 'Laventville', the view is from the hill on the east side of Port of Spain,[9] where the city's poorer districts are located. The poet looks down 'on the hot, corrugated iron sea / whose horrors we all / shared' (*Castaway*, 33) and reflects that little has changed in the situation of 'the inheritors of the middle passage', who now find themselves 'stewed / five to a room, still clamped below their hatch, / breeding like felonies' (*Castaway*, 32). Despite having been 'rescued from original sin' (*Castaway*, 34) by Christianity, they remain typical Walcott protagonists in that they are caught between worlds: 'We left / somewhere a life we never found' (*Castaway*, 35). In 'Veranda' Walcott turns to the opposite end of the Caribbean social spectrum for the vantage point, for a poem about the end of Empire[10] which provides an interesting companion-piece to 'Ruins of a Great House'. As in the earlier poem and as in 'A Far Cry from Africa', 'Veranda' initially adopts a critical attitude towards Empire, in this case treating its various 'grey apparitions' with punning irony rather than overt hostility:

Colonels, hard as the commonwealth's greenheart,
middlemen, usurers whose art
kept an empire in the red,

Upholders of Victoria's china seas ...

To the tarantara of the bugler, the sunset furled
round the last post. (*Castaway*, 38)

Again, however, as in 'Ruins of a Great House' and 'A Far Cry from Africa', this mood is replaced by a gentler, more elegiac tone and an overriding compassion. As in 'Laventville', the poet contemplates a sea crossing which seems to be both the Middle Passage and the process of living itself and this collapsing together of historical and existential conditions has the effect of breaking down the distance between colonizer and colonized. Midway through the poem Walcott again introduces an 'I' persona who invokes the ghost of a white grandfather in a spirit of tenderness which has a healing effect. Although, as in 'The Almond Trees', burning is the central metaphor for the passage of Caribbean history, the 'I' protagonist finds beauty in the house which represents the survival of this strain of his – and the Caribbean's – ancestry:

Your house has voices, your burnt house,
shrills with unguessed, lovely inheritors,
your genealogical roof tree, fallen, survives,
like seasoned timber through green, little lives.

(*Castaway*,39)

While *The Castaway* continues to explore many of the same concerns as Walcott's earlier verse, its poems, although still highly personal at times, generally have external correlatives, such as shared social concerns. The result is a movement away from the often cryptic subjectivity of his 'apprenticeship' period, which had continued to characterize several of the poems in *In a Green Night*, towards verse which is generally both more accessible and more powerful.

After the publication of *The Castaway*, Walcott seems to have, at least temporarily, lost interest in the Crusoe figure. In 1968 he told the Jamaican writer Dennis Scott, 'two, three years ago I was attracted to the Robinson Crusoe idea … but I am not interested in that idea anymore'.[11] The controlling image of his next collection was, however, again indicated by its title, *The Gulf*, a signifier which also has multiple resonances. In the title-poem the gulf is most obviously the Gulf of Mexico – the poet is on a flight above Texas – and Gulf gas-stations are also mentioned, but more generally the poem discusses the social divides that are threatening an impending apocalypse in the United States of the 1960s:

> The Gulf, your gulf, is daily widening.
>
> each blood-red rose warns of that coming night
> when there's no rock cleft to go hidin' in
> and all the rocks catch fire …[12]

and then moves beyond this to suggest the more general sense of psychological displacement felt by a poet who feels he has 'no home' (*Gulf*, 29) as long as religious and racial divisions promote a clamour for revenge.

American experience is equally important in a number of other poems in the volume. 'Blues', an untypically direct piece, describes an inter-racial encounter in which the poet sees himself as being beaten 'black and blue' because of his in-between situation, here specifically his skin-colour; 'not too bright / for a nigger, and not too dark' (*Gulf*, 34). The ostensible occasion for 'Elegy' is the assassination of Robert Kennedy, but more generally it is a lament for America and Walcott reflects on the contemporary social inequalities in the country:

> Still, everybody wants to go to bed
> with Miss America. And if there's no bread,
> let them eat cherry pie. (*Gulf*, 31)

and the impossibility of a Natty-Bumppo-like retreat from the collective cover-up of the dark side of the American Dream:

> the old choice of running, howling, wounded
> wolf-deep in her woods,
> while the white papers snow on
> genocide is gone. (*Gulf*, 31)

The poem echoes another classic elegy, Whitman's lament for Abraham Lincoln, 'When Lilacs Last in the Dooryard Bloomed', before suggesting how contemporary media images of dead Native Americans and Puritan settlers construct binaries that perpetuate violence:

> the cherry orchard's surf
> blinds Washington and whispers
> to the assassin in his furnished room
> of an ideal America, whose flickering screens
> show, in slow herds, the ghosts of the Cheyennes
> scuffling across the staked and wired plains
> with whispering, rag-bound feet,
>
> while the farm couple framed in their Gothic door
> like Calvin's saints, waspish, pragmatic, poor,
> gripping the devil's pitchfork
> stare rigidly towards the immortal wheat. (*Gulf*, 31)[13]

The implications would seem to be that the contemporary assassin is a product of the gulf dividing contemporary American society, a situation which belies the ideals on which the nation was founded, but the poem also questions whether these ideals *ever* really obtained.

In a sense this may seem to replicate the Manichean situation in which Walcott had felt he was growing up in colonial St. Lucia and which he had related to revolutionary Haiti; and 'Elegy' begins with a passage in which it is the Caribbean that is seen as existing in a gulf, as a 'hammock swung between Americas' (*Gulf*, 31). The range of references to the Americas as a whole is also extended by a parallel with the death of Che Guevara and the poem, like several others in the volume, charts a restless movement between 'north' and 'south',[14] an axis that becomes central in Walcott's later verse, particularly after he took up appointments in the United States. Throughout, *The Gulf* is notable for its emphasis on journeying which leaves the persona perennially between worlds. Its poems move between the Caribbean, America and England and it is the first Walcott collection in which the figure of the Odyssean traveller that dominates his later verse becomes a leading protagonist.[15]

So the stasis engrained in the trope of the Caribbean artist as a contemplative Crusoe is replaced by an emphasis on the constant movement and migrations of this travelling protagonist, and while this is most vividly expressed in the mid-air predicament of the title-poem, it is a situation which informs the whole of *The Gulf*.

In his 1968 interview with Dennis Scott, Walcott also spoke of his sense that his writing was becoming 'terrifyingly plain', saying that he now found himself 'writing so directly that I wish I were ... more "important" or complicated'.[16] However, although the language of *The Gulf* may be superficially simpler than his earlier poetry, it has lost nothing in metaphorical density. In fact, to an even greater extent than hitherto, metaphor becomes the subject of much of the poetry, since it is about transformations of one kind or another, a subject which is linguistically enacted through metaphor, the language of transformation. While some of the poems are again intensely personal, generalized metapoetic concerns are also very much to the fore. In 'Moon', a poem in an early sequence entitled 'Metamorphoses', the poet dons the role of Orpheus and envisages his body transformed first into a vowel and then a whole poem – and more generally the poem is about revitalizing a range of experience through a practice rooted in metaphorical transformation. Thus in 'Hawk' there is the same kind of analogy between the eponymous bird and human counterparts as one finds in Ted Hughes's *Hawk in the Rain* (1957), but the human counterparts occupying the role here are *both* Carib Indians and white planters and a further metamorphosis is anticipated at the end, where:

> Slaves yearn for their master's talons
> the spur and the cold, gold eyes,
> for the whips, whistling like wires, (*Gulf*, 16)

while an actual hawk circling in the sky over a Trinidadian beach is said to 'have no music' (*Gulf*, 17), as it were to exist (paradoxically, since the poem has transformed it through metaphor) in a world beyond poetry.

In 'Mass Man' the link between metaphor and transformation, this time in the context of carnival masquerading is
explicit:

> Through a great lion's head clouded by mange
> a black clerk growls.
> Next, a gold-wired peacock withholds a man,
> a fan, flaunting its oval, jewelled eyes,
> What metaphors!
> What coruscating, mincing fancies! (*Gulf*, 19)

although no opinion is given on whether such role-playing
contains real potential for change or whether it is mere escapism,
offering only temporary release. In 'Junta' the theme of Carnival
transformation is given another wry, metaphorical twist as a
masquerader who has won the title of Individual of the Year,
playing the role of the barbarian king Vercingetorix, turns his
talents to politics.

Ultimately, however, the transformations of *The Gulf* are
more concerned with the poet himself than with social issues.
'Mass Man' depicts a split persona, who can stand outside
himself even as he appears to be caught up in the frenzy of
Carnival:

> But I am dancing, look, from an old gibbet
> my bull-whipped body swings, a metronome!
> Like a fruit-bat dropped in the silk cotton's shade
> my mania, my mania is a terrible calm. (*Gulf*, 19)

and several other poems stage a similar conflict between active
involvement and the detachment of the onlooker. This two-way
movement relates to the theme of Odyssean wandering, as the
poet finds himself, for example in 'Homecoming: Anse La Raye',
torn between north and south, between exile and ambivalent
'homecomings without home' (*Gulf*, 51). The theme comes to a
head in the final poem 'Hic Jacet', which responds to the
question, asked in its opening line, 'why did you remain?'
(*Gulf*, 70). In a reference which is suggestive of a comparison
with V. S. Naipaul's attitude to the Caribbean, the poet says he
has stayed:

> Not to spite some winter-bitten novelist
> praised for his accuracy of phlegm,
> but for something rooted, unwritten
> that gave us its benediction,
> its particular pain. (*Gulf*, 70)

He commits himself to 'the power of provincialism' (*Gulf*, 70) and the poem concludes with his portraying himself seeking 'more power' (*Gulf*, 71) than the Caribbean's expatriate writers through this commitment – a goal which would be achieved by his creator, at least in one sense, when Walcott became a Nobel Laureate. In the closing lines of 'Hic Jacet' he achieves the volume's ultimate act of transformation, a quasi-spiritual 'second birth' (*Gulf*, 71) made possible by remaining within the region rather than becoming an exile. Although the poems of *The Gulf* wander more widely than Walcott's earlier verse and dramatize the sense of in-betweenness that characterizes all his responses to experience in a wider range of contexts, they remain rooted within a Caribbean world-view and, although they are major work in their own right, provide a fitting prolegomenon to *Another Life*, the work in which he has most fully fulfilled his vow to realize St. Lucia on the printed page.

As will be clear from the discussion above, there had been a strong autobiographical thrust in all Walcott's poetry thus far and this impulse came to a head in *Another Life* (1973), ostensibly a poetic autobiography of the same kind as Wordsworth's *Prelude* in that its central subject is the 'growth of a poet's mind'. However, while the poem is very personal in some respects, particularly in its treatment of an early love affair, and it is certainly about the development of the poet's artistic sensibility, it is again a work about the problem of tradition and its canvas expands to incorporate a consideration of Caribbean history and aesthetics more generally. Later, Walcott would subsume autobiographical elements into his epic poem *Omeros*, sometimes revisiting personal territory he had already mapped out in *Another Life*; here the movement is in the opposite direction, with autobiography incorporating history and epic, as Walcott relates the situation of the artist to the cultural life of the society at large. The main emphasis in the discussion which follows will, however, be on the way he uses the autobiographical form for a continuing exploration of the problem of constructing a Caribbean tradition.

Initially the main focus of *Another Life* is on the poet himself, represented as a 'divided child'[17] torn between the undocumented experiences of the St. Lucian landscape and the *other* life offered by European literature and art, but as the poem proceeds the growth of the individual artist's mind is located within the supposedly 'history-less' (*AL*, 76) predicament of the Caribbean and a more general response to the situation of the artist who is, at least potentially, 'growing up stupid under the Union Jack'.[18]

Another Life adopts an intertextual approach to auto-biography, devoting more space to examining Walcott's formative artistic influences than to attempting to provide a transcription of 'lived' experiences. Such an approach has much in common with the view of autobiography taken by post-Barthean 'death of the author' theorists. In Julia Kristeva's words: 'any text is constructed as a mosaic of quotations; any text is the absorption and transformation of another. The notion of intertextuality replaces that of intersubjectivity.'[19] While, in one sense, all Walcott's work could be seen to be moving towards such a view of textual production, *Another Life* involves a more comprehensive and searching account of his discursive formation than his other poetry and so particularly lends itself to such an intertextual reading.

From the outset the stress on the 'divided child' marks a departure from the practice of conventional autobiographies which attempt to recapture the essence of a unitary self. Instead the poem presents its subject as an intertextual construct: less a 'divided child' because of his mixed racial ancestry than because of his split responses to the two kinds of discourse which influence his character from an early age: the vernacular, hitherto extra-literary discourse of the St. Lucian people and landscape and the much more traditional 'literary' idioms of

European culture. While the poem dramatizes a split between these two discursive spheres, it gradually erodes this, creating its own syncretic continuum from a fusion of elements. The title of the whole poem encompasses several meanings and prominent among them is the notion that the world of art is 'another life' away from the island location in which the child is growing up. However, even as the poem portrays the child as a construct of different discourses, it is itself creating an image of him and this image is 'another life', another textual construct, which exists at the interface of the various discourses that are being combined together in the text.

The poem's concern with investigating the processes by which autobiography comes into existence is immediately apparent in the metaliterary opening lines:

> Verandahs, where the pages of the sea
> are a book left open by an absent master
> in the middle of another life –
> I begin here again,
> begin until the ocean's
> a shut book, and, like a bulb
> the white moon's filaments wane.
>
> Begin with twilight, when a glare
> which held the cry of bugles lowered
> the coconut lances of the inlet,
> as a sun, tired of empire, declined. (*AL*, 3)

As in 'Veranda', the moment is the twilight of Empire, but the particular force of the passage relies on the reader's making out certain associations, recognizing how other texts, phrases and images are being redeployed to produce the distinctive effect of this 'mosaic of quotations'. The line 'in the middle of another life –', alludes to the opening of the *Divine Comedy*,[20] and in so doing immediately suggests a debt to one of the greatest of European allegories, while changing a word to make it clear that it describes *another* life, one which has an ambivalent relationship to European cultural codes. As in *Dream on Monkey Mountain*, the white moon image suggests a European muse – a meaning which becomes clearer as the poem develops – and the

reference to its waning filaments anticipates the gradual movement away from this Muse that will occur in the poem as a
whole. The 'verandahs', 'bugles' and 'lances' all confirm the
moment of the opening as the twilight of Empire; and the
'absent master' seems to suggest the 'cultural absenteeism'[21]
which was a legacy of the Caribbean plantocracy that persisted
into the late colonial period and beyond. So the problem of
tradition is introduced in the opening sentence and the reference
to 'pages' and 'book' provide a clear index of the poet's awareness of the extent to which his perception of his natural
surroundings is mediated by his colonial, 'literary' upbringing.
At the same time the self-referential dimension is accentuated
by the analogy that is being drawn between the act of perceiving
the natural world and that of reading a text. It soon becomes
clear that the poet is creating a pictorial tableau, 'a landscape
locked in amber', but there is irony since this 'clear/glaze of
another life' has been produced by a 'monster / a prodigy of the
wrong age and colour' (*AL*, 3).

Subsequent details repeatedly stress how the child's vision
has been shaped by European texts, phrases and imagery: his
mother's brooms remind him of 'drooping ostrich crests' and
the Prince of Wales's motto, 'ICH DIEN, I SERVE' (*AL*, 10);
washday bubbles bring on envious thoughts of the Bubbles
frontispiece of *Pears Cyclopedia* (*AL*, 12); he sees 'autumn in a
rusted leaf' (*AL*, 41). In short, a concern with tradition informs
the description of even the most routine everyday occurrences.
Sometimes the poet's response to the world of his youth seems
to be entirely shaped by imported language and imagery:

> I saw, as through the glass of some provincial gallery
> the hieratic objects which my father loved:
> the stuffed dark nightingale of Keats,
> bead-eyed, snow-headed eagles,
> all that romantic taxidermy. (*AL*, 41)

At the same time the landscape is depicted as 'virginal,
unpainted' (*AL*, 152), awaiting Adamic naming by its artists and
Another Life embarks on this project. So, although the colonial
filter threatens to colour the poet's vision to the point of

distortion, another lens offers an entirely different perspective:

> no one had yet written of this landscape
> that it was possible, though there were sounds
> given to its varieties of wood;
>
> the *bois-canot* responded to its echo,
> when the axe spoke, weeds ran up to the knee
> like bastard children, hiding in their names,
>
> …
>   trees and men
> laboured assiduously, silently to become
>
> whatever their given sounds resembled,
> ironwood, logwood-heart, golden apples, cedars,
> and were nearly
>
> Ironwood, logwood-heart, golden apples, cedars,
> men. (*AL*, 53–4)

In passages like this which establish the validity of particular signifiers, the poem is very obviously performing the Adamic task, but in making an 'unwritten' landscape 'possible'[22] it is also doing so in its entirety. Throughout, *Another Life* documents a tension between metropolitan and local St. Lucian influences, but although Walcott seldom forsakes European verse forms – pentameters predominate even towards the end – there is a gradual movement away from 'romantic taxidermy'.

The Russian formalist critic Boris Tomashevsky has spoken of tradition as the problem which confronts all writers: 'The writer constantly tries to solve the problem of artistic tradition which in literary experience is like the encumbrance of an ancestral heirloom'.[23] *Another Life* uses the image of the heirloom very similarly in a passage which once again foregrounds Walcott's ambivalent colonial situation:

> I had entered the house of literature as a houseboy,
> filched as the slum child stole,
> as the young slave appropriated
> those heirlooms temptingly left
> with the Victorian homilies of *Noli tangere*. (*AL*, 77)

While, like Tomashevsky, Walcott envisages tradition as an ancestral heirloom, it is not one which has been bequeathed to the colonial 'houseboy' and so he has to steal and appropriate for his own uses. In so doing he is not assimilated, but rather assimilates for his own ends. And this is exactly how *Another Life* works, with potent images of the local landscape gradually supplanting those of European literature. Formerly he has seen autumn in a rusted leaf, but this process is reversed when he finds the smell of local hogplums, 'exuding / a memory stronger than [Proustian] madeleines' (*AL*, 76).

Another Life is unequivocally a Caribbean poem, but the intertexts that contribute to its making are primarily European in origin. A consideration of the poet's account of his early love for a woman called 'Anna' illustrates this further. This narrative is once again less an attempt to give the illusion of transferring a past reality to the page than an exploration of the ways images of self are constituted – in this case an investigation of the discourse of love. This functions in two ways: the poet foregrounds the extent to which 'Anna' is a construct of the text, formed by his own memory and perceptions and by the act of writing, but in addition the love which is now being transformed through writing is seen as having originally been a product of the two young St. Lucians' image-making. Where the poet himself is concerned, love appears to be an intertextual creation long before he turns to rendering it in his writing. His love for 'Anna' clearly owes something to literary texts when he imagines her as Anna Christie and Anna Karenina (*AL*, 96) and earlier in the poem he has approached her through the mediation of the Book of Hours and the Biblical figures of Ruth and Judith (*AL*, 60–1).[24] There is an interesting moment when 'Anna' resists such analogical categorization, turning on the poet and complaining: 'I became a metaphor, but / believe me I was unsubtle as salt' (*AL*, 101). However, since the method of the whole poem is once again founded on metaphorical transformation,[25] this seems to be an alternative viewpoint in a dialectical debate which is not finally endorsed. The main thrust of *Another Life* suggests that all discourse is metaphorical and

this particularly comes in a passage where the young lovers are
seen walking beside the sea:

> Where they now stood, others before had stood,
> the same lens held them, the repeated wood,
> then there grew on each one
> the self-delighting, self-transfiguring stone
> stare of the demi-god.
> Stunned by their images they strolled on, content
> that the black film of water kept the print
> of their locked images when they passed on. (*AL*, 94)

Here the photographic metaphors seem to be less a formulation
of the text than a product of the imaginations of the lovers (as
characters *within* the text). As they realize that they are re-
enacting their own version of the behaviour of other lovers, they
in effect become engaged in a form of role-playing which is
analogous to the transformations of the intertextual process,
even if no earlier *written* texts are explicitly mentioned at this
point. Clearly they can conceive of their love as achieving the
stasis of art, as the camera-like water appears to perform the
function of a modern-day grecian urn. At the same time, of
course, the fluidity and transience of the water cannot preserve
their image for posterity; on the other hand, the poem *Another
Life* can, and does, do exactly this.

So, even when the subject of tradition is not overtly to the
fore, *Another Life* still suggests that fictions of self are original,
but derivative reworkings of received fictions. The particular
creative tension of the poem emerges from its auto-referential
dimension, its investigation of the processes of autobiography
and specifically of the ways in which images of self are generated. Walcott's conception of himself as a 'split writer' results in
the production of an autobiography that has more in common
with such works as *The Life of Giambattista Vico Written by
Himself* and Roland Barthes's *Roland Barthes*, texts which
question the notion of the unitary Cartesian self, than with
Wordsworth's *Prelude*, which may initially seem a more
obvious departure-point for *Another Life*. While he has never
shown any inclination to make common cause with post-

structuralist theorists, Walcott's practice in the poem effectively promotes a view of subjectivity as a discursive formation which has much in common with theirs. His problematization of issues of self-representation and his implicit distrust of transparent accounts of unitary selves seem to arise primarily from his awareness of writing from a hybrid heritage, but this makes his autobiography every bit as much a writerly text as those mentioned above – and as such it offers a radical challenge to versions of identity predicated upon linear, essentialist conceptions of the self.

Walcott's next collection, *Sea Grapes* (1976), is notable for its unity of tone and theme. Again the title-image is central to the whole volume, which offers Walcott's most sustained set of variations on his view, powerfully expressed in 'The Muse of History' published two years previously, that the American Adamic situation is a bitter-sweet predicament. A certain astringency of tone had been prominent in much of Walcott's previous verse. *Sea Grapes* develops this with bouts of acrimony, as when he writes about exiled novelists:

> You spit on your people,
> your people applaud,
> your former oppressors
> laurel you.
> The thorns biting your forehead
> are contempt
> disguised as concern … ('At Last',[26] *SG*, 88)

and mordant imagery such as:

> Desolate lemons, hold
> tight, in your bowl of earth,
> the light of your bitter flesh. ('Lemons', *SG*, 14)

From the outset, however, the title-poem makes it clear that this acerbity is a response to the island predicament of 'gnarled sour grapes' (*SG*, 9) and that the grapes image is being used as a metaphor for the New World experience.

In 'The Muse of History' Walcott says of the 'great poetry of the New World':

[I]ts savour is a mixture of the acid and the sweet, the
apples of its second Eden have the tartness of experience.
… It is the acidulous that supplies its energy. The golden
apples of this sun are shot with acid. The taste of Neruda is
citric, the *Pomme de Cythère* of Césaire sets the teeth on
edge, the savor of Perse is of salt fruit at the sea's edge, the
sea grape, the 'fat-poke', the sea almond.[27]

Like St.-John Perse's salt fruit, Walcott's sea grapes also 'set the
teeth on edge'. Through the volume the sourness outweighs the
sweetness, but the two are seldom extricable from one another.
In 'The Wind in the Dooryard', which is dedicated to the
Tobagonian poet E. M. Roach, who drowned himself in 1974, the
admixture of sour and sweet is particularly complex. Walcott
begins by speaking of the poem as an involuntary creation,
which he has not wanted to come either from his own 'torn
mouth' or Roach's 'salt body' (*SG*, 64). Initially, this reluctance
seems to stem from his grief at the drowning of a fellow island-
poet whose death, like Harold Simmons's, has provided a literal
instance of his early belief that the pursuit of an artistic career in
the Caribbean was tantamount to suicide.[28] However, as the
poem proceeds, the sense of possible identification with Roach is
problematized as he implicitly criticizes what Roach's poetry
'celebrated' – 'the wall with spilling coralita … and the clean dirt
yard' (*SG*, 64) – which seem to represent a sanitized version of
Caribbean social realities. And at this point, it begins to appear
as if Walcott's reluctance may result from a feeling that his
criticism is improper in what is, at least in one sense, another
Walcott elegy. However, the last stanza of the poem involves
another shift in direction, as it almost grudgingly admits:

sometimes, under the armpit
of the hot sky over the country
the wind smells of salt
and a certain breeze lifts the sprigs of coralita
as if, like us,
lifting our heads, at our happiest,
it too smells the freshness of life. (*SG*, 65–6)

So, although at the outset the poem seems to engage in a

repudiation of Roach's late Romanticism, still a significant strain in Caribbean verse when Walcott began his writing career in the 1940s,[29] by the conclusion it is conceding that such verse does express a particular, if limited, dimension of island experience; and in acknowledging the validity of Roach's 'freshness of life' amid the armpit smells, Walcott suggests a compound of tones that can be related to the mood of bitter-sweetness prevalent throughout *Sea Grapes*.

In much the same way as Crusoe had been the main protagonist in *The Castaway*, the related figure of Adam[30] is the central character in *Sea Grapes*. The first of several poems in which he appears, 'The Cloud', portrays him at the moment of the Fall possessed of a curious kind of innocence in that his initiation into the postlapsarian state *liberates* him from the Manichean binary of bondage to either God or the Devil, instead of sentencing him, as in orthodox Christian theology, to a world of sin and death. Demythologized, such an Adam is humanity able to discover the New World emancipated from the dualistic moral imperatives of Western thought and free to write its signature as it chooses on the *tabula rasa* continent. However, lest this vision of being able to name the world anew seem unduly optimistic, the next poem 'New World' immediately provides a counter-balance. It concludes by showing Adam and the serpent working together as capitalist entrepreneurs to invent the New World:

> Adam had an idea.
> He and the snake would share
> the loss of Eden for a profit.
> So both made the New World. And it looked good.
>
> (*SG*, 19)

Taken together, 'The Cloud' and 'New World' express Walcott's complex and ambivalent view of the American Adamic experience. As he constructs it, it is both a postlapsarian 'sour grapes' condition and a predicament which offers the possibility of liberation from the crippling moral dualism he here particularly associates with Europe.

In 'The Muse of History', where he argues the case for a cyclic view of history which will offer release from the determinism implicit in linear historiography with its emphasis on causality, Walcott relates such a view to the Adamic vision of the 'great poets of the New World, from Whitman to Neruda',[31] saying that it is their 'awe of the numinous, this elemental privilege of naming the new world [sic] which annihilates history in our great poets, an elation common to all of them, whether they are aligned by heritage to Crusoe and Prospero or to Friday and Caliban'.[32] In *Sea Grapes*, particular poems pay homage to Whitman and Neruda, but the Adamic vision is integral to the whole volume – and most of Walcott's other poetry – since, as discussed above, Walcott's poetic practice again performs the Adamic task of bestowing names. In a poem actually entitled 'Names', which is dedicated to Brathwaite (presumably as a response to his project of *Afro*-Caribbean renaming), Walcott argues the complex case that the 'belittling diminutives' (*SG*, 41) of the names bestowed upon slaves by exiled European courtiers were gradually dignified by later creolization, in which 'The African acquiesced, / repeated, and changed them' (*SG*, 42). And 'Sainte Lucie', in which the poet attempts to reclaim the folk speech of his youth, offers an inventory of Caribbean signifiers, which, if it does not exactly name the world *anew*, nonetheless contributes to the Adamic project by putting a distillation of aspects of the island's speech (and its natural phenomena) on the printed page for the first time:

> Pomme arac,
> otaheite apple,
> pomme cythere,
> pomme granate,
> moubain,
> z'ananas
> the pine apple's
> Aztec helmet,
> pomme,
> I have forgotten
> what pomme for
> the Irish potato,
> cerise,

the cherry,
z'aman
sea-almonds
by the crisp
sea-bursts,
au bord de la 'ouviere.
Come back to me my language. (*SG*, 43–4)

Where earlier Walcott collections had referred to the onset of middle age,[33] in *Sea Grapes*, though still only in his mid-forties, Walcott looks forward to the approach of *old* age and asks himself, in 'To Return to the Trees', whether he will soon, like the venerable Jamaican poet John Figueroa,[34] who had been one of his tutors during his undergraduate days,[35] be 'a gnarled poet / bearded with the whirlwind, / his metres like thunder?' (*SG*, 93).

Ageing is important in the collection in another sense, as Walcott finds himself in the ironic situation of a former angry young man who is now beginning to be regarded as insufficiently radical by a new generation of highly politicized poets. His reaction to their rhetoric comes out most clearly in the poems 'The Brother' and 'Dread Song'. The savage imagery of the former is not untypical of *Sea Grapes*, though its language is more uncompromisingly direct than that of most of the volume:

That smiler next to you who whispers
brother

knife him

That man who borrowed your coat
the one of many colours

reclaim it as yours. (*SG*, 23)

While the poem's biblical references, such as the allusion to Joseph's coat here, suggest that false brotherhood is far from being a peculiarly Caribbean phenomenon, the primary object of attack is the political exclusiveness of contemporary black 'brothers'. Questioned on this in a 1973 interview, Walcott spoke of having become disenchanted with the black revolutionary movement in Trinidad, because of the 'blacker than thou' character it had assumed:

> The rhetoric began to take over. And so the thing was deflected. But the validity of the young uprising and the unemployed people, it was a genuine and worthwhile thing. ... And a lot of people use the slogans, naturally, to cover up their own inadequacies and so on. So a guy who calls you brother, after a while if he's just saying the thing, you should watch out for him.[36]

'Dread Song' is a subtler poem which expresses a similar disillusion. Ostensibly it is a Rastafarian song of praise and it is not difficult to take the opening at face value:

> Forged from the fire of Exodus
> the iron of the tribe,
>
> Bright as the lion light, Isaiah,
> the anger of the tribe. (SG, 32)

After a few lines, however, the tone changes as Walcott tells how the 'tribe' now buys the lies of 'lizard-smart poets' (SG, 32), who have usurped the religious leader's role. As in 'The Brother', it is the subversion of a powerful ideal by cheap rhetoric which is the central object of attack and the point is neatly clinched in the final lines of the poem where the loss of true revolutionary fire is mirrored by a descent into incantatory banality.

Walcott is not completely unsympathetic towards either of the extremes represented by E. M. Roach and the Rasta rhetoric, but he eschews both for a middle style which ranges across the Caribbean linguistic continuum. This is not, however, simply the style of an 'ironic mulatto', who chooses to keep his distance from opposing poles of the Caribbean racial and cultural spectrum. It is once again a commitment to the plurality of Caribbean life and to a stance which rejects binary oppositions and the kind of thinking that precludes movement and dialogue between positions:

In the final poem, 'Return to the Trees', he reflects:

grey has grown strong to me,

it's no longer neutral,
no longer the dirty flag
of courage going under,

it is specked with hues
like quartz; it's as
various as boredom, ...

grey is the heart at peace,
tougher than the warrior
as it bestrides factions. (SG, 93–4)

This 'grey' is said to involve 'the toil that is balance' (SG, 94)
and *Sea Grapes* works towards such balance through its com-
bination of an acerbic manner and its expression of a reverential
attitude towards Caribbean life. Again there is a sense of 'obliterating hurt', but the bitter-sweet tensions are less often and
less comfortably resolved than hitherto and it is the image of the
acidulous sea grapes that lingers longest in the mind.

Renegotiating roles

COMPLEMENTING his various poems about the twilight of Empire and the castaway, Walcott's next play *Franklin* (1969) returned to the figure of the expatriate marooned at the end of Empire and in so doing laid the groundwork for the theme that was to dominate his drama of the 1970s and early 1980s: the renegotiations of roles occasioned by the coming of the various Caribbean independences. During the first part of this period, he continued to be engaged in the task of creating an appropriate theatrical practice for the region and the 1970s saw the first production of one of his finest and most popular 'Caribbean' plays, *The Joker of Seville* (1974), a creolized musical reworking of the original Spanish Don Juan play. However, it was the about-faces in social roles, a subject rich in dramatic potential, that most absorbed Walcott at this time; and the focus of his plays on this theme was often, but not always, on the former privileged classes, forced to don new roles if they were to continue to have a place in society.

In a programme note for the 1973 Theatre Workshop production of *Franklin*, Walcott saw the protagonist as 'man alone, stripped, a Crusoe facing a new beginning, someone who turns his back on Europe and the Empire and casts his lot with the Fridays of the village'.[1] He had first used the name Franklin in Chapter VII of his 'Tales of the Islands' sequence in *In a Green Night*, where the figure's diseased and disdainful vision isolates him from the local people:

Franklin gripped the bridge-stanchions with a hand
Trembling with fever. Each spring, memories
Of his own country where he could not die
Assaulted him. He watched the malarial light
Shiver the canes. In the tea-coloured pool, tadpoles
Seemed happy in their element. Poor, black souls.
He shook himself. Must breed, drink, rot with motion.[2]

In *Franklin*, a play which Walcott has rewritten several
times,[3] he is an altogether more complex and, finally, more
compassionate character, so much so that the play has been
criticized for the sympathy it displays towards its white,
'colonial' protagonist.[4] The setting is a St. Lucian estate house
and the opening stage direction is explicit about its significance:
'The house, white, ageing and neglected is an externalisation of
Franklin's character'.[5] As in 'Veranda' and the opening of
Another Life, the moment is sunset; off-stage the congregation
of the local Mission is singing the final verse of Kipling's
'Recessional'.[6]

Franklin's forerunner, *The Wine of the Country*, had suffered
from an obsessive engagement with the nuances of the politics
of racial identity, which failed to see the positive potential of
hybridity, and from some excessively melodramatic blank verse.
In contrast, *Franklin*, a tightly-knit prose play, succeeds on a
naturalistic level (even if elements such as the opening stage
direction which likens the house to Franklin himself suggest
expressionistic possibilities[7]), constructing a more credible set of
characters and inter-racial relationships which function as a
microcosm of the social and political changes occurring in the
Caribbean around the time of independence.

Franklin himself is a crippled former sea-captain, who
sustained his leg injury during a wartime U-boat attack on his
schooner, which killed his wife and daughter. While he is
inevitably cast in the role of master, and characteristics such as
his heavy drinking may suggest the stereotype of a European
going to seed in the tropics, he emerges as an ambivalent and
insecure character, who now occupies the role of colonizer with
little conviction. His major crime seems to be insensitivity and

at the end of the play he comes to terms with this, saying 'I took too much for granted, I was an empire of indifference' (*Franklin*, 61). Equally complex is the first mate (and *de facto* captain) of his current ship, the black Morris, a character who, like Franklin, finds himself caught in a dilemma occasioned by the coming of independence.

At the opening of the play, Franklin is planning a second marriage, to the Indo-Caribbean Maria, but ghosts from his past prevent him from sleeping with her when she moves into his house. Meanwhile Maria and *Morris* are drawn together, perhaps suggesting that *rapprochement* between Indo- and Afro-Caribbean cultures will be a more urgent agenda in the post-independence future. In *Franklin*, though, neither relationship succeeds. Pregnant (presumably by Morris) and cursed by her father Ramsingh, an interesting study in Hindu acculturation in the Caribbean, Maria commits suicide. With such tragedy in his own life and with the new politics personified by a local leader, Charbon, causing labour unrest on the neighbouring estate owned by his friend Willoughby, it looks as though Franklin's days are numbered. However, the play is neither tragedy nor elegy. It takes a very different view of the fate of the displaced expatriate from *The Wine of the Country*. There the protagonist Bemminger has resolved to leave the island he loves from the outset. *Franklin* is about 'staying on'.

The play builds towards a confrontation between Franklin and Charbon, who claims Franklin's estate, partly because its earlier French Creole owner had made a will leaving it to him before selling it to Franklin, but more fundamentally because he feels his people's suffering has made them the rightful owners of the land. Before her death Maria has given Charbon the deed to the house and in the dramatically powerful final scene, where with a group of followers Charbon sets fire to Willoughby's estate and conducts a 'siege of nerves' (*Franklin*, 58) against Franklin, he appears to hold all the cards. Franklin expresses the choices he is left with as follows:

> If I walk through you, right through that aisle of hatred that you'd make, and go down to that jetty to my ship …

and burn her again. Burn her with me aboard, many of
you will admire me. You'll think it glorious, proud,
unbroken, British! But to myself, I'd be a coward. I'm
familiar with cowardice, weakness, betrayal. But to me all
these things were human. I am incapable, thank God, of
any bravery. … On the other hand. If I come towards your
flag, acknowledge it, my own race, my countrymen may
see it as a contemptible compromise.

…

Well let me tell you now. Whatever I do, I do neither for
England or for this country, but for myself. For what my
heart compels. I do it in honour of Maria Ramsingh, in
memory of my son, my wife, and for myself. I'm part of
you now. And if the penalty I have to pay, to others like
humiliation, failure, cowardice, that is my choice.

(*Franklin*, 63–4)

Earlier he has told Willoughby that he is prepared to be a
'chameleon' and adapt 'to suit the scenery' (*Franklin*, 55). Now,
accompanied by Morris, he salutes the new flag and through this
gesture of allegiance to the emerging political *status quo* of the
future wins the respect of Charbon who returns the deed of the
property to him. Again the allegory is dramatically effective,
with the crucial Caribbean issues of land ownership and the
transfer of power being enacted on a personal level.

The success of *Franklin* is not, however, achieved through
schematic allegory, but rather from its convincing naturalistic
scenes and the complexity of its characterization, which is a far
cry from the stereotyping reductiveness of *The Wine of the
Country*. Michael Gilkes, who has directed two productions of
Franklin,[8] has said of the play, 'In almost every character there
is a contradictory quality, so you don't go as it were to a
superficial character portrayal …, each character has a complicated response to the Caribbean and to each other. And it is
played out on the stage of the great house of the Caribbean
which is our set.'[9] There remains the problem that *this* 'great
house' is not in ruins – as was the case with the similar house in
the poem in *In a Green Night*[10] – and Franklin remains its owner
at the end. Walcott's resistance to oppositional aesthetics is

usually refreshing, but here a narrative structure which leaves former power hegemonies undismantled, albeit humbled, does not seem to go far enough. In *Drums and Colours* Walcott had promoted the federal ideal through a thorough-going cross-cultural conclusion. Here his humanitarian concern for the predicament of whites threatened with becoming the new victims of what he perceives as characteristically Caribbean adversarial binarism operates against the ideal of racial integration towards which the play, at least sometimes, seems to be working. The identity politics implicit in Walcott's later versions of the same theme, such as *In a Fine Castle* and *Pantomime*, are more satisfying in this respect, but *Franklin* remains one of his most successful plays dramatically.

In 1973 Britain's Royal Shakespeare Company commissioned Walcott to adapt the original seventeenth-century Don Juan play, Tirso de Molina's *El Burlador de Sevilla*. He accepted the commission with the proviso that the Theatre Workshop be allowed to stage the play in Trinidad before its English premiere[11] and told a Trinidadian interviewer:

> I did not want to produce a play purely for the Shakespeare company or English actors and audiences. I wanted to write a play that could also be produced in the West Indies.
>
> So what I have done is put Don Juan, or the Joker of Seville, in a West Indian setting and, indeed, one of the runs in the story is: Don Juan was a stickman![12]

So, while the reworking of the Don Juan legend, with its associations with such names as Molière, Mozart, Byron and Shaw,[13] might initially suggest a play redolent with echoes of European culture, Walcott's musical adaptation, *The Joker of Seville*, creolizes the Spanish original and he justifies this practice by saying that 'Shakespeare creolized the Classic theatre as much as any Third World writer who re-invents these legends which are after all universal'.[14] Irrespective of whether the Don Juan legend *is* universal – one might see it as representing a particularly European inscription of myths about male sexuality

– *The Joker of Seville* draws extensively on very specific Caribbean folk forms to create its own particular hybridized fusion of elements. Once again it is a metatheatrical piece which concerns itself with, among other things, the creation of an appropriate local theatrical practice.

The main determinants behind the writing and production of *The Joker of Seville* would seem, then, to be threefold: a metropolitan commission; a European original; and a resolve on Walcott's part to creolize this original. In fact, the elements that went into the making of the play were more complex than this, not least because both Walcott and Ronald Bryden, the Royal Shakespeare Company's literary adviser, saw a relationship between Tirso's world and the contemporary Caribbean. Walcott's introductory note to the play says he was given the commission because Bryden felt that 'a West Indian poet, living in a country whose language and music have one form' (*Joker*, 3) could best render the spirit of the old Spanish play; and, as he himself puts it and his earlier plays had already amply demonstrated, 'the verse play is not a literary exercise in the West Indies' (*Joker*, 4). Moreover, as a product of the folk traditions of a late medieval society, Tirso's play lies outside the mainstream of classic European tragedy and Walcott comments specifically on the sound of flamenco and guitar to be heard in the verse of *El Burlador* and refers to Juan as 'a man who must have come from the folk imagination' (*Joker*, 4). The process of cultural cross-pollination is further complicated by Walcott's incorporation of folk elements which are themselves already hybrid. These are of two kinds: he suggests affinities between Trinidadian and Hispanic culture by drawing on Spanish elements in Trinidadian masquerades, such as the *burroquette* and *parang*;[15] and he utilizes syncretic elements from Trinidadian customs, such as the stick-fight and the mummers' play,[16] which have origins in both Africa and Europe.

Beyond this, the *Joker* discovers at least three thematic strands in Tirso's play which, as Walcott sees it, have a particular relevance to Caribbean society. First, although he calls his play *The* Joker *of Seville*, the title of *El Burlador* is more frequently translated as 'the *trickster* of Seville'[17] and, as a trickster of sex, Don Juan is clearly a possible, if dubious, folk hero in a society which relishes the picaroon exploits of Anansi, the wily spiderman of Akan folklore whom the slaves of the Middle Passage brought to the New World with them.[18] Second, Tirso's play provides Walcott with an opportunity to satirize the cultural legacy of colonialism through the medium of the earlier text's satire of the literary and social pretensions of the age of chivalry. Third, the play's representation of gender relations allows Walcott to explore similarities between the macho ethic embodied in *El Burlador* and attitudes in his own adopted society of Trinidad,[19] where male virility was celebrated in many classic calypsoes of the post-war period, particularly those of the Mighty Sparrow (Slinger Francisco).[20]

The calypso tradition is also manifest in the *Joker* in other ways: the score, for which the composer Galt MacDermot wrote the music to accompany Walcott's lyrics,[21] draws extensively on Trinidadian popular music, particularly calypso and related musical forms; and the play's use of sexual innuendo also has much in common with a certain kind of calypso discourse. Its metaphors for sexual activity include riding, bullfighting, stickfighting and swordplay; animal images for sexual virility include stallions, peacocks and cockerels.

Although Walcott's adaptation follows Tirso fairly closely, his representation of the Don Juan figure is more ambivalent than Tirso's. *El Burlador* is a Revenge Play, which can also be viewed as an early example of the tragedy of damnation, the genre of Marlowe's *Dr Faustus* and *Macbeth*. Walcott's creolization of its form is complemented by a similar thematic movement which interrogates the scheme of moral retribution at the heart of Tirso's play. Identifying some of the formal elements in the *Joker* and showing how they are accompanied by parallel thematic shifts – in the representation of the man-woman relationship and Juan's damnation – helps to show how this change is effected.

From the outset Walcott creates a Caribbean ambience by having a troupe of Trinidadian villagers stage the re-enactment of the Don Juan story which forms the main body of the play. This frame also makes it clear that, as in *Ti-Jean*, a legend is being reworked, as Rafael, the village elder, asks the Earth to allow Don Juan to be resurrected for one night, the eve of All Souls (*Joker*, 8). Juan is thus recreated, as it were by the collective authorship of the Trinidadian villagers who celebrate his Joker/trickster attributes in song:

> *Now of all the cards in the pack,*
> *Ace, King, Queen, Joker, and Jack,*
> *of all the royal cards in the pack,*
> *Ace, King, Queen, Joker, and Jack,*
> *The Ace is the dead man, of course,*
> *but the Joker is really the boss;*
> *He can change to elation each grave situation,*
> *sans humanité!* (*Joker*, 9)

From the outset, then, Juan's resurrection suggests a pattern which promises to challenge the ethic of Tirso's basically ortho-dox theological tragedy, in which he is condemned to Hell at the end, while the Jungian view of the Joker/trickster as a shaman-like figure who can metamorphose experience[22] – '*change to elation each grave situation*' – and initiate others into new states of awareness[23] further threatens to subvert the values of the source play.

The desirability of creating a Caribbean ambience is further stressed in a prefatory note in which Walcott suggests that, if possible, the *Joker* should be staged in the round and identifies the setting as a stickfight arena. This note on the play's staging goes on to add that 'The audience should sit on wooden bleachers close to the action, as in a rural bullfight, cockfight, or stickfight' (*Joker*, 5) and, when it was produced by the Trinidad Theatre Workshop for the second time,[24] the company not only mounted it in the round, but gave Sunday morning perfor-mances under natural light and at one of these encouraged the audience to make a celebration of the occasion by serving shark and bread, souse, coffee, oranges, sweetbread and juice.[25] Walcott saw such a production as an attempt to overcome both the traditional divide of the proscenium arch and mimicry of metropolitan theatre-going habits, unsuitable to Trinidad. The analogy between bullring and stickfight arena is an outcrop of one of the play's central themes, since bullfighting is a metaphor for Juan's sexual exploits which Walcott adapts from Tirso, particularly by using elements from the Trinidadian *burro-quette* masquerade, one form of which is Venezuelan in origin and which burlesques aspects of bullfighting.

More generally, stickfighting is used in the *Joker* as the equivalent of duelling in *El Burlador* and when, towards the end of the first of the play's two acts, Juan fights and kills Don Gonzalo, father of Ana, the third of the four women he seduces, Rafael and his troupe accompany their duel by singing a *kalinda* ('Better watch yourself, old man, / Nobody can beat Don Juan' [*Joker*, 83–4], a particular type of calypso which evolved from traditional Trinidadian stickfighting chants. Errol Hill has commented that stickfighting was as much musical performance as martial art and the *kalinda*, 'sung by the stickmen themselves with a supporting chorus [was] responsible for the warlike tradition in calypso repertory'.[26] The *Joker*'s *kalinda* has all the main features of the form – martial rhetoric, a shout-and-response structure and a rapid, accelerating pace – and also takes the form back to its stickfighting antecedents. It is followed by a song which belongs to a rather different genre of the music of the African diaspora. As the dead Don Gonzalo's body is borne off by stickfighters, this song introduces a theme which has no parallel in Tirso's play:

O Lord, let resurrection come
from this stickfight! …

We cannot believe that death is champion – …

In this stickfight! (*Joker*, 86)

This derives from the rhythm-and-blues music popularized in the 1960s by such American artists as Chuck Berry and Bo Diddley. So another element, possibly suggestive of the survival of African-based musical forms in the new World, is employed to reintroduce the resurrection motif. Act I ends ambivalently with Juan having killed Gonzalo, whose ghost will be the main agent of retribution in the second act, but also with suggestions of possible resurrection, nowhere to be found in *El Burlador*, and the potential for renewal offered by folk drama.

Walcott's other main departure from Tirso's play comes in his treatment of Juan's seduction of Tisbea, a rather idealized fishergirl who believes herself to be immune from love. In *El Burlador* she is encountered by a shipwrecked Juan on the coast of New Tarragon in the New World. Tisbea ostensibly epitomizes the virginal innocence of the Americas and in his attempt to find her 'New World'[27] Juan affects an air of religious piety, while telling her to hold his 'serpent' firmly so that they can 'bring the old gospel to the New World' (*Joker*, 41). The song which follows is, like much of the play's imagery, steeped in the kind of imagery which typifies post-war calypsoes about the man-woman relationship. Again Walcott draws on particular discourses of the black diaspora: his stage directions refer to the first part of this composition as a 'revivalist dance' (*Joker*, 42) and the latter part as a 'brimstone-and-hellfire meeting' (*Joker*, 43):

> Tisbea went and bathe,
> a swordfish take she maid.
> Tisbea, oh, oh!
> Fire in the water!
>
> […]
> Hold on to the rod,
> Sister Tisbea!
> hold on to the roh-oh-od!
> Though it turn like the staff of Aaron
> to a miraculous serpent,
> mind it jump out your hand! (*Joker*, 42–3)

Here the notion of 'fire in the water' derives from *El Burlador*,[28] but the main intertext is a calypso, 'Sophie went in the sea to bathe':

> Sophie went in the sea to bathe:
> Wild, wild Sophia,
> Cat-fish came an' make a raid:
> My! My! Sophia.[29]

The idea of the revivalist meeting would appear to be all Walcott's own, but it is very much in keeping with the religious motifs which loom large in both plays, being given serious expression in *El Burlador* and satirical treatment in the *Joker*. Again, the song represents an interplay of diverse elements, but the main emphasis is on the *folk* tradition.

There are numerous other instances of Walcott's lyrics and MacDermot's score creolizing the Don Juan legend. The *sans humanité* calypso of the opening, which introduces sentiments which will be prominent throughout the play, alludes to one of the earliest forms of calypso and, while the provenance of the term remains controversial,[30] sets the tone for the activities of the trickster of sex, which can effect transformations but are 'without humanity'. As Juan and his Moorish Man Friday, Catalinion, make the Middle Passage crossing, a wild sea shanty, touching on various aspects of the experience of the African diaspora, is sung while slaves dance the limbo, allegedly a product of the cramped conditions of their transportation,[31] as well as an apt metaphor for their deracination. When Juan comes across a peasant wedding in Act II, the rustics' mimicry of royalty relates closely to burlesque elements in Trinidad Carnival and Caribbean dance more generally;[32] and a 'bacchanal of the skeleton' (*Joker*, 133) performed by Rafael and his troupe appears to be based on the Devil Bands of Carnival.[33] In short, Trinidadian folk elements feed into the *Joker* at virtually every point.

The two most significant transformations of the themes of Tirso's play occur in the representation of the man-woman relationship and Juan's death and damnation. *El Burlador* is theological drama, in which the libertine Juan gets his come-uppance when a statue of the dead Gonzalo comes to life and kills him. In the *Joker* Juan is altogether more complex and is given an ideological justification for his predatory sexual behaviour: he sees himself as an opponent of the hypocrisy of chivalric society and as a liberator of its women:

> it's true what I do may undo a
> woman, but I renew her
> and honor her with dishonor. (*Joker*, 8)

This is clearly a contentious view, when according to one sensitive reading he is a 'desolate conquistador' who 'accomplishes his mission on a woman's body',[34] but Walcott has spoken of the issue in more complex terms, viewing Juan as 'the victim of a trick'[35] and emphasizing the extent to which he 'reinforces the flaws' of those whom he tricks:

> [...] Juan is a figure who is anti-conduct. He is anti-establishment, anti-concepts of the tradition that he comes out of. And those traditions are, of course, based on honour and chastity and faith ...
>
> The joke that Juan plays in each case is that he reinforces the flaw that exists in the people he plays his tricks on. ... It's a little sordid to think of him just deflowering women.[36]

Clearly the *Joker* goes beyond the moral scheme of the tragedy of damnation, rendering Juan, and with him certain Caribbean attitudes to sexuality such as those celebrated in many post-war calypsoes, an object of debate. His claim is that he is a force for renewal, the promulgator of a 'gospel' (*Joker*, 41), which can lead women into a new state of awareness, not only by bringing them sexual fulfilment, but also by releasing them from the society's gender stereotyping. According to the first of the women he seduces, Isabella, society simplifies women's roles to those of 'wife' and 'whore' (*Joker*, 19). In Juan's gospel the myth of the Fall is reversed to suggest an unguilty postlapsarian sexuality: he claims to embody the 'principle ... of the generating earth' and 'the freedom delivered / after Eden' (*Joker*, 138). After seducing Tisbea, he says '[T]he old world's dying' and speaks of his quest for 'one simple, unremorseful Eve'. He is disappointed when she responds that she hopes she will make him 'a good wife' (*Joker*, 47). Taken at his own estimate, then, Juan represents the positive potential of the New World figure, even if he is a fallen Adam in conventional terms. Viewed negatively, he is an exploitative colonizer. The play thus offers its directors and audiences the *possibility* of choosing between polarized interpretations of the character – callous libertine who threatens the civil order and interpersonal relationships based on trust and loyalty or creative trickster who liberates women and offers them opportunities for self-definition? – and arguably Juan embodies some of the dualities that Walcott finds in the Crusoe figure[37] and in Caribbean experience more generally. Consequently, perhaps the most satisfactory way of rendering Juan in performance is as a 'Manichean' force that challenges Cartesian divisions between mind and body and traditional Christian divisions between divine and secular love. Walcott's own comments suggest he favours such a view himself:

> The moral problem is sex; the moral problem is the body, the function of the body. What is the moral responsibility of the body created by God with its lusts? Now here is a Manichean question; here is a blasphemous question. If these lusts are created within us, this is the Devil's question. And each person is in himself or herself indulging in lust, even if it is chaste and courtly love, or honourable love.[38]

Seen in this way, then, the *Joker* provides another instance of Walcott's trying to dismantle the binaries that construct oppositions between areas of experience which, he suggests, are part of a continuum.

Juan's insistence that he is 'a force, a principle' (*Joker*, 48) and claim that he transcends conventional gender stereotypes also make it possible to see him as a folk hero associated with some form of ritual renewal. In this respect, the resurrection theme comes to be of especial interest. As already mentioned, it is implicit from the outset that he has achieved a kind of immortality through art, as Rafael and his troupe resurrect him and the epigraphs to the two acts of the play, taken from the *Pisan Cantos* of one of Walcott's earliest mentors, Ezra Pound,[39] directly raise the question of whether or not Juan is to be damned, as in *El Burlador*. Act I is prefaced by the line 'With a painted paradise at the end of it ...' (*Joker*, 7); Act II by the line 'Without a painted paradise at the end of it ...' (*Joker*, 87). Within the play itself the 'painted paradise' is associated with Rafael's troupe:

Here's your old troupe of mummers with their art,
their painted Heaven and their painted Hell. (Joker, 125)

So, in a manner typical of the play's metatheatrical practice, the decision as to whether Juan is to be consigned to Heaven or Hell is seen to lie within the prerogative of art; and his putative immortality is achieved not through his qualities of character, but through artistic re-presentation. The mummers reference is particularly significant since it invokes a secular folk genre which embodies values which are at odds with the Christian scheme of Tirso's play. The traditional English mummers' play takes as its concern the death and resurrection of the hero, which personifies seasonal renewal.[40] Since the mummers' play appears to derive from ancient fertility rituals, since the custom of mumming was taken over and creolized in the Caribbean, particularly in Jamaica as part of the Christmas Jonkonnu mas-querade,[41] and since folk practices culminating in resurrection lie at the heart of the mummers' play, there would seem to be a strong affinity between the mummers' play and the resurrection theme in the *Joker*.

Faced with the prospect of imminent death towards the end, Juan remains defiant, resolving to '*go down a living lover*' in the heat of a passionate tropical night, rather than find himself an aged lecher reminiscing over his debauchery in his memoirs like '*simpering de Sade and cretinous Casanova*' (*Joker*, 145). Juan's stepping out of the historical era of the main action in this anachronistic manner is one of several auto-referential passages which again foreground the fact that this is a treatment of an archetypal figure whose mythical status constitutes a kind of immortality; and Juan dies with the expectation of having 'a legendary name / beyond this life' (*Joker*, 137). The *Joker* remains faithful to Tirso's original in that Juan is claimed by the dead Gonzalo's statue and this is followed by marriages which reaffirm the moral positives of Seville society, but fittingly this is not the final conclusion to a play which has offered an altogether more ambivalent reworking of the archetype. Walcott furnishes a kind of epilogue in which Rafael and his troupe reappear and the 'Sans Humanité' calypso of the opening is repeated, sung this time by the Ace of Death who disclaims knowledge of whether Juan has 'gone down to Hell / or up to Heaven' (Joker, 150) and in so doing raises the possibility of resurrection. The play concludes with the whole company joining together in a song about the possibility of freedom for a caged bird (Joker, 151), which has also been sung earlier (Joker, 68). This suggests that Juan has been granted freedom from the constraints of the grave and this possibility seems to be confirmed by the final stage direction: the dawn rises as Juan's body is carried from the ring (Joker, 151).[42] The action, as staged by Rafael's troupe, has taken place during a single night, the eve of All Souls, and since this is the day in the Catholic calendar when prayers are traditionally offered for the souls of the faithful departed, this would seem to be the ultimate joke in the reworking of the traditional material: Juan, the trickster who has been tricked by Gonzalo, is now resurrected as one of the faithful departed!

After the success of The Joker of Seville, Walcott and MacDermot collaborated on several further musicals over the next two decades. The first of these collaborations, O Babylon! (1976), set out to do for Jamaica what The Joker of Seville had done for Trinidad, using reggae and related Jamaican musical forms instead of Carnival-related music.[43] It focuses on the culture of a particular sect, the Rastafarian community, which at this time in the 1970s was emerging from its origins as a localized West Kingston movement and being seen as a potential force for change throughout the Caribbean. As Rasta influence grew, the spiritual and political beliefs of a hitherto fairly private religious group were projected onto a world stage and along with other outward symbols associated with the sect's identity – dress codes, hair-styles and language among them – reggae found itself part of international popular culture, achieving an extra-Caribbean appeal which calypso, despite an American vogue for the music in the 1940s and 1950s, had never achieved. Walcott hoped that his reggae musical would be performed on Broadway and would provide him with the international recognition as a dramatist that had so far eluded him.[44] However, this hope was not realized and the first performances of the play were by the Theatre Workshop in the Caribbean.[45]

The play is set in 1966 at the time of the visit to Jamaica of the Ethiopian Emperor Haile Selassie, revered by Rastafarians as God incarnate. It deals with a small Rasta community who have established squatters' rights on a Kingston beach. The forces of 'Babylon', in the form of an alliance between a multinational corporation and local politicians, conspire to evict them so that they can build a tourist development on the site; they eventually succeed in doing so. On a more individual level, *O Babylon!* is about the conversion of Aaron (formerly Rufus) from gangster to Rastafarian woodcarver. Treating such a sensitive subject in the form of a popular musical was always likely to cause offence in the volatile Caribbean political climate of the 1970s and, although most of the play's initial audiences seem to have enjoyed it,[46] it received a mixed reception from critics, several of whom attacked it for its appropriation of Rasta culture and music and for its failure to capture the real spirit of the sect's beliefs and customs. Sule Mombara criticized it for its 'misunderstanding'[47] of Rastafarian music and choreography and its attempt to 'merge European musical forms on African movements and songs'.[48] Victor Questel saw it as out of touch with contemporary Jamaican society and felt that it drew on Walcott's student experiences of the 1950s;[49] and he took the Workshop's actors to task for failing 'to transcend the Trinidadian ethos of confronting Babylon with humour, whereas the Jamaican [sic] and especially the Rastafarians confront Babylon with dread and a flair for ritual.'[50] Questel's comment goes to the heart of what is wrong with the play. Transforming *El Burlador de Sevilla* into a musical rooted in the 'bacchanal' culture of Trinidad had proved a highly effective way of creolizing a European original. A comic, essentially carnivalesque, representation of the 'dread' culture of Jamaica simply did not have the same social appropriateness, especially if one agrees with Mombara's view that a European filter is being applied to the primarily Afrocentric culture of Rastafari. Walcott and MacDermot fail to show the same affinity for this culture as they had for the carnivalesque world recreated in *The Joker of Seville*. Walcott's Note to the printed text of the play acknowledges the particular problems Jamaican and Rastafarian speech posed him when he was writing the play and shows a keen awareness of the political implications of the choices a dramatist makes in rendering 'non-Standard' language:

> Jamaican is comprehensible only to Jamaicans. ... When I considered that, within that language itself, the Rastafari have created still another for their own nation, I faced another conflict: if the language of the play remained true to the sect, it would have to use the sect's methods of self-protection and total withdrawal. This would require of the playwright not merely a linguistic but a spiritual conversion, a kind of talking in tongues that is, by its hermeticism and its self-possession, defiantly evasive of Babylonian reason.
>
> The Rastafari have invented a grammar and a syntax which immure them from the seductions of Babylon, an oral poetry which requires translation into the language of the oppressor. To translate is to betray. My theater language is, in effect, an adaptation and for clarity's sake, filtered. (*Joker*, 156)[51]

However, despite his sensitivity to these issues, it is difficult to see Walcott's 'adapted' language as exempt from the betrayal of which he speaks. The fact that audiences, including a group of seventy Rastas who attended a performance of the play in Jamaica during its run at the Carifesta arts festival in 1976,[52] have generally enjoyed *O Babylon!* attests to its appeal as entertainment, but unlike *The Joker of Seville* it does little to further Walcott's aim of developing an appropriate Caribbean theatrical practice and this is perhaps hardly surprising considering his comparative unfamiliarity with the 'self-protective' world of Rastafari.

O Babylon! does, however, endeavour to broaden awareness of Rasta culture and to provide a sympathetic view of the sect. Walcott includes a fair amount of exposition, perhaps still necessary in the 1970s when the movement was not so well known as it has subsequently become. Thus, the significance of the Rasta colours of green, red and yellow are explained and the Biblical passage on which the belief in Selassie's divinity is based is cited (*Joker*, 169, 181–2). And if one reduces the dramatic conflicts of the play to the fairly stark moral contrast which lies at its centre, the Rastas' peace-loving ethic clearly comes across as preferable to the capitalist acquisitiveness and corruption of the forces that dispossess them. Nevertheless, critics such as Sule Mombara *have* felt that such sympathy fails to demonstrate any real grasp of Rasta metaphysics and ideals. He particularly attacks the ending of the play where, with the community now ousted from the beach, the recent convert Aaron resolves to join the others in a mountain camp and the final stage direction reads 'Exaltation. Their vision of glorious Zion' (*Joker*, 275). In Mombara's view this '"cloud nine" ending … is unrepresentative of the thrust of the Rastafarian culture'.[53]

However, whether such idealism is consonant with Rasta beliefs – the evidence suggests diverse responses to social problems among the sect's members – it is certainly in keeping with *Walcott's* earlier treatment of African revivalist belief in *Dream on Monkey Mountain*. The parallels between the two plays, which only Robert Hamner seems to have noticed,[54] are striking and help to show that Walcott's representation of his central Rasta figures involves more than well-intentioned, but not very credible, sentimentalization. Like Makak in the earlier play, Aaron has an apocalyptic vision of Africa, in which the desire for 'the Great Return' (*Joker*, 167) is instilled by four 'all white' horsemen:

> *I stood on the sand, I saw*
> *black horsemen galloping toward me.*
> *They were all white like the waves*
> *and turbanned, too, like the breakers,*
> *their flags thinning away into spume;*
> *white, white were their snorting horses.* (*Joker*, 166)

Like much Rasta lore, this passage has its origins in the Book of Revelation and when Aaron returns to the vision towards the end of the play, he likens himself to St. John the Divine, a figure whose response to his island predicament had suggested Caribbean analogies to Walcott ever since his early poem, 'As John to Patmos'.[55] So, as with Makak, the pull towards Africa, whether seen as physical or psychic, emanates from a complex Judaeo-Christian legacy which Walcott associates with the 'white' world. The four horsemen of the apocalypse are the equivalent here of the apparition of the White Goddess in *Dream on Monkey Mountain* and, again like Makak, after a period in jail, Aaron eventually resolves to seek Zion in a mountainous Caribbean interior. He abandons the 'white' apparition of African return in favour of a commitment to the local landscape. In this sense at least *O Babylon!* re-enacts characteristic Walcott concerns by moving outside the binary opposition of African atavism and Western (neo-)colonialism. However, it is dramatically far less satisfying than *Dream on Monkey Mountain* and the form does seem to have been compromised by the attempt to write a reggae musical for Broadway production. Even on this level it is dubious whether it succeeds, since MacDermot's lively score all too often seems to be at odds with the play's social agendas and songs are introduced in a manner which stifles rather than strengthens the dramatic development of the play. There had been no such problems with *The Joker of Seville*.

Walcott had previously collaborated with Galt MacDermot on a new version of his first musical play *The Charlatan* (1974),[56] and subsequent collaborations with the composer, whom he felt 'had created a form different from the American musical',[57] included *Marie Laveau* (1979) and *Steel* (1991). *Marie Laveau* took Walcott's drama into new territory by focusing on the historical figure of a voodoo queen who flourished in New Orleans in the early nineteenth century. It laid Walcott open to the charge of having sold out to white America,[58] but as Judy Stone points out provides another instance of his trying to bring 'classical and Creole cultures' together,[59] this time in a play which demonstrates the syncretist nature of African-based New

World religions. *Steel* began life as a lengthy screenplay for a film set in 1945, in which a love story is played out against the backdrop of the origins of steelband music. The film was never made and Walcott subsequently adapted the screenplay for a single-set stage version, which lacked the range that would have been possible in the film version[60] and received an unfavourable reception when it opened in Boston. Like *The Joker of Seville* it drew very heavily on the highly localized musical culture of Trinidad; unlike *The Joker of Seville* it did not prove a successful export.

Walcott's dream of achieving success on Broadway with a musical finally looked likely to be fulfilled when he subsequently collaborated with one of the late twentieth-century's most famous singer-composers to produce a Latino musical grounded in cross-cultural fusions central to the American melting pot. He joined forces with Paul Simon for *The Capeman*, a 1998 production about a cape-wearing Puerto Rican immigrant, Salvador Agron, who had stabbed two teenagers to death in 1959. The show appeared to have all the ingredients for Broadway success: Simon's previous record with albums inspired by South African and Latino musical forms, choreography by Mark Morris, lyrics by Walcott and a cast headed by singer Ruben Blades and other leading New York Latino musicians. However, *The Capeman* ran into problems even before its opening night; and numerous preview performances and a decision to delay its opening by three weeks failed to iron out the weaknesses in a production which received some of the worst reviews in Broadway history when it did eventually open in January 1998. Influenced by such reviews, audiences voted with their feet and the show closed after just sixty-nine performances, having incurred a loss of $11 million and in so doing earned the dubious distinction of becoming the most expensive musical flop in Broadway history, as well as having prompted protests from victims' rights groups, including members of the families of Agron's victims.[61] In the intervening years Walcott had, however, had rather more success with non-musical theatre.

In 1976 Walcott parted company with the Trinidad Theatre Workshop[62] and his next play, *Remembrance* (1977), was commissioned and premiered by the Courtyard Players in St. Croix in the US Virgin Islands. Theatrically it is far less ambitious than most of the Workshop plays: it has a single set and a smaller cast of characters; and the use of mime, myth and music is replaced by a series of dialogues which mainly serve to define the psychology of the play's protagonist, the retired Trinidadian schoolteacher and writer, Albert Perez Jordan. It has been suggested that this represents a compliance with 'demands characteristic of U.S. production'.[63] Whether or not this was intentional on Walcott's part, like *Pantomime* (1978) *Remembrance* demonstrates a marked shift away from the expressionist allegory of *Dream on Monkey Mountain* and the musical exuberance of *The Joker of Seville* and *O Babylon!* It is a sparer, more naturalistic play which, from the moment when the curtain rises on a fading lower middle-class drawing room in Port of Spain, has more in common with such tightly-knit post-war domestic dramas as Arthur Miller's *Death of a Salesman* (1949), John Osborne's *Look Back in Anger* (1956) and the Australian Ray Lawler's *Summer of the Seventeenth Doll* (1955). Since *Remembrance* was written and first staged some two decades after these plays, its similarities with them might seem to suggest that it is rather dated. In fact, any such suggestion is highly appropriate since anachronism is its *subject*. Walcott has referred to the play as 'a sincere and painful tribute'[64] to the figure of the colonial West Indian teacher. His own mother, Alix, had been just such a teacher and in his programme note for a 1979 New York production, he speaks fondly of this generation of teachers:

> Between their day and ours there is 'a great gulf fixed', and the tides of change have left them beached on their pensions, exaggerating lost glories. They laid foundations for those who went on to colleges and universities. They have become as anachronistic as their clothes. But they were not mere imitators, they believed in the Caribbean. They were honest. They were gentlemen [sic]. Their contribution is immeasurable, their example Roman.[65]

In the present of the play, Jordan is being interviewed by a reporter from a local paper, who tape-records his reminiscences. His act of remembrance is a complex mixture of supposed fact and fiction, which links episodes from his past with his two best-known short stories, which are themselves based on episodes in his life. Consequently, as Lowel Fiet has pointed out,[66] remembrance becomes a performative act and, as in all Walcott's work, there is the sense that, far from being securely settled, the past is a discursive formation, subject to multiple and serial rein-vention. As Jordan tells his story, contradictions abound: he avowedly rejects Creole registers for Standard English, but he uses them himself; he prefers the scribal to the oral and has resisted the idea of the taped interview, but the first act of the play is shaped by the interview-structure and his speaking voice is dominant throughout.[67] Initially, Jordan seems to be a study in colonial alienation, a character who has rejected his local world, but has failed to establish a successful relationship with the metropolitan culture he has championed; and his alienation can be seen in the retelling of his story, in which he sometimes refers to himself in the third person and takes shelter within the personae of his fictional protagonists. A 'radical critic' of his stories has accused him of having 'avoided the realities of our society'[68] and this charge seems reasonable since, both in literature and life, he has failed to deal with the death of his son in the 1970 Black Power riots and with the values represented by such protest against the *status quo*.

Reflecting Jordan's cultural orientation, *Remembrance* employs numerous intertexts from English literature. Central among these is a sustained parallel with Gray's 'Elegy', which seems to suggest that, like the uncommemorated villagers buried in the poem's churchyard, the colonial Jordan has been a flower 'born to blush unseen'.[69] He himself comes to the conclusion that his anglophilia has rendered him a misfit and the sense that he has lived an unfulfilled life is endorsed by 'The War Effort', one of his two autobiographically-based stories, which is re-enacted in the play. During the war he has fallen in love with an Englishwoman, but when she has finally responded to his courtship, he has proved unable to fulfil his desire for England by marrying her. Instead he has married the Trinidadian Mabel, his wife of thirty years in the present of the play. A self-styled 'plain downright Trinidadian from Arima' (*RP*, 20), she appears attuned to the Creole world that he denies.

So Jordan seems to exist in a 'gulf', not simply because he is an anachronistic figure, 'beached' in the Caribbean present, but also because he was unable to consummate his love-affair with England in the late colonial period. However, as *Remembrance* progresses, audiences are invited to engage with a more complex assessment of his character, as satire gives way to elegy. Like so much of Walcott's work – from early poems such as 'Ruins of a Great House' and 'Veranda' through plays such as *Franklin* to the figure of Major Plunkett in *Omeros* – *Remembrance* illustrates the injurious psychological effects of colonialism, but also evinces nostalgia for some of the values it has instilled. The Gray parallel is central to this mood. In the second act Jordan identifies with the 'obscurity and missed opportunities' (*RP*, 75) of the lives of the villagers in the 'Elegy', and gradually his act of memory strips away his 'grinning mask' (*RP*, 29) to reveal not only his underlying honesty, but also a vein of pragmatism. His second son, Frederick, a painter, is his obvious counterpart in the post-independence era and in the other Jordan story staged in the play, 'Barrley and the Roof', he is offered the opportunity to sell his work to a visiting American (a predicament which, one feels, parallels Walcott's own situation at the time of writing). Initially the work of art in question, a Stars and Stripes painted on the roof of the family house, seems a travesty of art and Jordan's attitude to it is heavily satirical, but as Frederick refuses to sell out to Uncle Sam a more serious, if rather obvious, allegorical significance emerges. He, too, chooses to remain a flower that will blush unseen.

Act II confirms this decision, when he is seen in a neo-colonial equivalent to his father's wartime relationship. Although given the opportunity to go to the United States with Anna, an American dancer whom Jordan identifies with his wartime lover, Frederick decides to remain in Trinidad and at the end of the play has, in Jordan's words, 'chosen a slower death in this place – art' (*RP*, 85). Jordan's own choice has resulted from his timidity rather than a conscious rejection of the metropolis, but Frederick's decision seems to confirm that it has been the correct one. The play ends with Jordan acting out a scene from his classroom days, in which he glosses what Gray is saying in the 'Elegy' by telling his pupils: 'It doesn't matter where you're born, how obscure you are, that fame and fortune are contained within you. Your body is the earth in which it springs and dies' (*RP*, 86). Within the Caribbean, discourses of the body[70] have tended to be associated with carnivalesque festivities and Afro-Caribbean repossession. There is no such suggestion here – it would be completely out of keeping with Jordan's character – and yet the play uncompromisingly asserts Jordan's, and Frederick's, rootedness in the physicality of the Caribbean world; and this emphasis on the corporeal, like the stress on the natural world in so much of Walcott's poetry, again suggests a mode of being which exists outside colonial definition.

Remembrance is not one of Walcott's strongest plays from a performance point of view. It is more static and wordy than most of his drama and at times its allegory inclines towards the over-obvious. Yet it has generally been a success on stage. As monodrama, it relies heavily on the performance of the actor taking the part of Jordan and the role has been particularly well played in the most notable productions of the play;[71] and the tendency towards simplistic allegory is frustrated in the latter part of the text. The audience is kept guessing until the end and the neatly sentimental possibility of Frederick's reversing his father's apparent mistake by going to the United States with Anna is avoided when he makes the opposite choice. More importantly, the tone of the play becomes increasingly complex, as the satirical impulse gives way to the elegiac, forcing audiences and readers to mediate between different assessments of the generation of colonial educators that Jordan represents. Finally, the balance is tipped towards a sympathetic interpretation and the ending suggests that they *should* be seen as 'mute inglorious Miltons'[72] whose lives have been their own justification.

Walcott's next play, the frequently performed two-hander *Pantomime* (1978), has been published with *Remembrance* and is in many ways a companion-piece to the earlier play. Dedicated to Wilbert Holder, who played the part of Jackson in the original Port of Spain production,[73] it again explores some of the personal reverberations of Independence in a theatrically compact form. The action takes place in the cliff-top gazebo of a Tobago guest-house where the two protagonists, the owner Harry Trewe, a retired English music-hall performer, and his 'factotum' Jackson Phillip, a former calypsonian, enact a series of improvised variations on the Crusoe-Friday relationship that had fascinated Walcott at least as far back as the time when he was writing the poems of *The Castaway*.

Despite its single set and small cast, *Pantomime* is dramatically more vibrant than *Remembrance*. Like *Remembrance*, it has a tape recorder on stage at the opening, but here the machine provides background music for a song-and-dance routine by Harry and this establishes the mood for a play which makes much greater use of performance elements and in which cut-and-thrust repartee and character interaction have replaced monologue. Although *Pantomime* does not make extensive use of Caribbean folk forms, it is indebted to the topsy-turvy, carnivalesque conventions of *English* pantomime and the use of this genre – and the Robinson Crusoe motif – as an intertext underlies a series of reversals in which the cross-dressing gender inversions of pantomime are replaced by playful exchanges of racial roles. As in much of Walcott's work, the exploration of Caribbean identity issues is largely androcentric, but here the parallels drawn between race and gender, particularly in the latter stages of the play where Jackson acts the part of Harry's English wife, suggest that gender and racial binaries often intertwine. Such a position is, however, implied rather than developed and the parallels are far less suggestive than they are in a text such as J. M. Coetzee's *Foe* (1986), which takes a female refugee with origins in another Defoe novel, *Roxana*, as its narrator and in so doing destabilizes male-female paradigms and the counter-discursive relationship with *Robinson Crusoe* in a more radically unsettling way.[74]

The two protagonists of *Pantomime* emerge as doppelgänger figures who complement one another perfectly, engaging in witty ironic repartee which sustains dramatic tension throughout. Thus Jackson says of the guest-house:

> This hotel like a hospital. The toilet catch asthma, the air-condition got ague, the front-balcony rail missing four teet', and every minute the fridge like it dancing the Shango ... brrgudup ... jukjuk ... brrugudup. Is no wonder that the carpenter collapse. Termites jumping like steel band in the foundations. (*RP*, 98)

and Harry is only slightly less colourful in his satirical comment on the difficulty of committing suicide in this environment:

> Attempted suicide in a Third World country. You can't leave a note because the pencils break, you can't cut your wrist with the local blades ... (*RP*, 97)

Such comedy obviously stages the renegotiations of roles of former colonizer and colonized taking place in the post-independence Caribbean but, characteristically, Walcott is less concerned with chronicling the about-faces generated by political and social change than with foregrounding the inadequacy of binary paradigms. Far from allowing the two characters to swap roles in a simple process of post-colonial reversal, he has them play out an extended repertory of variations on the Friday-Crusoe relationship, which problematizes the very idea of hierarchical positioning. *Both* characters act the part of Crusoe, a figure who in *Pantomime* has almost as many incarnations as in Walcott's 'Figure of Crusoe' essay, among them those of Adamic discoverer, emotional isolate and pragmatic Creole. Schematism is also avoided through the introduction of several other references to acting parts: Harry takes on the roles of Al Jolson and the Ancient Mariner, while Jackson plays a number of stereotypical black roles, including those of Noble Savage, 'stage nigger' (*RP*, 140) and Uncle Tom, all roles which may be seen as expressions of the ambivalent mimicry engendered by colonial discourse.[75] At one point Jackson, in uncharacteristically solemn vein, says, 'This moment that we are now acting here is the history of imperialism; it's nothing less than that' (*RP*, 125) and clearly the play's title can also be seen to suggest ambivalent colonial mimicry. As in *Dream on Monkey Mountain*, the image of ape-like imitation is used on a number of occasions and in a calypso, a genre associated with Carnival and its numerous modes of mimicry, Jackson claims that Crusoe '*make Friday a Good Friday Bohbolee*' (*RP*, 117).[76]

Through all this a playful emphasis on the possibility of transformation predominates and *Pantomime* avoids heavy-handed political agendas. What emerges most forcefully is that identity is a series of roles, to be donned and doffed at will in the post-independence period, just as they have been previously in the pantomime instituted by colonialism. Ultimately the play propounds a view of character as a fluid, endlessly mutating process rather than an essentialist entity, a view which can be seen as a post-colonial conception of subjectivity irrespective of the period under consideration. Like the Trinidadian novelist Sam Selvon, who had carnivalized the Friday–Crusoe relationship in *Moses Ascending* (1975), Walcott rejects an oppositional approach in which the roles of master and servant are simply reversed, but arguably goes further than Selvon in subverting the possibility of fixed positioning. The isolation of the two characters in the cliff-top gazebo suggests a suspended, liminal environment in which a more radical interrogation of power hegemonies can be conducted. Walcott's Friday and Crusoe create their own comic post-colonial space, which has an affinity with the milieu of Carnival as described by Mikhail Bakhtin:

> carnival celebrated liberation from the prevailing truth and from the established order; it marked the suspension of all hierarchical rank, privileges, norms and prohibitions. Carnival was the true feast of time, the feast of becoming, change and renewal. It was hostile to all that was immortalised and completed.[77]

Within the Caribbean Carnival has often been viewed as a politically ambivalent site, being variously seen as licensed escapism and as a vehicle for genuine revolutionary change,[78] and *Pantomime*, with its emphasis on a fluid transformational exchange of identities in a liminal environment, lends itself to a similar debate. One commentator, Biodun Jeyifo, acknowledges the play's 'radical relativism in its complete deconstruction of Eurocentrism and nativism', but asks whether such relativism has force 'when it evades or occludes the violence of the power relations between them by tacitly assuming an equivalence of either actual power consolidation between them, or the will-to-power of their pundits and adherents?'[79] Lurking behind such a question is a still larger one about the merit of post-colonial and postmodernist theories which valorize cultural translation and hybridity without addressing the socio-political factors which determine the lives of the socially immobile wretched of the earth, who have little or no sense of the positive dynamics of living between cultures.

There can be no simple answers to such questions. What one can say is that Walcott's practice in *Pantomime* seems to be grounded in the belief that language is central to debates about subjectivity. Like Homi Bhabha, who has spoken of Walcott's poem 'Names'[80] as the most profound evocation of 'the concept of the right to signify'[81] that he has found in contemporary post-colonial poetry, Walcott sees the moment of enunciation as crucial to cultural transition and in his drama theatrical speech seems equally to offer a means for such change. He has said that *Pantomime* is as much about theatre as society at large:

> It is basically, I suppose, about two actors, and their different racial and cultural origins creating whatever conflicts exist from their approach to theatre, its ritual, its meaning, its style. It may also be saying that the self-torturing schizophrenia that precedes the resolution of an identity can achieve a resolution with dignity. It may be a political play, with its subject, independence, but that process first has to become human before it can become political.[82]

The play makes extended use of theatrical imagery and although both characters are in flight from the world of entertainment – Harry from the English 'theatuh' (*RP*, 161) which has destroyed his confidence while making his wife a star; Jackson from the 'show business' (*RP*, 102) aspects of Trinidad's Carnival culture – they remain performers to the core and engage in a self-referential comic debate about what kind of play the pantomime should be.

At the beginning of the second act, Jackson is amused as he remembers an auditioning actor who has claimed 'I do all kind of acting, classical acting. *Creole* acting' (*RP*, 131) and this becomes a motif that runs through the remainder of the play. Jackson's amusement appears to stem from his surprise that anyone could envisage such a split and Walcott's text, again characteristically, creates a continuum in which both characters subvert the idea of such an opposition by creolizing the 'classical'. Harry has been a former pantomime dame and, despite some maudlin moments towards the end, is the initiator of the project to use Defoe's classic text for the purpose of post-colonial satire. Jackson is at first reluctant to take part in such revisionist role-playing, but quickly enters into its spirit and begins to take control of the script. As he does so, he interrogates Harry's self-projection of Crusoe as an emotional isolate, insisting that he be reconstructed as a pragmatic Creole: 'If he is not practical, he is not Robinson Crusoe' (*RP*, 146); 'Robbie is the First True Creole' (*RP*, 148). Again, as in Walcott's 'Figure of Crusoe' essay and as in his creolized reworkings of Adam, Don Juan and Odysseus, the emphasis is on refashioning 'classical' archetypes so that they have a valency which erodes the crude binarism of colonizer–colonized, European–'Other' dichotomies. In *Pantomime* the theatrical fusion of 'classical' and 'Creole' enacts a similar continuum of experience and the characters' meta-theatrical debate about what kind of play the pantomime should be once again shows Walcott wrestling with the question of what kind of theatrical practice is appropriate for the Caribbean.

Pantomime ends with Harry and Jackson working towards a man-to-man relationship and humanized by the stripping away of former stereotypes. Both men have boasted of violent, macho actions in their past, but both their claims appear to be bogus and Harry emerges as a decidedly ambiguous colonizer figure, when he confesses to having no belief in ownership. Acting remains central to this process of reconciliation and, while this can be interpreted as a metonym for the renegotiation of roles in the post-independence period, it also bears testimony to Walcott's belief in the role theatre has to play in the evolution of a new Caribbean culture.

A Branch of the Blue Nile (1983), a play centred on the squabbles of a Trinidad theatre group staging a production of *Antony and Cleopatra*, which inevitably invites speculation that it grew out of Walcott's experiences with the Theatre Workshop, took a similar, if less comic, approach to the role of drama, linking acting with role-playing more generally. However, two other Walcott plays dealing with aspects of post-independence change, which were subsequently to be published with *A Branch of the Blue Nile*,[83] appeared prior to this: *Beef, No Chicken* examined the impact of modernity – or more accurately what Bruce King has referred to as 'pseudo-Americanization'[84] – on rural Trinidad; *The Last Carnival* (1982) was a reworking of a play written in response to the short-lived 1970 Black Power Revolution in Trinidad.[85]

The first part of *Beef, No Chicken* provides an often farcical portrayal of the effects of modernization on the small town of Couva. The play's central symbol of 'progress' is the new highway that is coming to Couva, but fast food, television and the culture of the shopping mall are all seen as part of the same phenomenon. The play operates through broad humour, but, with occasional notable exceptions, this humour lacks the comic force of *Pantomime*. Its various productions have elicited a range of responses from commentators[86] and, as with so many of Walcott's plays, it has undergone multiple revisions. However, on the evidence of the printed text, its striving for comic effect is only intermittently successful and rather too much of the comedy relies on forced puns. Thus, after a road accident:

> *Otto.* I tell the sign painter mark DRIVE IN, DASH, then FAST FOOD SERVICE. Not he! DRIVE-IN FAST, a big comma, FOOD SERVICE.
> *Franco.* So you're in a coma because of a comma. (*TP*, 132)

and of a roti-cook, who begins most of her sentences with the word 'because':

> *Euphony.* Sumintra has resigned. She too insubordinate.
> *Franco.* You find so? She began every sentence with a
>   subordinate clause.   (*TP*, 122)

Similarly, the satire of the commercialism of contemporary Trinidadian life is over-obvious and the tendency to play everything for laughs that predominates until the last part has the effect of occluding the social criticism.

However, as the play progresses, it moves beyond comedy and its most effective moments are those which lament the passing of an older way of life. Just as *Remembrance* uses Gray's 'Elegy' as an intertext, *Beef, No Chicken* alludes to a similar eighteenth-century landscape poem, Goldsmith's 'Deserted Village',[87] to provide commentary on the despoliation of the rural Trinidadian world. Again the mood is elegiac and Walcott's sympathies are clearly with those characters who resist the homogenizing modernity which he feels is swamping Trinidad. Foremost among these is Otto, a restaurant owner and mechanic who, given the opportunity to profiteer from the coming of the new highway, resists corruption and, like Frederick in *Remembrance*, chooses the local over the American. Yet the most powerful statements about the urban blight which is sweeping the country are placed in the mouth of a minor character, Deacon, an ordained preacher who now leads the life of a vagrant. He is an apocalyptic prophet of ecological doom:

> Pretty soon there'll be no country left. Nowhere to walk,
> nowhere to sit in the shade, whole place one big concrete
> suburb. Oh! Yes! It's about McDonaldizing everything,
> it's Kentucky Frying everything, it's about going modern
> with a vengeance and televising everything, it's hamming
> up everything, traffic-jamming up everything, it's about
> neon lighting up everything, urban-blighting everything.
> I'm warning you. I seen it with my own two feet. (*TP*, 204)

Conducting a wedding-service at the end of the play, he makes a plea for the retention of personal distinctiveness. He believes this is fast being eroded by the replacement of substance by image which he sees as characteristic of the new religion of television:

> All you hold hands tight before you disappear.
> From reality to shadow, from the substantial
> to the insubstantial, we believe in our images
> instead of ourselves until everything that lives
> ain't holy no longer but fully photographed,
> and the test of our creed is: 'I saw it on TV.' (*TP*, 199)

In *Pantomime* shadow existences are associated with the colonial predicament; here the emphasis has shifted to global consumerism and the postmodern image-fetishism which replaces selves with simulacra, leaving ordinary people – in the Caribbean and elsewhere – as disempowered as ever. However, while *Beef, No Chicken* is an elegy for the older rural Trinidadian world, symbolized at one point by an 'honest' road which '[s]ometimes, in the afternoon, when it had no traffic, … would lie down and roll over on his back, like a pothound warming his belly in the sun' (*TP*, 196), it acknowledges the inevitability of its demise. Although the forces of corruption are defeated in the main action of the play, a brief final scene provides a *coda* in which four of the main Couva characters, each representing a slightly different point of view, have become television performers, and Deacon who has previously refused the offer of a television, watches them on a set which 'glows like a bomb' (*TP*, 207).

In a Fine Castle (1970), the first version of the play that was to develop into the now better-known *The Last Carnival*, had offered a fairly stark dramatization of the contrast between its black revolutionaries and a decaying French Creole family, which has affinities with the Vertlieu family of *The Wine of the Country*. Its central figure is a journalist, Brown, who occupies the middle ground between the two factions and has been seen by Judy Stone as 'the familiar Walcott mulatto in his sensitivity to two cultures',[88] even though he is black. While the concerns of the play go beyond the racial binaries that lie at its centre, it was perhaps not surprising that its earliest critics and audiences saw little else in the politically charged aftermath of the Black Power uprising. Initial responses were not generally favourable and the first Trinidadian reviewers were unimpressed by the play's depiction of racial issues, feeling that neither French Creoles nor blacks were flattered by the way Walcott had represented them.[89]

The Last Carnival offers a much more complex treatment of revolution and Carnival than *In a Fine Castle*, locating them in a longer historical context. Perhaps distance helped Walcott to situate the events of the Black Power Revolution within a broader framework. In any case, whereas *In a Fine Castle* focuses on 1970, *The Last Carnival* devotes the first of its two acts to events in 1948 and includes a brief scene set on the day of Trinidad's Independence in 1962, before moving to 1970 in its second act. It has a more extensive cast, which includes one completely new major character, Agatha, a Cockney governess employed by the French Creole De La Fontaine family.[90] Her arrival in Trinidad marks the beginning of the action and she offers an interesting working-class outsider's perspective on the De La Fontaines' life-style and their relationship with the Trinidad populace, as well as being an important protagonist in her own right.

The new title of the play focuses attention on its central concerns, which, as in *The Wine of the Country* and *Franklin*, have to do with issues of ownership and belonging around the time of political independence. It is a title which has several resonances. In the first act, the artist Victor De La Fontaine is painting a copy of Watteau's 'The Embarkation for Cythera'[91] and in the penultimate scene of this act, he stages a fête based on Watteau's painting at the family's estate house, Santa Rosa. When Agatha and his more creolized brother, Oswald, threaten to subvert his intentions by introducing a bawdy element, he declares that this is Santa Rosa's 'last Carnival' (*TP*, 49). In the second act, the Revolution takes place against the backdrop of Carnival and a government minister says that the uprising means that 'this could be the last Carnival for years' (*TP*, 67);[92] and when Sydney, one of the revolutionaries is shot, he is said to have 'played his last Carnival' (*TP*, 97). So the title variously suggests: the French Creole fêtes that were a partial source for later Trinidad Carnival; the contemporary people's festival; and the Revolution, which involves a carnivalesque inversion of the social order, albeit one which is intended to be neither comic nor temporary.

Through this triple definition, the play effectively explores the issue of who owns Carnival and, in a society where it is not only the most important cultural festival but has also been seen as an expression of the national psyche, this raises issues about ownership more generally. Victor's Watteau masque suggests a modern-day version of what Errol Hill views as the earliest form of Trinidad Carnival, the pre-Lenten masquerades and festivals of the French plantocracy who became a significant component of Trinidad's population when they settled on the island after the Haitian Revolution.[93] There is, of course, another genealogy for Trinidad Carnival, which places more emphasis on forms which evolved from the folk culture of the Afro-Caribbean majority population. Most notable among these in the nineteenth century was *canboulay*, a ritual which developed from the practice of slaves' extinguishing plantation fires[94] and which after Emancipation became associated with the changed condition of the ex-slaves. Significantly, this ritual was not held in the pre-Lenten period but on 1 August, Emancipation Day. This clearly suggests another provenance and it is clear that by the end of the nineteenth century, 'carnival had become a symbol of freedom for the broad mass of the population and not simply a season for frivolous enjoyment'.[95] Today Carnival is held in the pre-Lenten period and is often considered to have been co-opted by commercial forces, but *The Last Carnival* suggests the ambiguities that remain at the heart of the festival. As in *Pantomime*, Walcott addresses a central question concerning Carnival: 'Is it simply an amoral "bacchanal", a time of licensed escapism or does it contain genuine revolutionary potential?' Predictably, his implied answer erodes the binary opposition contained in such a formulation by blurring the dividing-lines and suggesting a shared creolized heritage with commonalities that span class, race and gender difference.

At the same time Walcott exhibits a particular imaginative engagement with the predicaments of the various members of the De La Fontaine family and once again the element of elegy for the former ruling classes looms large. The play provides Walcott's most incisive analysis of the impact of francophone culture in the Caribbean, though the nuances of this are not fully developed and are consequently unlikely to be accessible to the average audience. They centre on the use of the Watteau allusion and a range of other 'French' cultural intertexts: to the paintings of Toulouse Lautrec, to Baudelaire's 'Voyage to Cythera' and to the Paris-based German composer Meyerbeer's opera *L'Africaine*. In Victor's masque in Act I, Oswald plays Toulouse Lautrec and Agatha takes the role of Jane Avril, an English performer at the Moulin Rouge whom Lautrec painted during his Paris period; Victor himself takes the role of Watteau and George, a family servant, plays the traditional, though by this time neglected, Pierrot Grenade[96] figure of Carnival. Earlier Victor has painted Agatha in the guise of a Watteau shepherdess and now in the masquerade Oswald is to recite the Baudelaire poem[97] and a parang band is to appear in Watteau costume.

The use of Watteau's 'Cythera' is fascinating, not simply because it invokes the masquerade performances of the early French plantocracy, but also because the artist was noted for his paintings of *fêtes galantes*, 'in which exquisitely dressed young people idle away their time in a dreamy, romantic pastoral setting',[98] or, to put it another way, enter an escapist, carnivalesque space where the exigencies of everyday life cease to exist.[99] Cythera in Watteau's paintings is an idealized fantasy landscape for lovers; subsequent responses have often 'picked up that mood of sadness (even resignation) which the images strangely convey'.[100] Within the play the exact significance of Cythera is far from obvious, but it clearly represents a questionable form of Carnival escapism, associated with a European Romantic vision of the Tropics. In a poem entitled 'Watteau' included in *Midsummer* (1984) Walcott comments on Cythera as a product of a diseased francophone longing for a paradise amid alterity:

The amber spray of trees feather-brushed with the dusk,
the ruined cavity of some spectral château, the groin
of a leering satyr eaten with ivy, in the distance, the grain
of some unreapable, alchemical harvest, the hollow at
the heart of all embarkations. Nothing stays green
in that prodigious urging towards twilight;
in all of his journeys the pilgrims are in fever
from the tremulous strokes of malaria's laureate.
So where is Cythera? It, too, is far and feverish,
it dilates on the horizon of his near-delirium, near
and then further, it can break like the spidery rigging
of his ribboned barquentines, it is as much nowhere
as those broad-leafed islands, it is the disease
of elephantine vegetation in Baudelaire,
the tropic bug in the Paris fog. For him, it is the mirror
of what is. Paradise is life repeated spectrally,
an empty chair echoing the emptiness.[101]

One way of reading this is to say that the embarkation for Cythera involves an impossible kind of exoticization of the Caribbean world, analogous to a form of Orientalism, even if languor and disease are part of this construction. Agatha arrives in Trinidad fascinated by its smells and light, and feeling it may offer the possibility of a second Eden ('It's as if the world were making a fresh start', *TP*, 6). Victor tries to paint it as a paradisal place, but significantly his canvases remain unfinished. Cythera remains a place to be approached through multiple embarkations; the notion of arriving at a settled condition is as elusive in the play as it is in V. S. Naipaul's *The Enigma of Arrival* (1987), which also turns to European art for an intertext that points up the impossibility of reaching a definitive end-point or discovering an originary moment.[102] Unable to achieve this vision or, it would seem, to live with the uncompletedness that can be seen as a positive aspect of the post-colonial situation, Victor commits suicide in the years which elapse between the two acts. While the theme of artistic suicide is not uncommon in Walcott's work, here it seems to relate specifically to the conception of the Caribbean artist that Victor personifies. The more pragmatic Agatha quickly grasps the discrepancy between the imagined paradise of her preconceptions and the actuality of the socially divided world in which she finds herself and sets about providing its have-nots with a political education. In so doing, she is responsible for the making of a future government minister and one of the revolutionaries. Victor has no interest in such pragmatism. He realizes the impossibility of Watteau's vision:

> He painted
> his whole culture as if it were a sunset,
> because all embarkation is a fantasy. You see
> those pilgrims in the painting? They can't move.
> It's like some paralyzed moment in a carnival. (*TP*, 17)

Yet he remains committed to the frozen moment, to the attempt to arrest social processes, movement, life itself, through art. In a sense this is a version of the classic dilemma faced by most pictorial and scribal artists, who find that by immortalizing the fugitive nature of experience in artistic form, they, like Keats's grecian urn, deny movement and process. It is, however, a dilemma that takes on a particular urgency in a Carnival culture such as Trinidad's where the emphasis is on 'becoming, change and renewal'[103] rather than stasis and completion. Victor's view of art and experience is, then, an inappropriate, European – and, it would seem, specifically French-inscribed – response to the changing social and artistic world in which he finds himself, and his failure to acknowledge the value of process, as opposed to product, proves suicidal.

Victor's son, Tony,[104] a Carnival designer who has created a Watteau band for the 1970 Carnival but is committed to a more creolized artistic practice, sees his father as the embodiment of a particularly French colonial sensibility:

> I suppose, although I loved my father, I detested him. He made us cherish taste, and it was the wrong taste for this country, and that makes us useless. The French are shitty colonizers. They create this longing for the metropole in their colonials. But what's worse is that they also create this longing for paradise in *their* metropole.
>
> ...

> In the end he was delirious and kept calling himself
> Watteau. ... Well, after many doctors, he had one of his
> lucid periods, and in one of those rational periods, he did
> the rational thing. No more illusions. No more Cythera!
> He killed Antoine Watteau. (*TP*, 73)

His father has sought the idealized perfection of classical landscapes, but Tony represents Walcott's acknowledgement of the positive side of hybridity and his 'mongrel'[105] predicament.

Several other issues figure prominently in *The Last Carnival*, but the remainder of the characters are not developed with the same degree of complexity as Victor, Oswald and Agatha and the off-stage revolution which hastens the end of their world itself seems a doomed fantasy. Consequently it is difficult to disagree with the verdict of the finest of literary commentators on Carnival, Earl Lovelace who, reviewing the 1982 Trinidad production of *The Last Carnival*, praised the play as 'strong and textured', but took Walcott to task for his failure 'to press home, indeed plunge into those truths that are there within the fabric of the play'. Lovelace particularly criticized the 'incomplete characterisation'[106] of the black militant Sydney, the journalist Brown and Victor's daughter, Clodia, who like her brother seems to be committed to the society at large but leaves the island at the end, in a neat reversal of Agatha's arrival at the beginning. Certainly, *The Last Carnival* suffers in comparison with Lovelace's representation of Carnival and related forms of Trinidadian popular culture in *The Dragon Can't Dance* (1979) and *Salt* (1996), both of which handle a broad gallery of character types, including a French Creole in the case of *Salt*, with great assurance. Nevertheless the play remains memorable for its vivid characterization of Victor, Oswald and Agatha and for its very precise depiction of a particular kind of French Romantic psychology, shipwrecked in the Caribbean; and the portrayal of this mentality offers commentary on idealized European constructions of alterity more generally.

A Branch of the Blue Nile returned to the issue of the relationship between the Creole and the classical which had exercised

Walcott's imagination since the beginning of his career. As in *Pantomime*, a European intertext provided a departure-point, but the use of such a framework is far less comic in *A Branch of the Blue Nile*: a group of Caribbean actors rehearse *Antony and Cleopatra* and debate the appropriateness of performing such a play in Trinidad. *Antony and Cleopatra* is not, however, the only play-within-a-play: one of the actors, Chris, has written a Creole comedy, which provides an obvious contrast to the Shakespearean tragedy, and towards the end he composes another play, which is also called *A Branch of the Blue Nile* and which appears to be the same as the main play: when an extract is performed, it is a verbatim transcription of an episode that has occurred within the frame-play.[107] Such self-reflexiveness foregrounds the extent to which Walcott is once again engaging with the issue of what constitutes an appropriate Caribbean theatrical practice. While *A Branch of the Blue Nile* has widely been seen as having a basis in real-life events, including Walcott's break with the Trinidad Theatre Workshop, popular Trinidadian dramatist Freddie Kissoon's attempt to create a theatre for ordinary West Indians and the Workshop actor Albert Laveau's endeavour to make a career in the United States[108] and while it *is* doubtless indebted to some of these factors for its origins, it is a more profound metatheatrical piece about the nature and role of theatre in the Caribbean.

On one level the conflict between the Creole and the classical seems once again to reflect the schizophrenia which Walcott had felt from early on in his career and which he had expressed particularly memorably in a 1970 essay:

> I am a kind of split writer: I have one tradition inside me going in one way, and another tradition going another. The mimetic, the Narrative, and dance element is strong on one side, and the literary, the classical tradition is strong on the other.[109]

The pivotal character in this respect is the white director, Harvey St. Just, who resolves the problem of whether to privilege the classical or the Creole by deciding that the company will perform both *Antony and Cleopatra* and Chris's 'dialect piece'

(*TP*, 223), just as Walcott had tried in his own dramatic practice and his involvement in the choice of the Theatre Workshop's repertory to bring the two strands together. By the second act *Antony and Cleopatra* is undergoing creolization with the clown's speeches in his exchange with Cleopatra about 'the worm'[110] being rewritten in 'dialect', much to the chagrin of a highbrow local theatre critic. However, the play engages in a more searching enquiry into the relevance of the classical in the Caribbean by problematizing the significance of a text such as *Antony and Cleopatra*, and this comes out more forcefully through the character who originally takes the part of Cleopatra, Sheila Harris.

The play opens with Sheila reciting the speech Cleopatra makes as she prepares to kill herself in the final act of the play.[111] Harvey, an exponent of Lee Strasberg's school of Method acting, complains that her performance suffers from 'sexual hesitation' (*TP*, 213); her response to the dead Antony's corpse lacks passion. She replies that she is not Cleopatra and this raises the issue of what Cleopatra might represent both to her and for the Caribbean more generally. Harvey's attack on her and references to the affair she is having with Chris in real life rouse Sheila to give a completely different, inspirational interpretation of the lines. The whole cast is moved by the metamorphosis that has taken place and one of the other actors, Gavin Fontinelle, who has spent time in the United States, expresses his admiration through a 'Sammy Davis number' (*TP*, 220):

> Man, can't you see this elegant black fox
> smothered in furs, up to her throat in sables,
> these fingers flashing starlight like hot ice.
> Can't you hear sirens, babe? Now, come on,
> turn on a white grin, wide as a marquee,
> and blind them screaming fans; come on, man, walk!
>
> (*TP*, 219)

Even Sheila herself is moved by the transformation that has taken place and feels that for a moment at least she has received a special 'gift' and has become Cleopatra.

In this sense Sheila is a branch of the blue Nile and her

coming alive as a brilliant actress is related to her African origins. She subsequently recounts a visit to an old African prophetess who has read her palm and implied that her connection with Africa is inescapable:

> She said that she saw implicit in my palm
> a river with seven branches tracing it.
> That my past was connected with that river
> and I couldn't avoid it any more than I could
> remove the tributaries in my open palm. (*TP*, 240)

Later, however, she turns her back on the theatre for what the play presents as another kind of performance arena, the Adventist church, saying that the 'congregation' is a more appropriate place for an 'ambitious black woman' (*TP*, 284) than the stage and she has killed off Cleopatra, because:

> She was killing me
> My body was invaded by that queen. …
> I found myself walking in pentameter. (*TP*, 285)

In her view, then, while certain forms of Christianity have become totally absorbed by Afro-Trinidadian society, Shakespeare remains an alien discourse. At the same time, another level of complexity is involved, since both 'Cleopatra' and 'Egypt' are presented as ambivalent signifiers.[112] Resisting Gavin's view that her success in playing Cleopatra has come from portraying the Egyptian queen as an 'elegant black fox', Sheila tells Harvey that another actress, the racially-mixed Marilyn, will play the part more satisfactorily, because Cleopatra 'wasn't black, / she was like Marilyn, Mediterranean' (*TP*, 284). At this point, then, the prospect of a cross-cultural Caribbean theatre seems to be breaking down because of self-imposed racial stereotyping, which perpetuates the binary exclusions of colonial discourse. Gavin has encountered the typecasting of black actors in the United States and appears to have become a master of operating within the available possibilities, by reconstructing himself as a 'reflection' (*TP*, 225), which fits the society's 'definition' (*TP*, 226) of what a black actor can be. The less urbane Sheila makes no such compromises and takes the view that the theatre remains a white preserve in the post-independent Caribbean.

A Branch of the Blue Nile clearly works to dismantle such assumptions, suggesting that talent is a 'gift' which crosses racial and ethnic boundaries and, through its own dramatic practice, treading a middle path between the modes of classical tragedy and local realism. As in Walcott's earliest plays, there are several Shakespeare allusions[113] and images,[114] but these are now subsumed into a style which, while it moves between different registers as part of its metatheatrical project, seamlessly suggests the continuum aspects of Caribbean discourse and does nothing to threaten the psychological credibility of the characters.

The focus on quarrels between the actors, Sheila's decision that she does not belong on the stage and the company's eventual break-up might suggest a pessimistic conclusion on the future of Caribbean theatre, possibly a product of Walcott's mood after *his* break with the Theatre Workshop. In fact, *A Branch of the Blue Nile* does not come to such a conclusion. The play ends with a new generation of actors acting Chris's second play (the inner *Branch of the Blue Nile*), which suggests continuity is being achieved through Walcott's own play, and an exchange between Sheila and a hitherto minor character, Phil, a 'derelict', holds out further promise for the future. Like Sheila, Phil is a man who has had a 'gift' which has deserted him. He has been the lead singer of a 1960s group, which enjoyed a brief period of success before subsequently falling into obscurity and now he loiters outside the theatre complaining about the way Caribbean society treats its artists. Phil is the Lear or 'Mad Tom' (*TP*, 247) of the play, the supposed madman who speaks more sense than sane society:

> I sorry I does scream outside when all you does be rehearsin'. ... This walking I does do all over town is like some fellows who does catch the spirit and start preaching to the traffic. Some of them mad, they look mad, they talk mad, but what they saying, sometimes it ain't always madness. That the government ain't care, that this one in a racket, this one is a thief, this one forget where he come

> from, that there is a spirit overhead does guide us and does
> catch us safe in his palm, like my hand could catch this
> drop of rain. (*TP*, 299)

He wishes he could 'sprinkle benediction' on all actors and
entertainers, whom he sees as Christ-like scapegoats who
'incorporate man's suffering inside their own' (*TP*, 300) and
when he speaks to Sheila at the end, it is once again to affirm the
'sacred' quality of acting and the extent to which the gift which
they have received is something 'God lend you for a little while'.
In his case inspiration seems to have deserted him completely,
but he urges Sheila whom he believes still has the gift to
continue '[f]or all our sakes' (*TP*, 312). The play ends with Sheila
returning to the stage alone and beginning to do breathing
exercises. So again there is the suggestion of continuity, both in
terms of the specific contexts that have been evoked and for
Caribbean theatre more generally.

Throughout the 1980s and 1990s Walcott continued to be
prolific as a dramatist and, in addition to the plays and musicals
mentioned above, wrote a number of other unpublished
plays,[115] among them *The Ghost Dance* (1989), which depicted
the last days of the Sioux chief Sitting Bull and drew parallels
between genocidal episodes in North American and Caribbean
history,[116] a subject which Walcott would return to in *Omeros*,[117]
and *Viva Detroit* (1990), a comedy about an inter-racial love
affair set in St. Lucia, in which a local man and an American
tourist engage in role reversals reminiscent of *Pantomime*. Two
other plays of the 1980s, both originally written as screenplays
for films which were again never made,[118] looked at moments of
national political change with an emphasis on the perspectives of
particular individuals: *The Haytian Earth* (1984) returned to a
subject which had fascinated Walcott since his youth, the
Haitian revolution; set on a small island off the north-east coast
of Trinidad at the moment of the 1983 American invasion of
Grenada which toppled Maurice Bishop's socialist government,
To Die for Grenada (1986) used the backdrop of the invasion as
a focus for consideration of a range of American–Caribbean

encounters. Despite the difference in period, the two plays have much in common and revisit several of the central themes of Walcott's drama, while once again demonstrating his distrust of macro-historical accounts. *The Haytian Earth* is especially interesting in this respect, since Walcott's representation of the events of the black Jacobins' revolution in this play moves away from the Elizabethan and Jacobean dramatic conventions and the heroic characterization, which had informed his attempt to invest Caribbean historical figures with the stature of European tragic protagonists in his first treatment of the Revolution, *Henri Christophe*. Instead it employs an approach which has more affinities with his emphasis on ordinary Caribbean experience in *Drums and Colours*, where he had returned to the subject of the Revolution for one of the episodes.

The Haytian Earth was premiered in St. Lucia in 1984 as part of the island's sesquicentennial celebration of Emancipation. Again Walcott exploited correspondences between revolutionary Haiti and the contemporary St. Lucian situation, particularly through the use of francophone Creole and references to local folk practices.[119] In one sense the play is Walcott's most pano-ramic account of the Haitian Revolution and its aftermath: it opens in 1790 before the first phase of the Revolution and closes, at the end of Henri Christophe's reign, in 1820; and it certainly offers the most extensive *dramatis personae* of Walcott's three treatments. Each of the three main protagonists of the historical events of the cataclysmic thirty years that completely changed the course of Haitian history – Toussaint L'Ouverture, Jean-Jacques Dessalines and Henri Christophe – is individualized and developed in some depth. The play also provides snapshots of numerous other historical figures, among them Ogé and Chavannes, the mulatto 'Friends of the Blacks' who led the first uprising against French rule, Baron F. De Wimpffen, the French author who wrote a travel-journal of his visits to Haiti in the years immediately before the Revolution,[120] and Boukmann, the *papaloi* (or voodoo high priest) who led the first black rebellion. However, any illusion of comprehensive historical coverage is undermined by the inclusion of a number of fictional or heavily fictionalized characters, most of whom had previously appeared in the Haitian episodes of *Drums and Colours*. These include the French planter, Calixte-Breda and his adopted son, Anton, a typical Walcott 'bastard ... mulatto' (*HE*, I, 4) caught between the conflicting claims of the white and black sides of his ancestry, and quick to see his own psychic duality as an expression of the Apollonian/Dionysian binaries that have surrounded constructions of race in Western society at least as far back as classical Greek discourse.[121] Anton associates thought, here linked with Enlightenment philosophers, with whiteness and action with blackness:

> I'm tempted to write out my thoughts, but thought
> is like a thicket without a clearing,
> and I begin, then my wrist is paralysed.
> I look at my hand and abhor my own colour,
> it is mixed, a compound like the colour of the earth.
> And I put my pen aside, and I live apart
> from thought. I have read all of them,
> Rousseau, Voltaire, but it is as if I'm not entitled
> to thought, to ideas. Entitlement, entitlement,
> enlightenment, enlightenment. White,
> is the colour of thought, black of action.
> and I'm paralysed, Madame, between thought and action.
> Perhaps I should not be a writer but a soldier. (*HE*, 1, 4)

The play even includes brief scenes set in France, which allow for representation of Napoleon's perspective on the Revolution and the betrayal of Toussaint, and an account of the death of Toussaint in a prison cell in the Jura mountains. Its sweep is therefore altogether broader than that of *Henri Christophe*, where Walcott had primarily focused on the second phase of the Revolution and its aftermath, and *Drums and Colours*, where the treatment had of necessity been more summary, since there events surrounding the Revolution formed only one of four episodes in a historical pageant which ranged across five centuries.

Notwithstanding the breadth of its coverage, the historical events of *The Haytian Earth* seem more remote than those

Henri Christophe. The main action concerns itself with the psychological plights of individuals and the emphasis is on ordinary Haitians, particularly two other figures from *Drums and Colours*: Pompey, the shoemaker who had appeared in the nineteenth- and twentieth-century sections of the earlier play, and Yette, a member of Mano's group of contemporary masqueraders in *Drums and Colours*. Both characters point towards a realm of Caribbean possibility which transcends the political power struggles of the Revolution.

ıst as *Drums and Colours* had replaced a view of history red on the lives of great men with a *people's* history well ated to the nationalist and federalist mood of its period, *The Haytian Earth* makes *its* contemporary point by arguing that Caribbean folk culture is more enduring than the exploits of political leaders, whether they be tyrants or visionaries or both. As in *Dream on Monkey Mountain* and *Another Life*, Walcott stresses the importance of the landscape as a site offering release from the divisive dualities of Caribbean history; the play is no longer concerned, as *Henri Christophe* had been, to mediate between the different possibilities represented by Toussaint, Dessalines and Christophe, but rather to stress the abiding qualities of the folk imagination. Walcott's representative Caribbean man, Pompey, is transformed from a shoemaker (in *Drums and Colours*) to a peasant farmer for whom the land is a place of peace, offering a different – and, it is suggested, more enduring – vision of Haiti from that created by the warring factions. For Pompey the land is personified by the whore Yette who becomes his wife, Walcott's representative Caribbean woman:

> Why I want you? Because I want to see you
> with your arms brown and shining picking the
> corn that will die if you do not come. I want
> to hear you laughing like the water when you
> washing the two clothes we have. Because it is
> the time of peace. The war will finish. ...
> I will walk by the mule I have outside one thousand
> hundred miles, and we will reach to the old house.
> ... you and I, we is Hayti, Yette. (*HE*, 2, 7)

The trope of the land as woman is a cliché which frequently denies women autonomous selfhood and the play's represent-ation of Yette moving between the roles of whore and wife runs the risk of further stereotyping her. Arguably, however, Yette is more than a stereotypical madonna-whore figure. Her union with Pompey symbolizes a coming together of mulatto and black West Indians in a space outside the domain of the planto-cracy and the despotic revolutionary leaders; and, far from being simply a Muse figure for Pompey's (and Walcott's) imaginings, she is accorded a degree of complexity shared only by the other significant mulatto character in the play, Anton.[122] Walcott's revisionist reading of the Revolution is at odds with the cele-bration of the revolutionary struggle that one finds, for example, in the classic Caribbean study of the revolution, C. L. R. James's *The Black Jacobins*.[123] Toussaint, Dessalines and Christophe, to whom Walcott had been most sympathetic in *Henri Christophe*, are all seen as betrayers of their people, men who are corrupted by power and lose sight of the causes that have motivated them in the first place. Dessalines forces Yette to sleep with him; an ailing Christophe subsequently has her executed in the final scene. However, she defiantly voices her love of the local earth as she goes to her death and the play ends with an affirmation that ordinary Haitian identity will outlive tyranny, as the Chorus sings:

> HAYTI, HAYTI, I SHALL LOVE YOU
> I SHALL NOT JOIN THE HAYTIAN EARTH
> SUNS SHALL SET AND RISE ABOVE YOU
> SUNSET DEATH AND SUNRISE BIRTH. (*HE*, 2, 36)

Yette emerges as a more complex character than Pompey, whose loyalty to the earth and the view of Haiti this represents is unswerving. Her mulatto identity ensures that, like Anton and as is invariably the case with Walcott's mixed characters, she is mentally torn between conflicting forces. In this case the psychic split is primarily related to a rural-urban opposition:

> The white part of me is the town,
> the black part of me is the country. (*HE*, 1, 36)

and for much of the play she is torn between the two milieux, which are in turn related to the roles of whore and wife. Finally, she finds peace by choosing the country over the town and through so doing seemingly achieves emancipation from her inner angst which, as always in Walcott, is a correlative of the political, historical and ethnic divisions of the country at large. Pompey, in contrast, is consistently and uncomplicatedly associated with the land from first to last.

The Haytian Earth is a problematic play dramatically. There are too many short, disjointed scenes; too many characters pass across the stage too rapidly; and the action is difficult to follow without prior knowledge of the events of the Revolution. It is far from being Walcott's most successful play, but it does nevertheless bring divergent strands from his ideological armoury together in a way that none of his earlier plays had quite succeeded in doing. These include the need to evolve a different historiography, a reading of the mulatto predicament and its relationship to Caribbean society and an attempt to find a space outside the power hegemonies of Caribbean history and politics through emphasis on the resilience of the folk imagination and the land itself. All of these issues are sensitively explored within *The Haytian Earth*, but the sheer range and pageant-like quality of the action prevent any of them from being developed in a sustained way.

To Die for Grenada has clear affinities with *The Haytian Earth*, although it is finally a much slighter play. For its setting Walcott employs a variation on a locale he had used in such plays as *Franklin*, *Pantomime* and *The Last Carnival*, a house which serves as a focal point for reflections on Caribbean social change, played out in relation to the views and actions of a small group of characters. Just as the 1970 Black Power Revolution in Trinidad had provided the occasion for parts of *In a Fine Castle*, so the American invasion of Grenada which overthrew the ruling socialist New Jewel Movement, following a *coup* in which the Prime Minister Maurice Bishop and several of his cabinet were killed, provides a background for the events of *To Die for*

Grenada. The setting for the action of the play is Monos, a small island facing towards Grenada, near Chaguaramas in north-eastern Trinidad, where Walcott had a beach house and which he has celebrated as a natural environment untainted by the divisions which, in his view, have poisoned Caribbean political and social life.[124] In the play Monos serves much the same function: characters as different from one another as an older black Captain and a white expatriate American government employee, Christine, both see Monos as an Edenic refuge from society at large, whether it be Trinidad, Grenada or post-Beirut Washington. The tension between the desire to live an apolitical existence in a safe place such as Monos and the inescapability of political involvement provides the central dynamic on which the play turns. Christine and her Trinidadian lover, Noel, debate the morality of American political involvement in the Caribbean, with the lawyer Noel proclaiming himself a neutral 'Switzerland',[125] a man who prefers the 'higher fiction of the Law' to 'truth' (*TDG*, 1, 38) and tries to avoid commitment, and Christine, who opposes the invasion, reluctantly acknowledging the need for moral choices and commitments. The play includes other interesting characters: among them a local poet Nabo, a self-styled 'parasite', 'lizard' and 'chameleon' (*TDG*, 2,10), who nevertheless espouses Walcott-like ambivalence in his belief in creative doubt, his refusal to be coerced into choosing between the 'two madnesses' of Russia and America (*TDG*, 2,10) and his rejection of Old World mind-sets in favour of the view that 'The whole world is one age' (*TDG*, 2, 8); and an East Indian radical, Rafiq 'Max' Mohammed, another ambivalent character whose two names suggest a mulatto-like oscillation between different political positions and who is eventually killed when his house is blown up, possibly, as in Grenada, as a result of American involvement. *To Die for Grenada* frequently suggests loose analogies between personal and public events, but finally lacks the clarity and narrative momentum to make it a success for audiences or readers unfamiliar with Walcott's views on Caribbean culture and society While it shares the desire expressed in *The Haytian Earth* to inhabit an apolitical space and while it is structurally more compact than the earlier play, it lacks the range and complexity of the Haitian epic which, perhaps as a result of Walcott's life-long fascination with the subject, finally has more to say not, only about Caribbean history, but also about the renegotiation of roles in the post-independence period.

Odysseys

SINCE his very first collection of verse, 25 Poems, Walcott has repeatedly found Homeric analogies for his Caribbean experience and virtually all his published volumes of verse to date contain references of one kind or another to *The Iliad* or *The Odyssey*. From the outset the Caribbean is seen as a 'New Aegean'[1] and the poet and the St. Lucian companions of his youth as 'Afro-Greeks';[2] and by the time *Omeros* appeared in 1990, the figure of Odysseus had come to provide a personification of Walcott's view of Caribbean artistic subjectivity – and one might argue of Caribbean identity more generally – as a migrant predicament perennially poised between restless journeying and a longing for home. Subsequently the premiere of his stage version of *The Odyssey* by the Royal Shakespeare Company in Stratford in 1992 and the publication of the text of this play in the following year further cemented his reputation as a Caribbean Homer, to a point where, as Paula Burnett points out, it has now become something of a cliché for the press to refer to him in this way.[3]

This chapter examines the significance of the Homeric parallels in Walcott's work with particular reference to *Omeros* and *The Odyssey*, in an attempt to show how the analogies he draws between contemporary Caribbean and ancient 'Greek' culture function. While the allusions to Homer sometimes suggest affinities between the two cultures, Walcott equally frequently frustrates the imposition of any pattern of neat correspondences or oppositions between the two worlds and in so doing problematizes issues of post-colonial subjectivity more generally. The chapter also argues that the travelling Odyssean protagonist, an important figure in Walcott's work from *The Gulf* onwards, increasingly becomes a vehicle for expressing his sense of the need to escape static, essentialist constructions of personality and sees the character as the central figure in all Walcott's later collections, even though he is only sometimes specifically identified as Odysseus. As a ceaseless wanderer – though not a man who has ceased to believe in the values of home – Walcott's Odyssean protagonist is a metonym for his complex beliefs about cultural affiliation; and, although his Odysseus never reaches an Ithaca where he can settle with any secure sense of belonging, he also provides some kind of resolution to Walcott's quest for an aesthetic practice appropriate to the Caribbean region. He is a figure who not only crosses lines of longitude and latitude at will, but also engages in a similar movement along a discursive continuum which offers emancipation from the Manichean binaries that had stifled Walcott's earliest attempts to create an art which would both be uniquely his own and an expression of the distinctive hybrid legacies that had shaped anglophone Caribbean culture.

So how is the ostensibly European influence of Homer redeployed in Walcott's writing? Does he, as some of his detractors would claim, adopt a Eurocentric viewpoint by shaping Caribbean subject-matter in a Greek mould? Or should the Homeric parallels be viewed as mock-heroic? If so, are they being used as in, for example, *The Rape of the Lock*, where Pope points up the shortcomings of his society by measuring them against a classical yardstick; or are they employed as in Joyce's *Ulysses*, a text which acts as a mediating lens for Walcott's response to Homer in *Epitaph for the Young*, to suggest an altogether more ambivalent mock-heroic relationship, with the present being rendered as 'ordinary' – at times even comic – *and* heroic? Or does Walcott simply adapt Homer for the Caribbean, creolizing him in much the same way as he had creolized the Don Juan figure in *The Joker of Seville*? Or do the Homeric analogies operate in an oppositional way, as a counter-discourse that undermines or contests the force of the original? The range of possible interpretations is considerable.

Perhaps the simplest short answer to these questions would be to say that, like his Crusoe, Walcott's Odysseus has a multiplicity of identities and is finally Proteus. As with Crusoe – and Friday – in *Pantomime*, the figure undergoes so many metamorphoses in his hands that it is finally futile to try to ascribe any unitary identity to him. Nevertheless Walcott is clearly pursuing certain particular agendas in his use of Odysseus and in his Homeric references more generally.

At first sight *Omeros* may well seem to constitute itself in terms of a derivative relationship with Homer's epics, in this case particularly *The Iliad*. The title certainly invokes Homer, albeit by using a Greek form of his name, and protagonists such as Achille, Philoctete and Helen clearly have Homeric names. However, the relationship between *Omeros* and Homer's epics is not simply one of derivative homage; nor is it an adversarial counter-discursive riposte in which the post-colonial text simply opposes the master-narrative of a colonial original; nor does it fit either of the mock-heroic paradigms outlined above. Walcott creates a Caribbean world of parallel status and originality with comparatively little sense of vicarious dependence on Homer. Although characters' names point to *The Iliad* as an intertext, few of the episodes are closely patterned on the earlier epic; and the names mentioned above are not at all extraordinary in St. Lucia, which has long been known as the 'Helen' of the West Indies,[4] and where slave-names derived from classical culture, such as Hector and Philoctete, are not uncommon. As one reads the poem, these characters claim an autonomy that sets them apart from their Greek namesakes and in an interview Walcott has spoken of them as archetypes that transcend particular cultural origins:

> Odysseus, the Eternal Wanderer; or Helen, the Eternal Beauty; or, in this case, Achilles, the Eternal Warrior, or Hector … These are just magnified, very ordinary symbols … Household names, really. I don't know the history of Achilles' activity in *The Iliad*. Maybe I was scared of *The*

Iliad. Because – I don't want to be swallowed up, in a sense, by Homeric comparison.[5]

Within the text Walcott is extremely ambivalent about acknowledging any debt to Homer. In the closing pages his poetic persona explicitly rejects Homeric correspondences, representing his Helen as an Afro-Caribbean woman with eyes that 'never betrayed horned Menelaus / or netted Agamemnon in their irises'.[6] Then the very last section effectively reverses this and reinstates the Homeric analogy by referring to Achille as 'a triumphant Achilles' (*Omeros*, 324). The poem also demonstrates its ambivalent relationship to the putative Homeric theme by moving between episodes focused on fishermen who bear Homeric names and at one point feud over a local Helen, and sections where this emphasis is forgotten as Walcott engages with other characters. Most prominent among these is the 'I' persona of a poet who bears a clear resemblance to Walcott himself. Where *Another Life* transforms autobiography into epic, *Omeros* moves in the opposite direction, interlinking epic with autobiography. Both poems – and for that matter all of Walcott's work – fuse the poet's own personal odyssey with that of the Caribbean more generally. Consequently, while *Omeros* may give the impression of being a loosely-structured text that roams across a broad range of subjects in a fairly capricious way, the dimensions of Caribbean epic and autobiographical odyssey are both part of the same quest for personal and regional self-definition in non-essentialist terms.

Over the years Walcott has frequently denied having read Homer's epics in their entirety[7] and *Omeros* appears to be the culmination of his attempt to produce a Caribbean equivalent of the Greek poet's epics while trying to resist the complicity implicit in entering into a discursive relationship with them, an endeavour to assert a parallel spatial collocation rather than a linear temporal debt. Even the title operates in this way: on the one hand it reclaims Homer from his assigned role at the headwaters of *Western* European culture by reassigning his *Greek* name to him; on another level it propounds an altogether different etymology for 'Omeros':

and *O* was the conch shell's invocation, *mer* was
both mother and sea in our Antillean patois,
os, a grey bone, and the white surf as it crashes

and spreads its sibilant collar on a lace shore. (*Omeros*, 14)

So, at the same time as Homer is reclaimed as Greek 'Omeros',
he is also reinvented as a Caribbean poet. Moreover, another
level of Caribbean reference may suggest itself to the reader who
knows that one of Walcott's earliest friends was Dunstan St. Omer,
the Gregorias of *Another Life*.[8] In short, Walcott uses the play of
the signifier to suggest that words have multiple origins and in
so doing frustrates the attempt to assign them to a single *culture*.

Most of *Omeros* does legitimize a reading that allows its St.
Lucian protagonists and the poem itself to stand on their own,
independent of any relationship to their Homeric counterparts
and yet the very use of Homeric names inevitably suggests at
least a residual sense of need for classical validation. At the same
time, the nature of the cultural brokerage involved here is
complex, since the significances attached to 'Homer', a poet (or
poets) of indeterminate identity are also arguably multiple and
the poem hovers between assigning Omeros/Homer the familiar
role of a first Western poet, a precursor for all who follow[9] and
rescuing him from his positioning in Western European
versions of classical culture. The very notion of Homer as the
first European poet is predicated upon a set of assumptions
which invite interrogation from a post-colonial point of view:[10]
the Homeric stories surfaced in Asia Minor as an oral collection
of unascertainable authorship, as a layered repository of legends
that appear to have been circulating in the region for a period of
time; and while classical Greece defined itself in contra-
distinction to Asia in such histories as Xenophon's *Anabasis* and
such plays as Aeschylus's *The Persians* and Euripides' *The
Bacchae*,[11] Greek culture over the centuries has been a hybridized amalgam which arguably owes more to 'Eastern' elements
(such as Byzantine architecture, Turkish music and cuisine)
travelling westwards than it does to 'Western' elements travelling
eastwards. *Omeros* promotes an awareness of this from early

on: the passage quoted above which suggests a Caribbean etymology for the name 'Omeros' is prompted by an encounter
with a modern-day 'Antigone' whom the poet meets in the
United States and whom he characterizes in terms of her 'Asian'
features and her love of islands:

> I saw how light was webbed
> on her Asian cheeks, defined her with a black
> almond's outline, as Antigone turned and said:

> 'I'm tired of America, it's time for me to go back
> to Greece. I miss my islands.' I write, it returns –
> the way she turned and shook out the black gust of hair.
>
> (*Omeros*, 14)

and in addition to relocating Homer by using the Greek version
of his name, creolizing this name and problematizing the nature
of Greekness, Walcott also provides Homer/Omeros with an
African ancestry in identifying him with a blind St. Lucian
Odysseus figure, Seven Seas, also called St. Omere.[12]

The metamorphosis that Homer undergoes in the poem is,
then, a product not only of changes wrought by the passage of
time, which seems to be the primary emphasis in Modernist
reinscriptions of Odysseus, such as those of Joyce and Pound,
but also of a spatial relocation; and Walcott effectively displaces
Homer and reinvents him as an extra-territorial traveller, who is
the common property of different periods and cultures, as well
as a protagonist who can particularly embody the cross-cultural
genealogies that have gone into the making of the Caribbean
melting-pot. *Omeros* makes explicit a view of the Odysseus
figure which has been implicit in Walcott's work from early on.
This view sees him as a type of the migrant subjectivity of the
New World poet, a Protean traveller endlessly journeying
between past and present, north and south, east and west, a
protagonist constantly endeavouring to elude entrapment in the
nets of nationalism, historiography and influence.

Omeros provides the finest example to date of Walcott's
strategy of seeking self-definition and regional definition through
a practice, grounded in layer upon layer of metaphorical trans-

formations, which resists the possibility of unitary, essentialist definition, a practice which suggests that identity will always be process and never product. On the one hand, like all Walcott's work, it is riddled with influences; from another point of view it rejects the very notion of influence, at least as conventionally constructed – as operating through *time*. Such a seemingly paradoxical stance is, of course, entirely consonant with the view of history expressed in 'The Muse of History', where Walcott pleads the case for an aesthetic which goes beyond 'a literature of recrimination and despair, a literature of revenge written by the descendants of slaves or a literature of remorse written by the descendants of masters', arguing that the historical slate should be wiped clean so that a fresh start may be made.

Idealistic though such thinking may seem, *Omeros* actually evolves a procedure which provides an imaginative enactment of it. It challenges the authority of history by employing geographical tropes (in much the same way as post-colonial writing and theory can be seen to challenge the former ortho-doxies of literary studies based on historiographical paradigms). In Book Five of the poem, the Odyssean 'I' persona travels to Europe, at first specifically to Lisbon, whose name, according to one version of its etymology which sees it as a contraction of 'Ulissibona', derives from Odysseus. The Book opens with the persona declaring 'I crossed my meridian' (*Omeros*, 189) and the complex web of associations which follows contains references to other meridians, specifically Greenwich and the meridian of Pope Alexander VI who, at the end of the fifteenth century, decreed the line of demarcation that divided the New World between Portugal and Spain. In a section set in post-imperial London in the same Book, the poet asks, 'Who decrees a great epoch?' and immediately answers, 'The meridian of Greenwich' (*Omeros*, 196). Meridians, then, come to stand for the Eurocentric metanarratives on which the mappings of history of recent centuries have been based. By crossing his own meridian – a highly personal meridian, but one which obviously relates to and reverses the Middle Passage crossing and other voyages of Empire – the persona both steps inside the former colonizer's space and at the same time disturbs the hegemonies instated by the Greenwich project and decreed by Pope Alexander. Crossing meridians is thus an act of migrancy that dismantles the historically constructed borders that separate Caribbean space and subjectivity from Europe, and the poem *Omeros* operates in a very similar manner throughout, confounding history with new cartographies which have their origins in the migrant restless journeying of the Odyssean traveller. The text itself moves through a sea of discourses and, while very firmly rooted in St. Lucian specifics on the one hand, is equally committed to an eclectic textual procedure which articulates a poetics of migrancy on the other.

Homeric intertexts in Walcott's early poetry sometimes seem more Eurocentric in orientation. Thus 'Roots', a poem first published in *In a Green Night*, begins by suggesting that St. Lucia will remain uninscribed, except in the inferior mode of the 'naturalist's notebook', until such time as 'our Homer with truer perception erect it' (*IGN*, 60). In *Another Life* the most memorable of a number of Homeric parallels is an 'alphabet of the emaciated' (*AL*, 22) mainly based on Homeric analogues. This is ushered in by a schoolteacher's question which suggests the Eurocentric nature of the colonial educational curriculum: 'Boy! Who was Ajax?' (*AL*, 16). The 'alphabet' finds several Homeric correspondences for ordinary St. Lucian life. Ajax is a cart-horse that achieves heroic greatness when he becomes 'a thoroughbred / on race-days, once a year' (*AL*, 16–17); Helen is 'Janie, the town's one clear-complexioned whore' (*AL*, 19); a 'frog-like crippled crone' becomes Cassandra (*AL*, 17), a tattooed ex-merchant sailor' (*AL*, 18) Odysseus himself and Castries 'Troy town' (*AL*, 18, 20). Underpinning all of this is the poet's identification with Homer – and Milton – as he enviously watches a blind man and decides himself to 'practise blindness' (*AL*, 18). Although later in the poem Walcott will depict himself as a houseboy, siren child or slave stealing from 'the house of literature' (*AL*, 77), the effect of these analogies is hardly subversive. It is equally difficult to see them as straightforward heroic parallels, even though Walcott concludes the 'alphabet' by referring to the

e opening poem of the collection, 'The
ni-epic which prefigures *Omeros*, that
st probing, poetic exploration of the
ce outside the Manichean binaries of
d its post-independence legacy. The
yled 'red nigger'[18] Shabine, is Walcott's
es figure thus far in his career and an
the Odysseus of his 1992 play. Shabine is
and tells his tale in a verse that moves
Standard registers; he emerges as both a
, who is self-conscious and at the same time
representative possibilities – in the poem's
e says 'either I'm nobody, or I'm a nation'
gure who seems to have particular affinities
he opening of the poem sees him leaving the
Trinidad,[19] looking back on both himself and
duality of vision typical of his creator:

he rearview and see a man
he, and the man was weeping
s, the streets, that whole fucking island.
                                    (*SAK*, 4)

        and I, Shabine, saw
slums of empire was paradise. (*SAK*, 4)

abine, the poem takes ship, immersing itself in
eafaring as liberation and an ideal of poetry which,
is History', turns away from the complexities of
orical existence:

        when I write
n, each phrase go be soaked in salt;
v and knot every line as tight
in this rigging; in simple speech
mon language go be the wind,
es the sails of the schooner *Flight*. (*SAK*, 5)

ows is a journey though geography and history, in
bine takes on the role of a Caribbean Kilroy, travelling
os, St. Lucia and Dominica and revisiting two of the

individuals concerned as 'the stars of my mythology' (*AL*, 22).
Edward Baugh has called the section a 'comic odyssey'[13] and
arguably it is best regarded as mock-heroic in the Joycean
sense.[14] Shortly afterwards *Another Life* further problematizes
the issue of the heroic status of such St. Lucian figures by
foregrounding the temporal distance between the poet's former
child's-eye view and the perspective of his present persona:

Provincialism loves the pseudo-epic,
so if these heroes have been given a stature
disproportionate to their cramped lives,
remember I beheld them at knee-height. (*AL*, 41)

Although this may seem to suggest a repudiation of the child's
idealization of such figures, and with this a denial of the idea
that they have genuine epic status, the case for constituting
them as heroes is not entirely undermined. The conditional 'if'
leaves open the question of whether or not they have been
disproportionately inflated; and the word 'heroes' is left
unchallenged as the term used in the *present* text; it is not
presented as a product of the knee-high sensibility. So once
again it becomes difficult to dogmatize about the nature of the
relationship involved and the Homeric parallels seem to function
simultaneously as genuine and 'pseudo-epic' comparisons, but
arguably there is more dependence on Europe (or Asia Minor?)
than one finds in the later Walcott.

Along with the use of such Homeric references as a way of
'locating' the ambivalences of Caribbean culture, Walcott's earlier
poetry also displays the first manifestations of his fascination
with the figure of Odysseus. In 'A Map of the Antilles', a poem
first published during the short-lived existence of the West
Indian Federation,[15] Walcott uses a Donne-like metaphysical
conceit (a compass is actually involved![16]) to question cartographical constructions of Caribbean cultural identity, main-
taining that 'men invent those truths which they discover'
(*IGN*, 55). In opposition to such constructions the poet declares:

Mariner or minister, I am none of these,
My compass keeps avoiding all the facts

> To find that South is its magnetic mover;
> By force of the separation it directs
> All active interest towards your shores,
> [...]
> And by such licence damns a federation
> Which can condone my extradition. (*IGN*, 55)

Into this situation of contrasted separation and union Walcott inserts a reference to Odysseus:

> And so an emerald sea, wild as this one
> Seemed to Odysseus a destructive ocean,
> Even as he lingered in Circean seas;
> Since in no magic port was there such peace
> As where his love remained. (*IGN*, 55)

Most obviously, the Odysseus presented here is a migrant poet, but the passage also suggests Caribbean subjectivity more generally, trying to escape the continuing divisiveness of a history that isolates individuals and groups from one another. As such it anticipates Walcott's representation of the travelling Odyssean protagonist in the collections of poetry he published in the late 1970s and 1980s: *The Star-Apple Kingdom* (1979), *The Fortunate Traveller* (1981), *Midsummer* (1984) and *The Arkansas Testament* (1987). In each of these volumes the figure of the traveller is very much to the fore and, anticipating *Omeros* and *The Odyssey*, provides an escape-route from the binaries of Caribbean history and identity politics.

The Star-Apple Kingdom is particularly notable for three longer poems which offer panoramic overviews of Caribbean history and geography. In 'The Sea is History' Walcott develops an idea he has already articulated in 'The Muse of History' and *Another Life*,[17] that the Caribbean natural world – in this case the sea itself – offers an alternative history which has far more relevance to the lived experience of Caribbean peoples than the linear records of colonial society or attempts at an adversarial counter-discourse. In *Another Life* this idea is expressed particularly powerfully in the image of a boy putting a shell to his ear and receiving a more profound understanding of the Middle Passage than any historian:

It is, however, in th
Schooner Flight', a mi
Walcott offers his m
attempt to find a spa
colonial discourse a
protagonist, the self-s
most developed Ulys
obvious forerunner o
both sailor and poet
between Creole and
Caribbean Everyma
sceptical about his
most-quoted line, l
(*SAK*, 4) – and a fi
with his creator. T
Carnival world of
the society with a

and I look in
exactly like n
for the hous

when these

Along with Sh
the notion of s
as in 'The Sea
social and his

this poer
I go dra
as ropes
my con
my pag

What foll
which Sha
to Barbad

o
th
in
hea

A

yes, i
...

And th
accepts

'The Sea is I
by drawing
Caribbean pas
seen as the reg
bondage' (*SAK*,
the most import
'Jonah' (*SAK*, 26
that such parallel
they are presented
(*SAK*, 25) which ca
plays such as *The Se*
ocean appears to be
schisms of Caribbean s
mood informs the titl
which the eponymous
functions more generall
whole. Again there is em
outside the divisions cre
imperatives, whether they
(*SAK*, 47) that underlies
pastoral' (*SAK*, 46) or the
independence Caribbean polit

One morning the Caribbea
by seven prime ministers wl

most traumatic episodes in Caribbean history, the Middle Passage and the genocide of the indigenous Amerindian population. Shabine has two ghostly visions of slave ships and on Dominica projects himself into the persona of one of the Sauteurs, a group of Carib Indians who on Grenada in 1651 chose to jump over a cliff-top to their death to elude capture by the French colonizers who had pursued them there.[20] Such nightmares and the traumas of his own personal past are, however, left behind in the activities of seafaring and writing poetry. Shabine is a typical Walcott migrant protagonist in that his 'flight' releases him from the political and aesthetic binaries of Caribbean life, seen once again in terms of the mulatto predicament:

> I had no nation now but the imagination.
> After the white man, the niggers didn't want me
> when the power swing to their side. (*SAK*, 8)

Yet he is also a traveller who is plagued with a sense of *spiritual* exile:

> Where is my rest place, Jesus? Where is my harbor?
> Where is the pillow I will not have to pay for,
> and the window I can look from that frames my life?
>
> (*SAK*, 8)

and from the beginning of the poem, which appears to allude to the opening of Chaucer's *Prologue*, his journeyings take on the quality of pilgrimage. He is an Odysseus, torn between the twin compulsions of wishing to return home and wanting to escape from the entrapments of social life through restless travelling. The poem ends, after a storm, in a mood of quiet benediction, with Shabine blessing various aspects of island life, but still finding the possibility of reaching a fixed point of prelapsarian harmony as problematic as ever:

> I have only one theme:
>
> The bowsprit, the arrow, the longing, the lunging heart –
> the flight to a target whose aim we'll never know,
> vain search for one island that heals with its harbor
> and a guiltless horizon, where the almond's shadow
> doesn't injure the sand.

...

But things must fall, and so it always was ...

(SAK, 19–20).

So the possibility of reaching an Edenic port remains elusive, once again as enigmatic a possibility as anything in V. S. Naipaul. However, the longing for a healing harbour, where almond trees, as always in Walcott an image of the Caribbean capacity for endurance, will make emancipation from a cycle of guilt and displacement possible, is equally intense.

The figure of the exiled Odyssean poet, perennially moving between northern and tropical worlds and between solitary contemplation and a sense of the need for active involvement remains the central persona in Walcott's next collection, *The Fortunate Traveller*. In a poem entitled 'North and South' this persona refers to himself as 'a colonial upstart at the end of an empire, / a single, circling homeless satellite' (*FT*, 11) and throughout the volume he can, like Walcott's other Odysseuses, be seen as either a representative post-colonial subject or as a rootless contingent individual resisting this and other such categorizations. In the title-poem, the ironically named eponymous narrator displays the nervous disquiet typical of the travelling protagonist ('There is no sea as restless as my mind' [*FT*, 95]), but less characteristically he is a spy, a Judas who has abandoned the 'pity' (*FT*, 91) he once found in academic research and is now making himself rich through Kurtz-like trading. His journeying takes him from Europe to a place 'where the phantoms live' (*FT*, 93). This is a church in the St. Lucian town of Canaries, where he finds a 'heart of darkness', not in the setting itself, but in the practices of the local Catholic church, which keeps the people poor and uninformed. Although this poem, with its use of a dramatized persona who cannot immediately be identified with Odysseus or Walcott, may at first seem to be off at a tangent from the main concerns of Walcott's later verse, the recurrent tension between detachment and involvement surfaces towards the end, as the protagonist wrestles with his conscience and a voice which repeats the Biblical refrain, *'and have not charity'* (*FT*, 97).

In 'North and South' the persona expresses a preference for
the 'raw' culture of the Tropics to the cooked 'culture' he finds
in Manhattan's 'heart of darkness' (*FT*, 12–13):

> How far I am from those cacophonous seaports
> built around the single exclamation of one statue
> of Victoria Regina! There vultures shift on the roof
> of the red iron market, whose patois
> is brittle as slate, a gray stone flecked with quartz.
> I prefer the salt freshness of that ignorance,
> as language crusts and blackens the pots
> of this cooked culture, coming from a raw one;
> and these days in bookstores I stand paralyzed
>
> by the rows of shelves along whose wooden branches
> the free-verse nightingales are trilling "Read me! Read
> me!"
> in various metres of asthmatic pain. (*FT*, 13)

These lines blur the distinctions between language and what it
supposedly represents: the Victoria Regina statue is an exclamation mark; the market roof has a patois 'brittle as slate'; the
shelves of the New York bookstores have 'wooden branches',
from which 'free-verse nightingales' articulate their pained
utterances.[21] This perspective reflects the complexities of Lévi-
Stauss's classic 'raw'/'cooked' paradigm[22] and erodes nature/
culture oppositions in much the same way as much of Walcott's
work interrogates the binarism of Manichean allegory. While
New York is ostensibly a 'cooked culture' and the Caribbean a
'raw' one, nature and culture prove to be subtly intertwined in
both spheres: the 'salt freshness' of the tropical world is
associated not only with the shifting vultures, but also with the
exclamation mark of the statue; the encrustations of language in
the United States are offset by the 'wooden branches' of the
bookstores' shelves, where the volumes of poetry are chattering
nightingales. Just as the travelling protagonist crosses meridians
in *Omeros*, so the imagery here suggests a similar porosity of
borders with regard to culturally defined oppositions.

The poems of *The Fortunate Traveller* are located in two
sections entitled 'North' which frame a longer central section

entitled 'South'. While this geographical dichotomy does point up distinctive differences between them, the sense of the 'other' place, whether it be the temperate North or the tropical South, is omnipresent. In the 'North' poems, which open and close the volume and include 'North and South' and 'The Fortunate Traveller', the persona presents himself as a man 'falling in love with America' ('Upstate', *FT*, 6), but finding her a tired Muse. In 'Upstate', '[h]er tired face is tired of iron fields' (*FT*, 5); in 'American Muse', she is likened to the emaciated women of Walker Evans's Depression photographs (*FT*, 7);[23] in 'Piano Practice', she pleads a headache when the poet calls on her and he speculates that she is 'shy at being seen / with someone who has only one climate' (*FT*, 10). All of these poems reflect Walcott's continuing ambivalence towards the American republic, which he feels has been founded upon 'broken promises' ('Old New England', *FT*, 3).

In the 'South' poems the protagonist habitually feels a sense of exile. Sometimes this seems very personal in origin and there are references to the 'disfiguring exile of [his second] divorce' ('The Hotel Normandie Pool', *FT*, 65),[24] but more frequently it relates to the predicament of the Odyssean artist. Classical analogies, both Latin and Greek, continue to abound. In 'The Hotel Normandie Pool', Walcott employs Ovid[25] rather than Odysseus as a metonym for artistic exile. The momentary resting-place of a Port of Spain hotel poolside provides an equivalent for Ovid's Black Sea exile and an occasion for a meditation on the competing strains in his own ancestry and socialization. Ovid, a poet who straddled different modes in his *Metamorphoses* and *Tristia*, is seen as a man mocked by the opposing camps of 'slaves' and 'Romans' for displaying 'the fickle dyes of the chameleon' (*FT*, 69). As in another of the 'South' poems, 'The Spoiler's Return',[26] the Caribbean parallels are clear and Walcott's identification with the figure of Ovid clearly has a good deal to do with his own sense of the exile visited upon a poet who believes that 'art obeys its own order' (*FT*, 69) but finds himself constructed in diametrically opposing ways by others.

At the centre of the 'South' section there are a number of poems, in which 'Greece' once again provides a sustained parallel for the Caribbean. Anticipating *Omeros*, Walcott presents Greece in a range of guises and it is no longer simply the classical site that had fascinated him since his schooldays. In 'From This Far', it is the country of George Seferis, winner of the 1963 Nobel Prize for Literature and, as one of the century's finest poetic chroniclers of alienation, a precursor for Walcott in another sense. Elsewhere it is mediated through the eyes of commentators such as Robert Graves, who in 'A Map of the New World' is quoted as saying 'Only in a world where there are cranes and horses … can poetry survive', and it is this which calls the wandering poet home (*FT*, 27). It also appears to sanction the view that the Caribbean contains the potential for epic composition at a time when its possibilities appear to have been played out in the Old World. In the first section of the poem:

> A man with clouded eyes picks up the rain
> and plucks the first line of the *Odyssey*. (*FT*, 25)

As with *Omeros*, this suggests that the poem about to be written is actually *The Odyssey*, not a derivative Caribbean by-product. Just as in Jorge Luis Borges's 'Pierre Menard, Author of the Quixote', where the fictional Pierre Menard produces his own verbatim version of Cervantes's novel without any indebtedness to it,[27] so the implication here is that a completely new work is about to be undertaken. The moment of the poem is the end of the Trojan War and so perhaps Walcott is suggesting that it is the post-independence period which makes epic possible in the Caribbean at a time when its possibilities have been diminished elsewhere. Alternatively, it could be his own Shabine-like predicament of feeling torn between the twin compulsions of restless wandering and the desire for homecoming that provides the originary impulse for the new *Odyssey*.

At the same time, Greek myths are humanized in 'Europa', a poem which takes as its departure-point the Phoenician princess Europa's seduction by Zeus in the form of a bull. This is achieved partly through the demythologizing assertion that stories of 'gods as seed-bulls, gods as rutting swans' were simply 'an overheated farmhand's literature' (*FT*, 33), but also through Walcott's vivid verbal rendition of the visual as, for example, in the opening lines:

> The full moon is so fierce that I can count the
> coconuts' cross-hatched shade on bungalows,
> their white walls raging with insomnia.
> the stars leak drop by drop on the tin plates
> of the sea almonds, and the jeering clouds
> are luminously rumpled as the sheets. (*FT*, 33)

Here the intensity of the pictorial imagery effectively realizes the specifics of the Caribbean world on the printed page, arguing for its autonomy and instating it as a fit subject for poetry more effectively than any intertextual mediation, from Greece or elsewhere, ever could.

Of the various poems in *The Fortunate Traveller* which explore the anxiety of influence that Walcott feels concerning the symbiotic relationship he traces between the Caribbean and Greece, a poem actually entitled 'Greece' does so most probingly. Here the 'I' persona climbs the Parnassus of a local promontory, carrying 'a body round [his] shoulders' (*FT*, 35). There are the usual correspondences between Caribbean and Greek worlds: olives 'gnarled as sea almonds' and 'boulders dry / as the calcareous molars of a Cyclops'; the protagonist carries 'a saw-toothed agave' as a 'blade'; and 'rooted phalanxes of coconuts' are seen as Trojans and Spartans (*FT*, 35). He reaches the top of the promontory, where, instead of the 'original story' he has expected to discover, he finds 'nothing' other than 'stones and light', the 'emptiness of sea and air' (*FT*, 35). Throwing the body he has been carrying down, he realizes that it is not really a body at all, but a copy of *The Iliad*. The wind blows 'Hector's and Achilles' rages' away and in the final stanza of the poem the persona liberates himself from 'the old Greek bull' which is threatening to subsume his identity by killing it with his blade. He rejects 'the dead end of the classic labyrinth' for signifiers which have a more immediate local reference: 'I wrote the sound for "sea," the sign for "sun"' (*FT*, 36). The killing of the Minotaur is clearly an epiphanic moment, an equivalent act of cultural emancipation to Makak's beheading of the White Goddess in *Dream on Monkey Mountain*, and the poet feels that after fifty years 'My head was scoured of others people's monsters' (*FT*, 36). Paradoxically, this act of wiping the cultural slate clean also ushers in the possibility of a local *Iliad*: the quarrel between a St. Lucian Achilles and Hector provides the starting-point for *Omeros*.

Walcott's next volume of poetry, *Midsummer*, comprises fifty-four short poems, only two of which run to more than a page and only three of which have titles. The poems encompass a year, from one summer to the next, and at first sight may appear to be occasional responses to very particular experiences. The volume is, however, far more unified than this and makes up a sequence revolving around the motif of 'midsummer' which proves to be more than a seasonal moment. In the early poems midsummer heat is to be found in both South and North. In Port of Spain, a mood of bored languor envelops the city:

> Midsummer stretches beside me with its cat's yawn.
> Trees with dust on their lips, cars melting down
> in its furnace. Heat staggers the drifting mongrels.
> …
> Monotonous lurid bushes
> brush the damp clouds with the ideograms of buzzards
> over the Chinese groceries. The oven alleys stifle
> …
> And one waits for midsummer lightning as the armed sentry
> in boredom waits for the crack of a rifle.[28]

New York seems equally tropical at the height of summer: 'The hemispheres lie sweating, flesh to flesh, / on a damp bed', hucksters 'have made the Big Apple a mango' and 'the dazed high-rises / rock to reggae and salsa'. Such Creole and mestizo fusions are an 'Aztec tango / of assimilation', a new chapter in the American melting pot (*Midsummer*, V). So it seems that 'midsummer' represents a crucible of hybridization, a time when divisions between cultures are eroded, even if the stasis which it generates is ambivalent. The poet finds summer as 'one-dimensional / as lust' (X) and on more than one occasion longs for the moment when the mood of torpor will be shattered by a flash of summer lightning (VI and IX). More frequently, however, it is associated with a spiritual radiance that provides the raw material of art. Several poems make direct reference to European painters[29] and, as Robert Bensen has pointed out, the pictorial impulse is always to the fore.[30] The eighth and ninth poems in the sequence crystallize the themes that lie at its centre.

Poem VIII opens with another picture of searing midsummer heat ('A radiant summer, so fierce it turns yellow') and goes on to liken this to the moment before a holocaust, a motif which will reappear in *Midsummer* in a variety of guises (the fall-out of a nuclear war, the genocide of the Nazi concentration camps and the post-Columbian predicament of the Americas) and a recurrent concern of Walcott's writing since his early radio-play, *Harry Dernier*.[31] As so often in Walcott, image is compounded with image, as the poet likens his act of composition to the activity of a general arranging lines (of troops?) and also to the 'peace … of a gold-framed meadow / in Brueghel or Pissarro'. The use of artistic analogies, whether with the work of writers or painters, is by this point in his career a staple of Walcott's self-reflexive verse, but *Midsummer* sees him moving away from such parallelism, even as he uses it. Poem VIII continues with the persona rejecting the frame of the Brueghel or Pissarro painting which he has initially invoked, saying 'let the imagination range wherever / its correspondences take it', proposing other artistic analogies and urging:

> let it [the imagination] come back to say that summer is
>   the same
> everywhere. …
> The heart is housebound in books – open your leaves,
> let light freckle the earth-coloured earth, since
> light is plenty to make do with. (*Midsummer*, VIII)

So while the tug-of-war between the attempt to render experience through direct, unmediated vision and the felt need to filter the subject-matter through the refracting lenses of intertexts which dominates so much of Walcott's writing continues, there is a clear exhortation to turn away from art in favour of the radiant light of midsummer, which seems to transcend cultural specifics ('summer is the same / everywhere') and which can illuminate 'earth-coloured earth' – far from being a tired use of language, the repetition of the word 'earth' in this phrase suggests the unchanging *quidditas* of matter until it is transformed by light and artistic activity. Although the imagination will persist in exploring 'correspondences', it is licensed to roam at will, as a kind of Odyssean traveller,[32] in the conviction that it will discover the underlying uniformity of the natural world represented by 'midsummer'. The poem concludes by seeing midsummer as the source of poetry and suggesting that it confers a quasi-spiritual benediction on the writer:

> Midsummer bursts
> out of its body, and its poems come unwarranted,
> as when, hearing what sounds like rain, we startle a place
> where a waterfall crashes down rocks. Abounding grace!
> (*Midsummer*, VIII)

In Poem IX Walcott's poetic persona returns to the subject of the difficulty of encompassing particular experiences in language, bemoaning the fact that 'everything I read / or write goes on too long' and longing for a transcendental signifier, such as 'God', which will synthesize everything 'in one heraldic stroke'. If at first this poem seems to be simply a finely wrought exploration of the signifier-signified gap, it becomes something more through the use of the image of lightning, which is seen as a conduit for the task of bridging this gap: 'Language never fits geography / except when the earth and summer lightning rhyme'. Lightning, it seems, is a vehicle for healing the post-Babel wound of the gap between 'language' and 'geography'. Like midsummer in the previous poems, it seems, at least sometimes, to offer the poet the power to heal the wounds inflicted by Babel.

How this relates to the post-colonial predicament is another question prompted by the poem. If language and *geography* never fit, is this because of the problems of rendering *any* place (or for that matter anything at all) in language or does it refer more specifically to Walcott's sense that his *Caribbean* world has hitherto lacked a language in which it can be adequately inscribed? Arguably the dichotomy implicit in such a question is finally bogus since, as in so many other respects, the post-colonial situation foregrounds a more general discursive problem. *Midsummer* repeatedly suggests that prelapsarian harmony has been lost as a consequence of language and the various ideologies it embodies. Elsewhere the persona asks whether an unnamed tropical world has experienced the Fall as a consequence of the advent of Christianity:

> the sea swift flew nameless in that wordless summer
> in the leafy silence before their christening language.
> [...] Was evil brought to this place
> with language? Did the sea worm bury that secret in clear sand,
> in the coral cathedrals, the submarine catacombs
> where the jellyfish trails its purple, imperial fringe?
>
> (*Midsummer*, XXIV)

On another occasion, he contrasts the healing powers of midsummer with the divisions and suffering generated by the political differences which inhere in language:

> Though they have different sounds for 'God' or 'hunger',
> the opposing alphabets in city squares
> shout with one voice, nation takes on nation,
> and, from their fury of pronunciation,
> children lie torn on rubble for a noun.
>
> (*Midsummer*, XXII)

Walcott's canvass is broad: he moves between the Caribbean, North America and Europe, reflecting on the various forces which perpetuate divisions between peoples, among them New England Puritanism, the holocaust of World War II and the wounds of the Trojan War. Whatever the setting, his poetic Odysseus is,

however, always questing for the artistic moment that will heal
the breaches inflicted by the warring forces of language:

> an old man wanders
> a pine-gripped islet where his wound was made.
> Entering a door-huge dictionary, he finds that clause
> that stopped the war yesterday ... (*Midsummer*, XXXIII)

And the poet himself is caught in the trap of language, as he
wonders whether his own compositions are themselves contri-
buting to the wounds inflicted by language. This theme comes to
a head in Poem XLI, in which he asks whether he would have
broken his pen when he began composing poetry forty years
before, if he had realized that 'this century's pastorals were
being written / by the chimneys of Dachau, of Auschwitz, of
Sachsenhausen'. In this poem he returns to a central theme of
Another Life, the sense of election and artistic vocation he felt as
a young man:

> Forty years gone, in my island childhood, I felt that
> the gift of poetry had made me one of the chosen,
> that all experience was kindling to the fire of the Muse.
>
> (*Midsummer*, LI)

Asked about these lines in a 1986 interview, Walcott reaffirmed
his belief that he felt it was his 'job' to give voice to the unwritten and unconventional beauty of the St. Lucian landscape
and people:

> I never thought of my gift – I have to say 'my gift' because
> I believe it is a gift – as anything I did completely on my
> own. I have felt from my boyhood that I had one function
> and that was somehow to articulate, not my own
> experience, but what I saw around me. From the time I was
> a child I knew it was beautiful. If you go to a peak
> anywhere in St. Lucia you feel a simultaneous newness
> and sense of timelessness at the same time – the presence
> of where you are. It's a primal thing and it has always been
> that way. At the same time I knew that the poor people
> around me were not beautiful in the romantic sense of
> being colorful people to paint or to write about.[33]

The midsummer moment is the central expression of such 'primal' beauty and timelessness, just as the healing Homeric sea and St. Lucian landscape have been in so many of his earlier poems and plays; and while 'midsummer' is presented as a phenomenon which traverses national boundaries, it is finally associated with the Caribbean and the quintessential Walcott setting of a St. Lucian beach.[34] America may offer its equivalents and the sequence is at pains to say that no culture has a monopoly of Edenic peace, but when the persona returns to New England at the beginning of the second part of the volume, a chilling wind makes him feel 'The *Fall* is all around us' (*Midsummer*, XXXI; my italics) and amid the shortening days of autumn 'the islands feel farther than something out of the *Georgics*' (*Midsummer*, XXXVIII). Wales prompts a similar sense of 'freshness lost'; crossing into England, he wonders why he thinks 'the crash of chivalry' is his 'own dispossession' (*Midsummer*, XXXV).

The longest poem in the volume, 'Tropic Zone', again contrasts the divisive forces of history, which the poet says 'will pierce your memory like a migraine' with blue skies which 'convert all genocide into fiction' (*Midsummer*, XLIII, ii) and he prays that he may be able to write:

> lines as mindless as the ocean's of linear time,
> since time is the first province of Caesar's jurisdiction.
> (*Midsummer*, XLIII, ii)

Here, then, 'midsummer' not only offers a space outside politics, but also outside the deterministic chains of linear historiography. However, the poet finds himself locked into *another* kind of bondage, memories of Caribbean 'laterite landscapes', which he drags 'behind [him] in chains' (*Midsummer*, XLIV).[35] Standing beside Boston's River Charles at the end of winter, his thoughts on the coming of spring are still haunted by the image of the timeless sea, as a black fisherman casts a shadow over the water (*Midsummer*, XLV). In one sense the notion of 'midsummer' as a timeless moment beyond both history and geography *is* retained to the last, but only in so far as it functions as

such in the poet's mind. Northern landscapes and cities are seen
to be riven with divisions: even when the early arrival of spring
in Ohio threatens to break the 'law' of the vernal equinox, 'the
arteries / of what was once the individual heart' are still blocked
by police patrolmen at a railway crossing gate with 'a crossed
black-and-white sign' (*Midsummer*, XLVI). So the poet's
imagination always returns to the image of peace within
Caribbean nature and this is where the notion of 'midsummer'
is finally located, not as provincial sentimentalization of the
world of his youth, but as a mental response to a world of
natural beauty which can sustain such an imaginative vision.
The Caribbean still has its reminders of martial division, among
them bickering gulls and foundered ships, but it nevertheless
offers 'blue spaces' unmarked by humanity and 'islets where our
shadow is nameless' (*Midsummer*, XLVII). Ultimately the
'midsummer sea, the hot pitch road, this grass, these shacks'
that have 'made' the poet are indestructible because 'they are in
the blood' and they provide the starting-point for a religion
beyond religion: 'the Word turned toward poetry in its grief'
(*Midsummer*, LIV).

Like *The Fortunate Traveller*, Walcott's next collection *The
Arkansas Testament* divides its poems between two locales,
'Here' and 'Elsewhere'. The Caribbean is 'Here' and so in one
sense at least it is privileged over other places, but again the
binary partition that structures the volume is an extremely
porous one and the two worlds are seen to interpenetrate one
another in both predictable and unexpected ways. In several of
the poems of the 'Here' section, Walcott revisits the St. Lucia of
his youth in memory, endeavouring once again to perform
'Adam's task of giving things their names'. Two of his most
memorable poems on this subject, 'Cul de Sac Valley' and 'A
Latin Primer', focus on the relationship between his 'craft' and
the landscape and people it strives to depict. In the former poem
he again sees himself as a carpenter,[36] working to fashion a style
which will provide an 'accurate' and 'honest' representation of
the specifics of the St. Lucian landscape and language:

as consonants scroll
off my shaving plane
in the fragrant Creole
of their native grain;

from a trestle bench
they'd curl at my foot,
C's, R's, with a French
or West African root

from a dialect throng-
ing, its leaves unread
yet light on the tongue
of their native road. (*AT*, 9)

'Cul de Sac Valley' also foregrounds the process of attempting mimetic representation of the external world in other self-referential ways: people, creatures and natural phenomena such as the sunrise 'enter' (*AT*, 11) the stanzas of the poem; trees are associated with consonants and a happy, barking mongrel with the vowels of the black populace that 'cannot write' the 'tongue they speak' (*AT*, 10). Throughout, the poem suggests Walcott's preference for the mongrelized language of St. Lucia and the extent to which the supposedly discrete areas of poem and observed world are interacting with one another. Again, it is an Odyssean composition which travels nervously across discursive boundaries, creating its own distinctive cross-cultural idiom as it does so.

'A Latin Primer', a poem which has its origins in the influence of Latin verse on Walcott's early poetic sensibility, is very similar. Once again the poet constructs parallels between the 'other' life of the world of art and his local experience ('The frigate bird my phoenix'; 'ploughing white fields of surf', [*AT*, 21]) and he writes about how he turned to 'the sand-crested kelp / of distant literatures' (*AT*, 21) for inspiration. However, the seaweed image used here points up the two-way nature of the process of adaptation in which the poem is engaging, as the *Caribbean* metaphor infiltrates the 'distant literatures'. Intermingling and cultural cross-pollination are everywhere. The 'I' persona hates Latin scansion, but finds it even permeates a boyhood activity such as 'skip[ping] a pebble / across the sea's page' (*AT*, 22); and the poem moves towards conclusion with a passage which brilliantly exemplifies the vibrancy of St. Lucian patois, even as it transforms it through the density of its imagery and its fusion of discourses:

> a frigate bird came sailing …
>
> named with the common sense
> of fishermen: sea scissors,
> *Fregata magnificens,*
>
> *ciseau-la-mer,* the patois
> for its cloud-cutting course;
> and that native metaphor
> made by the stroke of oars,
>
> with one wing beat for scansion,
> that slow levelling V
> made one with my horizon
> as it sailed steadily. (*AT,* 23–4)

So here metre, metaphor and lexical juxtaposition – of Latin and francophone Creole, within the primarily English vocabulary of the poem – enact the linguistic intermingling of Walcott's mongrelized practice and again help to shape a distinctive cross-cultural, Odyssean idiom, which paradoxically is at the same time very much *here* in the Caribbean.

These and other poems in the first part of *The Arkansas Testament* provide some of the most finely wrought expressions of Walcott's life-long goal of realizing St. Lucia on the printed page and are typical of his habitual emphasis on the interpenetration of Caribbean and metropolitan cultures. Other poems in the 'Here' section adopt a rather different stance, showing how cross-cultural comparison can work to the detriment of local folk forms. On two occasions parallels with Homer's Aegean are introduced to suggest the autonomy of Caribbean culture and selfhood: in 'The Villa Restaurant' the poet metaphorically strips a 'terra-cotta waitress' (*AT,* 25), preferring 'the living vase' to 'Greek urn or amphora' and, anticipating *Omeros,* stressing that the Caribbean 'has its own *Iliads*' (*AT,* 26); in 'Gros-Ilet' he concludes:

This is not the grape-purple Aegean
There is no wine here, no cheese, the almonds are green,
the sea grapes bitter, the language is that of slaves.

(AT, 35)

The first part of *The Arkansas Testament* also includes a group of poems which focus on Christianity and local folk beliefs and in so doing collectively contest the idea of definition through European analogy in a more adversarial manner than is usually the case in Walcott's verse. In 'St. Lucia's First Communion' the poet attacks the loss of innocence that Christianity has inflicted on the island; in 'Gros-Ilet' he asserts that 'There are different candles and customs here' (AT, 35). In 'The Whelk Gatherers' the moonlight fishermen of the title insist they have seen the devilish folk figure of 'Abaddon the usurper', not a devilfish, and reject 'the prelate's modern sermon / [which] proves there is no evil' (AT, 36).

This group of poems concludes with the powerful 'White Magic', which provides a summation of the concerns of the section. It invokes a number of St. Lucian folklore figures associated with magico-religious beliefs, among them the *loup-garoux* (or werewolf), the *gens-gagée* (or sorceress who flies by night, leaving her human skin behind) and the forest-god Papa Bois, whom Walcott had already given a prominent role in *Ti-Jean and His Brothers*. Christianity has failed to 'anachronize' (AT, 38) the hold these African-derived mythical figures exercise on the local imagination and the poem refuses the seductive possibility of validating them by identifying them with putative classical equivalents: Papa Bois is more than 'just Pan's clone, one more translated satyr' (AT, 38). Classical wood-nymphs are cleverly linked with the scribal – paper comes from wood:

Dryads and hamadryads were engrained
in the wood's bark, in papyrus, and this paper (AT, 38)

but the temptation of investing local myth with the status of Greek legend through drawing analogies is more or less resisted, although the poem coyly mention parallels it is not pursuing! 'White Magic' does perform the task of recording the oral in a scribal form (*The Arkansas Testament* engages with the Adamic role in relation to people and folk customs as well as landscape), but it nevertheless stops short of arguing that such transcription is a necessary way of providing status; and the poem concludes with the combative statement, 'Our myths are ignorance, theirs are literature' (*AT*, 39). As in *Ti-Jean*, Greek analogies are briefly introduced, but the folk culture becomes 'literature' in its own right.

The 'Elsewhere' poems of *The Arkansas Testament* are more eclectic than those in the 'Here' section. They include some particularly personal pieces, a poem about cultural translation between Wales and the Caribbean, where the emphasis is on the shared experiences of Methodism, bilingualism, coal and 'the colonial condition' ('Streams', *AT*, 81) rather than the distance between metropolis and colony and a number of poems in which Walcott adopts the persona of the Roman elegist Sextus Propertius. Other literary reference-points include W. H. Auden and Stephen Spender. Auden is the subject of a tribute Walcott delivered in New York in 1983, the tenth anniversary of the poet's death. 'Eulogy to W. H. Auden' is a *tour de force* in which Walcott deploys the full range of his poetic repertory: the 'fissured' landscape of Auden's face is likened to cartographical memories of countries (*AT*, 61) and 'the fissures made by speech' on 'the margin of a beach' (*AT*, 62–3); and the poem comes to rest expressing the view that poetry is a craft to which the privileged few are elected as spokespersons for humanity more generally and offering a prayer that the craft will confer 'the gift of peace' (*AT*, 65). Spender is the dedicatee of a poem entitled 'Elsewhere', which contrasts a secure world in which people have the freedom to espouse liberal causes, express anger at distant political outrages at conferences and become 'tired of torture stories' (*AT*, 66) and a world where state terrorism, censorship and murders are all too real, 'where nothing is free' (*AT*, 67). The poem is, however, less concerned with attacking political injustice than exposing the inadequacy of armchair liberalism and it ends with an attack on those who 'make a career out of conscience' (*AT*, 67).

The Arkansas Testament concludes with a longer poem which gives the collection its title and provides one of Walcott's most searching explorations of the American condition, in this case specifically the situation of the contemporary American South seen in relation to the historical legacy of the Civil War. 'The Arkansas Testament' is also a particularly fine example of Walcott's ability to infuse the most minute details with a welter of symbolic resonances which, for all his distrust of official historical and political discourses, suggest that history saturates everyday experience. What initially appears to be little more than careful poetic observation of a particular place, Fayetteville, Arkansas, on a particular winter morning, evolves, during the course of twenty-four gently paced meditative stanzas, into a full-scale indictment of the racially divisive legacy of the Old South. Towards the end the 'I' persona of the poem says 'only old age earns the / right to an abstract noun' and this provides the sanction for his Arkansas Testament, a quasi-religious state-ment on his 'people's predicament' (*AT*, 116), which is finally one of Walcott's most explicit abstract statements.

The poem opens with the persona checking into a cheap motel room in Fayetteville and contemplating the dead Confed-erate soldiers buried in a cemetery above the town. He reflects that the soldiers 'have no names' (*AT*, 104) and as he signs the motel register momentarily considers changing his own name, before deciding to keep up 'the game / of pretending whoever I was, / or am, or will be, are the same' (*AT*, 105–6). Identity is, then, as so often in Walcott, seen as a fluid construct, stabilized only by one's complicity in the social fiction of the unitary self. What follows is recorded in a low-key circumstantial manner which seems a marked departure from the customary meta-phorical density of Walcott's style:

> I dozed off in the early dark
> to a smell of detergent pine
> and they faded with me: the rug
> with its shag, pine-needled floor,
> the without-a-calendar wall
> now hung with the neon's sign,

no thin-lipped Gideon Bible.
[...]

I crucified my coat on one wire
hanger, undressed for bathing,
then saw that other, full-length,
alarmed in the glass coffin
of the bathroom door. Right there,
I decided to stay unshaven,
unsaved.

...

On a ridge over Fayetteville,
higher than any steeple,
is a white-hot electric cross.

It burns the back of my mind.
It scorches the skin of night. (*AT*, 106–7)

The apparently naturalistic mode of this passage is, however, an
illusion. The 'pine' in the motel room replicates the pine of the
hillside cemetery, suggesting the extent to which defining
moments from the national past permeate the mundane present.
The persona's crucifixion of his coat on the wire hanger links
with the 'white-hot electric cross' on the hillside and while this
is most obviously a memorial to the fallen soldiers, its scorching
qualities which burn 'the back of [the poet's] mind' suggest
another kind of southern cross, that associated with the
activities of the Ku Klux Klan. The persona's decision to stay
unshaven seems another commonplace detail, but its association
with the word 'unsaved' suggests it may be an image of the
unredeemed postlapsarian condition which figures prominently
in Walcott's verse from the outset, a suggestion which is confirmed as the poem proceeds. Cumulatively, the most ordinary
details assume profound significances; and as 'The Arkansas
Testament' develops, Walcott constructs a complex network of
images which relate to race, religion and history. The emptiness
of the motel room becomes a metonym for the spiritual vacuity
of the contemporary South; there is not even a Gideon Bible, but
the glare of the white cross still 'scribble[s] its signature' (*AT*,
105) on the bare wall.

Awake at dawn, the poet goes in search of coffee, walking streets where he feels the repressiveness of what he sees as the enduring Manichean racial binaries of the American South. Despite an appearance of Sabbath calm, the highway seems charged with a racist sub-text: he remembers 'the Trail of Tears' taken by dispossessed Cherokee warriors (AT, 108)[37] and feels a similar sense of personal dislocation, as he imagines silent hostility directed towards him because of his skin colour:

> In an all-night garage I saw
> the gums of a toothless sybil
> in garage tires, and she said:
> STAY BLACK AND INVISIBLE
> TO THE SIRENS OF ARKANSAS …
> Your shadow still hurts the South,
> like Lee's slowly reversing sword. (AT, 109)

Even breakfast is colour-coded, as he watches 'the shell / of a white sun tapping its yolk / on the dark crust of Fayetteville' (AT, 109–10) and identifies with 'the bubbling black zeros' of a decanter of coffee (AT, 110). The 'grey calm' of the town offers no relief – grey is the colour of the uniforms of Confederate soldiers – and he feels that the semblance 'of an average mid-American town' inhabited by 'simple, God-fearing folks' (AT, 112) and the platitudinous pretence that old divisions have been healed thinly veil a situation analogous to apartheid: curfew laws have only recently been repealed and the sunrise is linked with 'the doctrine / of Aryan light' (AT, 111). However, the poem also uses light imagery to suggest the possibility of an alternative transformative vision, which is associated with a form of *spiritual* illumination.

At the beginning of the poem, as the persona collapses on the motel-room bed, he likens himself to Saul on the road to Damascus and the notion of a Pauline epiphany recurs when he subsequently refers to the First Epistle of the Corinthians (AT, 108). So the 'testament' of the poem is an apostolic benediction which recognizes that it can do nothing to remedy the historic 'stripes and … scars' (AT, 117) perpetuated in the American flag, but nevertheless strives through art to offer its own kind of enlightenment. This enlightenment it offers is associated with the colour amber:

> The light, being amber, ignored
> the red and the green traffic stops,
> …
> like the lasers of angels, went
> through the pines guarding each slab
> of the Confederate Cemetery,
> piercing the dead with the quick. (*AT*, 113)

and the poem ends with television images of a journey across the United States in which the amber light spreads westwards, re-enacting the nineteenth-century American belief in Manifest Destiny. Typically Walcott poems about historic divisions move towards resolutions which 'obliterat[e] hurt'[38] but here the conclusion is more ambivalent since, while on the one hand the journey rejects 'the neon rose / of Vegas' and concludes with the shafts of light reaching the Pacific and 'huge organ pipes of sequoias' (*AT*, 117), the images that depict this are only media stills and it is a moot point whether they refer to the future or the past. The suspicion that America has forgotten its roots, 'its log-cabin dream' (*AT*, 114) of democracy, remains to the last. Yet the poem is itself an act of atonement, an artistic offering which offers the benediction of an inter-racial vision. Walcott likens the light to a mongrel which rushes towards the persona, displaying a warmth which is in marked contrast to the behaviour of the people he encounters:

> Abounding light
> raced towards me like a mongrel
> hoping that it would be caressed
> by my cold, roughening hand,
> and I prayed that all could be blest. (*AT*, 110)

This dog is perhaps as much the Odyssean protagonist of 'The Arkansas Testament' as the poet. Both cross boundaries and like the amber light resist the essentialism of static racial categories. This is the cautious religious benediction that the poem offers, but it remains far from sanguine about the possibility of redeeming society.

When it appeared in 1990, *Omeros* crystallized patterns that had been developed in the four collections Walcott published in the late 1970s and 1980s. Its larger scale quickly attracted recognition of a kind that Walcott had not previously received and was a major factor in his being awarded the Nobel Prize in 1992. In many ways *Omeros* really is Walcott's finest work, if only because of the sustained way in which it voices concerns which in many cases have now absorbed him for nearly half a century. Yet, seen from another point of view, it is simply the most condensed and extended version of these themes and there is a case for saying *Another Life* deserves to be ranked alongside it, as a poem which transforms autobiography into epic just as *Omeros* moves from epic to autobiography. Certainly one of the ways in which Walcott frustrates Homeric comparisons is by allowing his poem to grow beyond its initial impetus through the interweaving of a multiplicity of discursive strands which transgress Western generic boundaries and subvert the notion that an epic poem should have a single great theme.

The Iliad begins by invoking the Muse's assistance to 'sing' of the wrath of Achilles;[39] *Omeros* speaks of Achille's story as its subject, but includes *its* statement of the epic theme close to the end, almost as an afterthought, and relates it to the paean it has sung of 'our wide country, the Caribbean sea' (*Omeros*, 320). During its course *Omeros* has, in the tradition of classical epic, become an encyclopaedic poem which uses its narrative framework to comment on the Caribbean predicament and the wandering Odyssean poet who becomes its spokesperson. The poem conflates the genres of epic, nature poetry, autobiography, historiography and metaliterary poetic essay to create a hybrid form which, like the travelling poet, crosses meridians. Most obviously the poem is about the lives of St. Lucian fishermen and their rivalry for a local Helen, who is herself a person-ification of the island. It is, however, also the story of a white expatriate couple, Major Plunkett and his wife Maud, and the poet himself; and one of its most striking aspects is the way in which it merges these very different characters together to provide a kind of composite persona which suggests that, despite appearances to the contrary, Caribbean peoples have a shared history. If this seems over-idealistic, especially in its erosion of racial and economic differences which crucially determine St. Lucians' material circumstances, it can nevertheless be seen as an aspiration towards a healing process which is common to virtually all of Walcott's work.

Various characters in *Omeros* share the predicament of being wounded. Initially this condition is associated with the fisherman Philoctete who has a sore on his shin which has come from 'a scraping, rusted anchor' (*Omeros*, 10). However, Philoctete believes its resistance to healing suggests an ancestral origin:

> He believed the swelling came from the chained ankles
> of his grandfathers. Or else why was there no cure?
> That the cross he carried was not the anchor's
>
> but that of his race, for a village black and poor
> as the pigs that rooted in its burning garbage.
>
> (*Omeros*, 19)

At the opposite end of the social spectrum, Major Plunkett, who has sustained a wound in World War II feels a similar sense of primal hurt. So too does the poet, another Walcott protagonist who sees himself as a fallen New World Adam. These various characters begin to converge towards the end of the volume. Returning to St. Lucia and feeling a sense of blessing from the natural world in the closing pages, the poet feels an affinity with Philoctete which collapses the distance between author and character:

> Then Philoctete
>
> waved 'Morning' to me from far, and I waved back;
> we shared the one wound, the same cure. (*Omeros*, 295)

Along with the wound comes the cure and *Omeros* represents a departure from much of Walcott's writing, in that the source of the cure is to be found in the African heritage of the Caribbean. One of the most interesting migrant figures in the text is a sea-swift which, like the Odyssean poet and Achille who *dreams* of a return to Africa, travels east–west routes across the Atlantic.

The swift occupies much the same role as Athena, Odysseus's guiding deity in *The Odyssey*, but it traverses the Middle Passage, journeying not to Europe and the Homeric legacy but to Africa as a 'mind-/messenger' with a 'speed [which] out-darted Memory' (*Omeros*, 131). It becomes Achille's guide as he makes his imaginative journey back to the West Coast of Africa and the name of 'Afolabe' in an earlier incarnation. A swift is also the courier that brings a cure for Philoctete's wound to the New World. Centuries before, it has carried a seed, from which a weed with healing properties has grown, across the Atlantic. Philoctete is cured when the local equivalent of the sibyl of Cumae (*Omeros*, 245), the obeah-woman Ma Kilman, gives him a bush bath in a brew from the root of the transported African weed. This immersion cures Philoctete of his sense of ancestral wound, by reversing the trauma of the Middle Passage through an African-derived remedy.

While Africa plays a key role in this healing process, Plunkett too experiences a slow healing after the death of his wife Maud in the closing sections of the poem. She has spent her time in the Penelope-like activity of embroidering a quilt which becomes a tapestry that unites the divergent strands of Caribbean life, just as the poem itself increasingly insists on their consanguinity. Throughout his time in St. Lucia, Plunkett has been absorbed with the project of giving the island 'its true place in history' (*Omeros*, 64) and he has been particularly fascinated by the image of Helen as a symbol of the 'natural' world of the island. Now at the end he achieves a closer encounter with its folk culture as he visits Ma Kilman, seeking and receiving her help as a medium who can unite him with his dead wife.

In the later stages of the poem the poet himself increasingly becomes a character in his own design and the fictiveness of the work is strongly foregrounded. When Maud dies, he writes:

I was both there and not there. I was attending
the funeral of a character I'd created;
the fiction of her life needed a good ending. (*Omeros*, 266)

He compares his attempt to write history to Plunkett's project and sees the various characters of the poem merging together as 'interchangeable phantoms' (*Omeros*, 266). As they merge, he becomes the central Odyssean protagonist (in a text in which the *Iliad* references are increasingly swallowed up by the shadow of the *Odyssey*) and ultimately, despite the various journeys which the poem has shown him undertaking in Europe and North America, he is the most significant benefactor of the swift's legacy. *Omeros* concludes with a message which revitalizes Walcott's life-long preoccupation with classical epic and nervous engagement with the anxiety of influence. It once again stresses the need for porous cultural geographies which erode the static essentialism of binary classifications, but at the same time it admits the importance of African retentions in the Caribbean in a way that has hitherto been rare in Walcott's verse:

> I followed a sea-swift to both sides of this text;
> her hyphen stitched its seam, like the interlocking
> basins of a globe in which one half fits the next
>
> into an equator, both shores neatly clicking
> into a globe, except that its meridian
> was not North and South but East and West. One, the New
>
> World, made exactly like the Old, halves of one brain,
> or the beat of both hands rowing that bear the two
> vessels of the heart with balance weight and design.
>
> Her wing-beat carries these islands to Africa.
>
> <div align="right">(<i>Omeros</i>, 319)</div>

East–West meridians still continue to occupy a central role in the definition of Caribbean experience, but now Homeric epic and 'the meridian of Greenwich' cease to be the standards for measuring all other crossings of lines of longitude. Walcott's scepticism about the African revival in earlier works such as *Dream on Monkey Mountain* has now given way to a vision which heals the divisive binaries of Caribbean history more comprehensively by acknowledging that an odyssey, actual or psychic, across the Bight of Benin is as crucial a part of the process of reclamation and integration as any journey, real or imagined, to London or Homer's eastern Mediterranean.

By the time Walcott came to write his stage version of *The Odyssey* for the Royal Shakespeare Company, he clearly must have familiarized himself with the original epic, since his three-hour 'stage version' follows aspects of Homer's narrative closely. The programme notes for the play emphasize the numerous incarnations which Odysseus has undergone in Western literature, particularly stressing his 'quick-wittedness'[40] and the symbolic value his attempt to return to Ithaca has had for 'many later poets, especially Greeks and those in exile from their homelands'.[41] At the same time, the Odysseus of the play is recognizably the travelling protagonist of Walcott's later poetry, with whom he shares many attributes: he is again a man wrestling with the problem of trying to reconcile the values of home and family with an instinctive wanderlust, a personification of the poetic imagination and a force resistant to narrow, essentialist definition. Moreover, the RSC commission did not prevent Walcott from incorporating Caribbean elements into the play. As in *The Joker of Seville*, his earlier reworking of a European original for the RSC,[42] there is a definite attempt to creolize the European *Ur*-text, but whereas in *The Joker of Seville* this is central to the whole project, here it is more incidental. Thus a black storyteller, 'Blind' Billy Blue, provides a frame for the action, fairly obviously functioning, like Seven Seas in *Omeros*, as a Caribbean Homer.[43] Additionally there are other black characters – Odysseus's old nurse Eurycleia is a Creole-speaking Egyptian who retells 'Nancy stories'[44] – and references to a 'far archipelago' (*Odyssey*, 122) also suggest the Caribbean. Most obviously, the descent into the Underworld in the Circe episode is made possible through the performance of an Afro-Caribbean Shango rite, which like the Demeter-Persephone cult, briefly alluded to here, seems to offer release from the Apollonian tradition. Such parallelism is unforced and it is tempting to see the ease with which the play integrates different cultural traditions as an index of Walcott's having reached a position where he is able to move seamlessly and unselfconsciously between the two locations. However, if one considers the implications of these apparently effortless transitions just a little longer, it becomes clear that they have the effect of undermining the classic Western view of ancient Greece as the fountain-head of civilization – aspects of Homer's 'Greek' world are shown to have an Egyptian provenance and Egypt's genealogy is seen to contain elements from sub-Saharan African, even as the play points forward to the Caribbean – and that they introduce and assign equal status to non-'European' religious practices. And, given that they appear in a play drawn from the supposed precursor of all Western discourse[45] and were premiered in the former seat of Empire by a company associated with the Bard, the Caribbean elements of *The Odyssey* can be seen to constitute both a process of reverse colonization and, perhaps, an iteration of the multicultural nature of contemporary British and European societies.[46]

As in Homer's original, Odysseus's struggle to get home and the impediments that prevent him from doing so provide the plot with its central dynamic. 'Home' lies at the heart of the play and it has several resonances, among them a felt need for psychic belonging and security that offers deliverance from the uncertainties of wandering. Thus, when Odysseus eventually reaches Ithaca, he tells Penelope that his real home is his mind. Earlier he ostensibly yearns for a physical home – at one point he tells his helmsman Elpenor, 'I'd give up all this heaving for one yard of earth' (*Odyssey*, 39) – and yet, as in Homer, he 'stops off to plunder cities' (*Odyssey*, 38), spends seven years in Calypso's company and, even when the goddess Athena tells him at the end that the 'harbour of home' (*Odyssey*, 159) has given meaning to all his wanderings, he confesses that he may miss the wonders of the sea. In the Homeric original his return is prevented by Poseidon, the god of the sea. Here, while this motif is present, there is more emphasis on his being detained by monsters that represent human agency and these appear to be both external and internal: at the very end of the play Odysseus tells Penelope 'we make [such monsters] ourselves' (*Odyssey*, 160).

The identity of the play's monsters is heavily gendered: Odysseus encounters a range of female figures – Calypso, Circe, mermaids and sirens – who are all variations on the archetype of the seductress. These encounters form a sequence of erotic dalliance that offers an alternative to homecoming in Ithaca. Circe is explicit in telling him that he is at home in her brothel, which she refers to as 'A house men's desires built' (*Odyssey*, 82) and Odysseus's stay with her is fairly clearly a carnivalesque interlude which threatens to subvert the pattern of the linear Western quest towards an end which will resolve all complications. The notion of the travelling hero engaging in a single-minded quest to reach home and with it a unitary conception of fulfilment is problematized: Odysseus is torn between the attractions of picaresque philandering and the assumed constancy of his waiting Penelope; and the play briefly invites an interpretation that interrogates the gender stereotyping engrained in most versions of the Odysseus legend, when Penelope dissociates herself from the martial male behaviour represented not only by the Trojan War, but also by Odysseus's killing of the suitors who have besieged her while he was away.[47]

Two sections of *The Odyssey*, the Cyclops and Proteus episodes, shed further light on the ambivalent response to 'home' implicit in this pattern of erotic dalliance. Walcott's Cyclops, referred to in the play as 'the Eye', is a political dictator, a totalitarian nationalist who denies the value of art, the theatre and circuses. There is a hint that his regime may represent the Greece of the colonels and it could be related to repressive post-independence governments in the Caribbean, but more generally the Eye seems to represent a monolithic vision that not only denies freedom, but also cultural pluralism and polysemy, both of which of course are central to the play and Walcott's art more generally. In a conversation with him, Odysseus refuses to accept the logic of his one-eyed view of the world, arguing that 'God gave us two eyes because we're human'. Having two eyes, he claims, enables people to laugh and to cry, to have 'balance. Proportion. Contrast' (*Odyssey*, 68). So the Cyclops's monocular perspective, which negates the free play of thought and the possibility of other views of the world, is opposed to duality of vision. However, Odysseus is not happy simply to oppose monism with dualism. Still resisting the entrapments of binary models of culture and society, Walcott has his protagonist take refuge in a strategy associated with many earlier versions of Odysseus, but here reinvigorated through the highly individual way in which it is reworked: he takes refuge in disguise, a major motif in the play generally, which again suggests the fluid and plural nature of personality. Odysseus tells the Cyclops he is 'Nobody' and in so doing, like Shabine and Don Juan in *The Joker of Seville* who also refer to themselves as 'nobody',[48] he endeavours to elude not only unitary definition but any definition at all. As 'Nobody', he can be seen as a figure representing migrant resistance to entrapment in constricting identity labels and, a frame of reference which has particular resonance in the context of this play, a Protean capacity for transformation.

The episode in which Odysseus encounters Proteus is less extended than his meetings with some of the other 'monsters' of *The Odyssey*, but it is arguably the most interesting instance of a monster's being a product of his own mind. While, like all the other figures who delay Odysseus, Proteus represents entrapment, his shape-changing capacity obviously has its attraction for Odysseus, himself an Anansi-like trickster who dons disguises at will as a survival strategy. In the Mycenae scenes of the play, Menelaus says of Proteus 'He's fluent. He escapes' and goes on to add 'The gates of imagination never close' (*Odyssey*, 35). This suggests that Proteus is not simply a monster obstructing the hero's progress; he also represents the possibilities offered by a fluid, questing poetic imagination which resists closure, unitary definition and 'home'. As such, *like* Odysseus, he is another personification of migrant subjectivity refusing to be encased within the ideological strait-jacket of competing, opposed discourses. He also represents a view of language grounded in layer upon layer of metaphor, which opens up possibilities of carving new forms of identity from the dead wood of old conventions. Walcott's use of Homeric narrative works in just such a way. He provides a revitalized version of *The Odyssey* which creates its own discursive universe, resisting ensnarement in either a derivative relationship or an adversarial response which limits the possibility of creating a new imaginative space by locking its exponent into the agendas created by a discourse of resistance.

After *Omeros*, there was a seven-year gap before Walcott published his next collection of poetry, *The Bounty* (1997), in which he returned to the elegiac themes of his earliest verse, while once again employing the trope of travelling and worrying away at possible parallels between Caribbean and Greek cultures. *The Bounty* is also notable for a number of poems which propound a postmodern view of personality, but at the same time expound a quasi-religious view of experience, at odds with the relativism of much metropolitan postmodernism.

The collection opens with the title-poem, which is both an elegy for Walcott's mother, Alix,[49] and a meditation on his poetic vocation that intertwines itself with reflections on the representation of the Caribbean natural world. The central signifier is 'bounty' itself and it is variously Captain Bligh's ship, the ambivalent legacy conferred on the Caribbean, the gifts offered by the Caribbean natural world and the lesson the poet has been taught by his mother. The Caribbean staple of the breadfruit links several of these significances. Unknown in the region in the pre-Columbian period and during the first phase of colonialism, the breadfruit was being brought from Polynesia to Jamaica by the *Bounty* at the time of the mutiny. Captain Bligh is referred to as the 'white God' (*Bounty*, 9) and so the mutiny could be read as an anti-colonial act, but the poem adopts a more complex attitude. Addressing his mother and punning on Fletcher Christian's name, Walcott writes:

> Authority's argument
> diminishes in power, in the longboat with Captain Bligh.
> This was one of your earliest lessons, how the Christ-Son
> questions the father, to settle on another island, haunted
> by Him.   (*Bounty*, 9–10)

One form of colonialism is overthrown, but within the colonial period and despite European mythography of South Sea island paradises, there are no Edenic islands beyond Prospero's domain. In the contemporary Caribbean the breadfruit is part of the natural abundance which the poem celebrates and so there appears to have been a significant sea change, but the tree is still associated with the barbarity of the region's past:

> the breadfruit opens its palms in praise of the bounty,
> *bois-pain*, tree of bread, slave food. (*Bounty*, 3)

Transported to the Caribbean like the slaves of the Middle Passage, the breadfruit is, despite the very different associations of the Pacific islands from which it has emanated, an outcome of the same network of colonial sea routes which encircled the globe. Now in the present it is a hybrid, which offers the promise of transforming its transplanted past into an Odyssean identity rooted in the region's present. 'The Bounty' is equivocal about the luxuriance of Caribbean nature; it finds its 'vegetal fury' (*Bounty*, 13) a shocking contrast to the sense of grief the poet feels at his mother's loss, but like so many Walcott poems it reconciles its conflicting visions at the end, with the poet identifying his mother's legacy with the poetic process of breathing life into the familiar and praising her for:

> the lesson you taught your sons,
> to write of the light's bounty on familiar things
> that stand on the verge of translating themselves into
> news.   (*Bounty*, 16)

After *Omeros* and *The Odyssey*, one might have expected Walcott to have finally exorcized Homer from his poetic arsenal, but the travelling protagonist remains as central in *The Bounty* as in his previous volumes, here sometimes an Ishmael seeking the solace of a home which seems eternally to elude him, even though he has no doubt where it lies (within the Caribbean, and specifically in the St. Lucia of his youth);[50] and in the final poems of the collection the parallel between the Caribbean and Aegean continues to provide a pivotal focal-point. In Poem '29', the analogy is redeployed in the context of a comparison of cultural mythologies. This poem begins by asking whether more attention would be paid to the Caribbean islands if they were 'made from mythologies', implying that the levels of cultural inscription surrounding the Hellenic world invest it with a status not accorded to the Caribbean. However, as it moves on, the poem shifts its position by saying that the only 'patterned then unravelled threads' to be observed on the surf are those of the 'wanderer's shadow' (*Bounty*, 62). The suggestion is, then, that the only mythological figure to achieve any kind of permanence in the abiding natural world is the Odyssean traveller; neither Greek nor Yoruba gods (Hephaestus and Ogun are mentioned) have the same claim to longevity. Exactly what one is to make of this remains a subject for conjecture, but one possible interpretation is that the wanderer's fluidity ensures survival in contexts where less malleable gods might be 'forcefully forgotten' (*Bounty*, 62). Odysseus, like Proteus, can transform himself to blend with the shifting patterns of sea and surf.

In the very last poem of the collection Walcott once again returns to the figure of a wandering Greek: this time not to Odysseus but to Oedipus, the Oedipus of the third part of Sophocles' trilogy, who seeks atonement for his unwitting crimes in the healing world of Colonus. The poem provides a fitting conclusion to *The Bounty* and reiterates themes that are central to all Walcott's writing. It opens:

> After the plague,[51] the city-wall caked with flies, the
>   smoke's amnesia,
> learn, wanderer, to go nowhere. (*Bounty*, 78)

The injunction is, then, to put civil strife and a guilty past behind one and to find solace in an environment in which divisions are eroded. 'Colonus' quickly metamorphoses into a Caribbean site, with Walcott returning to his familiar theme of the healing properties of the sea. Along with Death, which casts a longer shadow over this volume than any of Walcott's collections since his very earliest work, the sea becomes a Leveller, which together with the Antigone-figure of a daughter, offers peace beyond binary divisions.[52] The poem moves towards conclusion in a mood of muted 'wonder':

> This is the right light, this pewter shine on the water,
> not the carnage of clouds, not the expected wonder

of self-igniting truth and oracular rains,
but these shallows are as gentle as the voice of your
    daughter,
while the gods fade like thunder in the rattling mountains.

(*Bounty*, 78)

This suggests a moment of spiritual arrival which offers an end
to the Odyssean traveller's restless journeying and could be seen
as a departure from the more characteristic predicament of
Walcott's later protagonists, Shabine's 'flight to a target whose
aim we'll never know'. However, homecoming remains an ideal
to be pursued, not a goal which has been reached, an exhortation
rather than an attainment, and Walcott's poetry in the collection
as a whole remains as poised between worlds, discourses and
value-systems as ever.

Throughout *The Bounty*, stress on the provisional, dialogic
quality of language and the fluidity of notions of self points
towards a postmodern view of personality and the impossibility
of achieving an essentialist vision of home and perfect peace; and
recent criticism of Walcott's work has drawn attention to the
extent to which his concern with cultural, linguistic and psychological displacement locates him as a postmodernist writer.[53]
Clearly such a categorization, resting as it does on the notion of
dislocation, relates closely to the physical realities of many
colonial and post-colonial situations, and supposedly more
'realistic' writers such as V. S. Naipaul may well be seen to share
the same concerns. Nevertheless, the very explicit foregrounding of metaliterary elements[54] in Walcott's writing justifies
viewing him as a postmodernist writer, despite his habitual
attempts at mirror-like transcription of physical phenomena,
particularly in his project of realizing the tactile qualities of the
St. Lucian natural world in print. Metaliterary elements are to
be found in all his work, but they are especially prominent in
The Bounty, where he frequently foregrounds aspects of his
artistic practice. In a section entitled 'Six Fictions' he wrestles
with his distrust of causality and linearity – 'Pray for a life
without plot, a day without narrative' (*Bounty*, 49) – and very
overtly deconstructs the notion of the unitary self. Throughout

this study I have tended to refer to Walcott's various poetic 'I' figures as 'the persona' or as 'the poet', even when they appear to share characteristics with their creator. The second of the poems in 'Six Fictions' confirms the necessity of taking such an approach, when the 'I' narrator of the poem explicitly identifies both the exiled protagonist that he is talking about and himself as constructs:

> He believed the pain of exile would have passed
> by now, but he had stopped counting the days and months,
> […].
> He wears black, his hair has grown
> white, and he has placed his cane on a bench in the park.
> There is no such person. I myself am a fiction,
> remembering the hills of the island as it gets dark.
>
> (*Bounty*, 50)

Such self-referential passages appear throughout *The Bounty* and a section entitled 'Signs' is particularly notable for the way in which it collapses the boundaries between European cityscapes and the literary and artistic genres that have described them. The novel form is seen as having 'an appetite for inventory' and becomes 'a market roaring with ideas' (*Bounty*, 20); elsewhere it is likened to 'seething' streets (*Bounty*, 21). What was once the Jewish quarter of a middle European city is presented through similarly self-conscious references to visual media:

> The shot elegiacally grieves
> and the sequel moves with the orchestration of conscience
> around the Expressionist corners of the Old Town.
>
> (*Bounty*, 22)

In addition to foregrounding artifice, such passages suggest the extent to which the scenes being rendered are actually being brought into being by the poetry, the extent to which art is its own subject. Ultimately, release from stultifying political and aesthetic binaries is not to be found in return to a comfortable Ithaca – or Colonus – but through the only 'nation' that Shabine in 'The Schooner *Flight*' feels he has left to him, that of the imagination. In the collection as a whole the poet remains an

Odysseus, torn between the complementary compulsions of wishing to return home and wanting to escape from the entrapments of social life through ceaseless travelling and this is reflected in an artistic practice, which alternates between an attempt to achieve the stasis of classical art and a realization that kinesis is inevitably the stock-in-trade of a postmodern, post-colonial poet.

Critical overview and conclusion

THIS chapter provides a brief summary of some of the main strands in Walcott criticism, with a particular emphasis on books and monographs about his work; it also attempts to locate the present study in relation to some of these strands. Criticism of Walcott's writing has moved through various phases during the fifty years of his writing career to date. Initially, reflecting the locations in which it was published or performed, responses came almost exclusively from within the Caribbean region; after his poetry was published in Britain and the United States, it increasingly attracted the attention of metropolitan critics; and the award of the Nobel Prize in 1992 substantially augmented the critical output on his work, particularly his poetry.[1]

From the outset, criticism of Walcott's writing has been dominated by discussions of its cultural politics. Early on, it was often reductively characterized as Eurocentric in orientation; more recently it has been embraced by post-colonial theorists, who have seen it as engaging with many of the preoccupations which they have brought to the fore during the last two decades. In one sense there is an appropriateness about both of these responses, in that, despite his rejection of conventional political discourses, Walcott's early work is centrally concerned with the divisions in Caribbean society and, in more recent years, the writing's Odyssean attempt to claim a space outside the political domain has offered a significant alternative to oppositional historiography and aesthetics. Moreover, despite his distrust of abstract theorizing, Walcott's emphasis on Adamic naming as a strategy for (re)claiming one's world from the colonizer, his career-long concern with eroding Manichean binaries and his development of a poetics of migration all strikingly anticipate subsequent developments in post-colonial theory.

However, to pigeon-hole his work in any of these ways *can* be to obscure the complex and subtle ways in which he approaches such issues and to occlude the cultural specifics from which and about which he writes. Emphasis on the supposed European orientation of his writing and the contrast frequently made with Edward Kamau Brathwaite invariably obscures the extent to which he creolizes European forms.[2] The present study has attempted to correct this misreading by showing that his reworkings of European pre-texts such as *Robinson Crusoe*, Tirso de Molina's *Trickster of Seville* and Homer's epics are neither complicitous nor adversarial, and by illustrating his increasing emphasis on the dismantling of binary structures through his exploration of the Odyssean predicament. So far, his poetry has been much better served by critics than his drama, though this has to some extent been remedied by the recent appearance of two important studies of the plays: Bruce King's detailed account of the Trinidad Theatre Workshop, *Derek Walcott and West Indian Drama: 'Not Only a Playwright But a Company': The Trinidad Theatre Workshop 1953–1993;*[3] and Judy Stone's chapter, 'Classical Theatre' in *Theatre: Studies In West Indian Literature,*[4] which, in addition to providing an assessment of Walcott's plays, is, like King's book, an extremely valuable source of information for details about performances of the plays. One area of his work still remains seriously neglected: his essays. Even though the essays may seem to be no more than an off-shoot of the verse and drama, Walcott is arguably the finest prose stylist the anglo-phone Caribbean has yet produced, though his distrust of narrative, which he associates with linear historiography,[5] has prevented him from attempting extended prose fiction and impeded recognition of his genius as a prose writer. Essays such as 'What the Twilight Says: An Overture', 'The Muse of History' and his Nobel Prize lecture, 'The Antilles: Fragments of

Epic Memory', are classic statements on the problematics of Caribbean theatre, historiography and culture, which not only merit serious critical attention, but also book publication to make them accessible to a larger readership.

Although Walcott's first volume of verse, *25 Poems*, was published in 1949, it was not until the late 1970s that his work received book-length attention. Prior to this, studies of his poetry in particular concentrated on issues of cultural affiliation and the contrast with Brathwaite had already become commonplace by the time Patricia Ismond produced her essay 'Walcott versus Brathwaite',[6] an important statement on a supposed opposition which echoed earlier antithetical pairings of writers such as George Steiner's 'Tolstoy or Dostoyevsky?'. In her essay Ismond contrasted Walcott's alleged 'humanism' with Brathwaite's 'mission of protest',[7] coming to the conclusion that Brathwaite's 'protest … remains weaker, in the final analysis, than Walcott's kind of assertion'.[8] After the publication of *Another Life* in 1973, commentators devoted a good deal of attention to the Adamic project which Walcott outlined in this volume, a vein of criticism which is well illustrated by Michel Fabre's 'Adam's Task of Giving Things Their Names: The Poetry of Derek Walcott'.[9] Through these early years Walcott's drama remained largely neglected in academic circles, while a considerable body of Caribbean reviews offered (very mixed) responses to performances of the plays, sometimes praising Walcott for his engagement with issues central to the development of an autonomous regional culture, sometimes taking him to task for his alleged obscurity.[10] At the same time, Walcott's own *Trinidad Guardian* reviews provide valuable insights into his practice, both by discussing it directly and also through their comments on other writers' work and the directions in which he feels Caribbean theatre and culture should be moving.[11]

Edward Baugh's monograph *Derek Walcott: Memory as Vision: Another Life*[12] was the first book-length study of any aspect of Walcott's work, when it appeared in 1978. It locates *Another Life* within the specifics of Walcott's St. Lucian upbringing and puts particular emphasis on the poem's subtle representation of how perception operates and how memory is shaped into 'vision'. Baugh provides factual information about the background to the poetic autobiography and sensitively sketches in several of the main concerns of the poem: Walcott's abandonment of painting for poetry, once he realized that his real gift lay in metaphor; his attempt to wipe the historical slate clean and create a new aesthetic from this *tabula rasa*; and his belief in the need for the Adamic project.

Another monograph followed shortly afterwards. As a by-product of Walcott's being awarded the Welsh Arts Council's International Writers Prize in 1980 and a conference on his work, held to mark this award at Gregynog in the same year, Ned Thomas produced a bilingual (English and Welsh) study of Walcott's poetry.[13] Like Baugh, Thomas takes pains to outline the social and geographical circumstances from which Walcott's poetry has emerged, while also stressing its international accessibility. He argues that while the poetry must be read against Walcott's St. Lucian background, this needs to be done in terms of the particular poetic vocabularies that inform it. In addition to discussing parts of *Another Life*, Thomas's monograph looks closely at two poems which have been favourites among Walcott commentators, 'Ruins of a Great House' and the then recently published 'Schooner *Flight*'. Although a brief study, it is notable for its attempt to develop parallels between Walcott and contemporary Welsh and Australian writers and represents a pioneering attempt to discuss Walcott as a post-colonial poet. Thomas also addresses the question of Walcott's indebtedness to European forms, problematizing the issue of whether borrowings leave the writer in danger of being assimilated in an interesting manner.

Robert Hamner's *Derek Walcott* (1981)[14] offers a general introduction to Walcott's life and work within the constrictions of the format of the Twayne World Authors Series. It is notable as the first study to offer a discussion of Walcott's published and unpublished plays and, although the information provided is sometimes sketchy, it was a landmark in Walcott criticism at the time when it appeared, predating King's and Stone's accounts of

Walcott's drama by over a decade. Hamner also offers useful information on other aspects of Walcott's work which remain neglected, especially his early Caribbean-published volumes of poetry[15] and his journalistic writing for the *Trinidad Guardian*. Like Thomas, he discusses the issue of Walcott's 'assimilation', taking the view that the multiple nature of the influences on which he draws enables him to avoid imitativeness. Hamner achieves flexibility within the format of the series in which he is writing and the book remains the most informative single-authored book on the first three decades of Walcott's writing, if not the most critically incisive.

Between the late 1960s and the late 1980s a number of collections of essays on Caribbean literature provided general introductions to Walcott's work. These included Kenneth Ramchand's essay in his own *An Introduction to the Study of West Indian Literature* (1976),[16] Mervyn Morris's essay in Bruce King's *West Indian Literature* (1979)[17] and John Thieme's and Stewart Brown's essays, on Walcott's plays and poetry respectively, in David Dabydeen's *Handbook for Teaching Caribbean Literature* (1988).[18] Earlier, Cameron King and Louis James had contributed a perceptive essay on the contemplative aspects of Walcott's verse to the first significant collection of essays on anglophone Caribbean writing to appear in Britain, James's *The Islands in Between* (1968).[19]

In the 1990s international interest in Walcott's work, which had gradually been growing, particularly in the United States after he had partly settled in Boston, dramatically increased with the publication of *Omeros* in 1990 and the award of the Nobel Prize in 1992. This paved the way for more specialist studies of his work. Stewart Brown's 1991 collection, *The Art of Derek Walcott*, includes twelve new essays on specific aspects of Walcott's work, mostly particular volumes of his verse, although there are also dedicated essays on the early and late plays which, like most of the articles published on the drama, lack the detailed background knowledge to be found in King's and Stone's subsequent books.

Robert D. Hamner's 1993 *Critical Perspectives*[20] is an attempt to provide an extensive archive of Walcott material within the pages of a single volume. It is the most useful source-book of writing by and about Walcott to have appeared thus far; and brings together several of Walcott's own essays and interviews, along with critical pieces by others, which range from fully-fledged academic articles to ephemeral but fascinating reviews. The selection from Walcott's own essays favours those that had hitherto had a limited readership. Thus 'Leaving School' is included, but not 'The Muse of History'; and Walcott's 1965 talk 'The Figure of Crusoe', which provides an interesting companion-piece to *The Castaway*, is printed for the first time. The critical pieces are grouped into four chronologically-ordered sections, ranging from the juvenilia to *Omeros* and although some of the selections are poor in quality, the sheer volume and diversity of the material included makes it possible to appreciate the range and development of Walcott's work, albeit through the mediating vision of critics, without having to call on the services of several specialist libraries. Hamner's partially annotated secondary bibliography is the most useful to have appeared to date; the primary bibliography supplements the more exhaustive listings provided in Irma Goldstraw's two thorough bibliographies of Walcott's own writings.[21]

Rei Terada's *American Mimicry* (1992)[22] advances the study of Walcott's poetry by demonstrating how its self-conscious use of language complements a vision which interrogates notions of geographical centres and ideas of originality. For Terada, Walcott's American 'mimicry … replaces mimesis as the ground of representation'.[23] Unlike most of the other books on Walcott, *American Mimicry* abandons any attempt at an introduction to Walcott's poetry as a whole in favour of a discussion which outlines some of its problematics and sees him as a postmodernist writer whose thinking displays affinities with post-structuralist theory. Such an approach is sanctioned by the numerous meta-literary references in Walcott's work, which have become particularly prominent in his poetry of the last fifteen years, but are to be seen in both the poetry and the plays from very early on. Terada's remapping of Walcott's cultural and geographical horizons sees him as promulgating a new cartography in which

New and Old Worlds exist in a symbiotic, mutually constitutive relationship.

The amount of critical writing available on Walcott is now very considerable and this survey only offers a brief overview of some of the landmarks and the more readily available material. As indicated above, significant criticism of the drama is still comparatively sparse and only Hamner, King and Stone have hitherto been prepared to engage with the difficulties of trying to survey his vast dramatic output, some of which is fugitive and much of which has gone through numerous revisions. King offers a minutely detailed account of Walcott's involvement with the Trinidad Theatre Workshop and includes a wealth of information on particular performances and reviews. His thoroughness has provided the groundwork for future studies. Stone's fifty-two page chapter on Walcott's 'Classical Theatre' is similarly informative and also deals with plays unconnected with the Theatre Workshop. Its location within a general book on West Indian theatre helps it to contextualize Walcott's dramatic art and it offers rather more by way of critical analysis than King does. Both books have made a major contribution to the study of Walcott as a dramatist, in some cases making a readership that was previously unaware of just how prolific he has been as a playwright familiar with the range and extent of his dramatic writing.

To a far greater degree than is the case with the poetry, Walcott seems to see his plays as 'works in progress' and he has constantly returned to them, either revising them or recasting aspects of them in new forms. Arguably this reflects the extent to which he regards his dramatic utterances as provisional, gestures towards statements rather than statements themselves; and this can perhaps be related to his stagings of identity,[24] which again always seems to be malleable and dialogic in his hands. Plays are, of course, always reinvented in performance, whereas poems take on the stasis conferred by print when committed to the page and so perhaps this is inevitable. However, it is noteworthy that Walcott has, as it were, pursued two almost separate and parallel careers in these two genres, since it would seem that neither has enabled him to pursue his imaginative concerns satisfactorily on its own.[25] This, too, can perhaps be read as an expression of the Odyssean tension in his work, now being enacted through his response to genre, with the kinetic impermanence of dramatic performance complementing the stasis provided by the printed poem, even when it is about restless journeying.

In dealing with aspects of both the poems and the plays in some detail and attempting to demonstrate their shared concerns, as well as the very significant ways in which they differ, the present book has endeavoured to see Walcott as a whole, while recognizing that what emerges from such an attempt to describe totality is a layered portrait of a writer who, more than most, thwarts attempts at essentialist categorization. Through the two interlocking theses which I have pursued in the course of this discussion – Walcott's attempt to erode Manichean binaries in favour of a continuum model of culture and identity; and the development of a poetics of migration – I hope to have shown the extent to which his artistic journeyings have provided a solution not only to his own personal dilemmas, but also to the problem of formulating an appropriate Caribbean aesthetic practice. Ironically, since his quest for such a practice began as a response to a very specific 'marginalized' situation, this has emerged as a position which seems to have global valency at the turn of the millennium, at a time when essentialist categorizations have been interrogated not simply by the collapse of empires and physical migration, but also by the emergence of strains of cultural theory which Walcott was anticipating in his very earliest work.

Notes

Chapter 1

1   See particularly Homi K. Bhabha, *The Location of Culture*, London and New York: Routledge, 1994.

2   See particularly Edward Said, *Orientalism: Western Conceptions of the Orient*, London: Routledge and Kegan Paul, 1978.

3   Walcott interviewed by Melvyn Bragg, *South Bank Show*, ITV, 1989.

4   Jamaica and Trinidad became independent in 1962; Barbados and Guyana in 1966. St. Lucia followed in 1979

5   For example, Gordon Rohlehr, *My Strangled City and Other Essays*, Port of Spain: Longman Trinidad, 1992, p. 245.

6   Dates of plays given in the text are those of first performance, not publication.

7   This is in January. Walcott is not the only, nor the first St. Lucian Nobel Laureate: Sir Arthur Lewis, who like Walcott attended St. Mary's College, shared the 1979 Nobel Prize for Economics.

8   I am indebted to Michael Gilkes for this joke.

9   The audience for Walcott's drama is, of course, broader, even if what Judy J. Stone refers to as the 'classical form' of his plays creates a 'distancing between the audience and the performance', *Theatre: Studies In West Indian Literature*, London and Basingstoke: Macmillan, 1994, 75 and 92.

10   See, for example, Patricia Ismond, 'Walcott versus Brathwaite', *Caribbean Quarterly*, 17:3/4, 1971, 54–71; repr. in Robert D. Hamner (ed.), *Critical Perspectives on Derek Walcott*, Washington: Three Continents Press, 1993, 220–36.

11   For example, in 'Tribal Flutes', a review of Brathwaite's *Rights of Passage*, *Sunday Guardian* (Trinidad), 19 March 1967, 2, repr. in

Hamner (ed.), *Critical Perspectives*, 41–4; and in comments made in a televised poetry discussion with Linton Kwesi Johnson, Fred D'Aguiar and Darcus Howe, *Caribbean Evening*, BBC2, 1986.

12 Subsequently published as The *Development of Creole Society in Jamaica, 1770–1820*, Oxford: Clarendon Press, 1971. *Folk Culture of the Slaves in Jamaica*, London and Port of Spain: New Beacon, 1971, is a pamphlet extracted from this longer study.

13 *In a Green Night*, London: Jonathan Cape, 1962, 7. Subsequent references cite *IGN*.

14 *The Arrivants* originally appeared as three separate volumes: *Rights of Passage* (1967), *Masks* (1968) and *Islands* (1969). Eliot's influence is particularly prominent in the drought and water imagery that pervades the trilogy, for example, the account of a desert crossing in the opening poem, 'Prelude', *The Arrivants*, London: Oxford University Press, 1973, 4–8.

15 *IGN*, 7.

16 'Leaving School', Hamner (ed.), *Critical Perspectives*, 26–7; this essay was originally published in *The London Magazine*, 5:6, September 1965, 4–14.

17 *Ibid.*, 26.

18 *Ibid.*, 26.

19 *Ibid.*, 28.

20 The 'Gregorias' *of Another Life*.

21 Walcott interviewed by Melvyn Bragg, *South Bank Show*, ITV, 1989. Also 'The Art of Poetry', Walcott interviewed by Edward Hirsch, Hamner (ed.), *Critical Perspectives*, 68; an interview originally published in *Paris Review*, 28, Winter 1986, 197–230.

22 See particularly Walcott's poem 'Self Portrait', *Tapia*, 2 January 1977, 3; repr. in *Caribbean Quarterly*, 26:1/2, 1980, 94 and included in *Another Life*, London: Jonathan Cape, 1973, 56–7. Subsequent references to *Another Life* cite *AL*. The influence of Van Gogh on Walcott is discussed in Clare Rosa de Lima, 'Walcott, Painting and the Shadow of Van Gogh', Stewart Brown (ed.), *The Art of Derek Walcott*, Bridgend, MidGlamorgan: Seren Books, 1991, 171–90.

23 *AL*, 59.

24 In his essay 'Meanings', Walcott writes 'I do a lot of drawing for my plays. In fact, I visualize them completely in terms of costume and staging, even certain group formations, before I go into production and while I am writing the play', Hamner (ed.), *Critical Perspectives*, 47.

25 Other Caribbean artists who have committed suicide include the Guyanese novelist Edgar Mittelholzer and the Tobagonian poet E. M. Roach.

26 *The Banjo Man* was originally scheduled for performance as the St. Lucian entry for the 1956 Federal Arts Festival in Trinidad, but was banned by the Vicar-General, with Roderick Walcott finding himself accused of profanity and blasphemy; see Stone, *Theatre*, 78.

27 *AL*, 152.

28 *Ibid.*, 53.

29 *Ibid.*, 152. The phrase originates from the Cuban novelist Alejo Carpentier's *The Lost Steps* and is quoted by Walcott as part of the epigraph to Book Two of *AL* (47).

30 *Ibid.*, 52.

31 Walcott interviewed by Melvyn Bragg, *South Bank Show*, ITV, 1989.

32 *Sea Grapes*, London: Jonathan Cape, 1976, 43–55, particularly 43–5. Subsequent references cite *SG*.

33 *The Arkansas Testament*, London: Faber, 1987, 10. Subsequent references cite *AT*.

34 Walcott interviewed by Melvyn Bragg *South Bank Show*, ITV, 1989.

35 *Ibid.*

36 Quoted in Gordon Lewis, The *Growth of the Modern West Indies*, London: MacGibbon and Kee, 1968, 150–1.

37 'Leaving School', Hamner (ed.), *Critical Perspectives*, 26.

38 *Ibid.*

39 This theme is discussed in my article 'A Style of Dying', *Sunday Chronicle* (Guyana), 5 May 1974, 7. See also Walcott's 'Society and the Artist', *Public Opinion* (Jamaica), 4 May 1957, 7; repr. in Hamner (ed.), *Critical Perspectives*, 15–17.

40 *Dream on Monkey Mountain and Other Plays*, New York: Farrar Straus and Giroux, 1970, 17. Subsequent references cite *DMM*.

41 See Bhabha, *The Location of Culture*, and Salman Rushdie, *Imaginary Homelands: Essays and Criticism, 1981–1991*, London: Granta, 1991.

42 See his discussion of this experience in 'A Latin Primer', *AT*, 21–4.

43 See the opening section of *Epitaph for the Young*, Barbados: Advocate Co., 1949, 1; 'A City's Death by Fire', *IGN*, 14; and *AL*, 83–5. Subsequent references to *Epitaph for the Young* cite *EY*.

44   For example, 'The Figure of Crusoe', Hamner (ed.), *Critical Perspectives*, 33–40, an edited version of a previously unpublished talk delivered at St. Augustine, the Trinidad campus of the University of the West Indies, in 1965.

45   Stone, *Theatre*, 93.

46   'What the Twilight Says', *DMM*, 20–4.

47   *AL*, 7.

48   Bruce King, *Derek Walcott and West Indian Drama: 'Not Only a Playwright But a Company': The Trinidad Theatre Workshop 1953–1993*, Oxford: Clarendon Press, 1995, 12.

49   King, *Walcott and Drama*, 12–13.

50   Stewart Brown attributes Walcott's 'technique of using metaphor as the prime vehicle of shape and meaning' to the influence of the metaphysicals, 'The Apprentice: *25 Poems, Epitaph for the Young, Poems* and *In a Green Night*', Brown (ed.), *The Art of Derek Walcott*, 30.

51   The Federation collapsed in 1961 when a Jamaican referendum resulted in a vote to discontinue membership.

52   'Meanings', Hamner (ed.), *Critical Perspectives*, 47–8; this essay was originally published in *Savacou*, 2, 1970, 45–51.

53   'On Choosing Port of Spain', Michael Anthony and Andrew Carr (eds), *David Frost Introduces Trinidad and Tobago*, London: André Deutsch, 1975, 45–51.

54   'Meanings', Hamner (ed.), *Critical Perspectives*, 46.

55   There have been at least four versions of *Franklin*, five if one follows Judy Stone in seeing the play as a reworking of *The Wine of the Country* (1956), Stone, *Theatre*, 107–8.

56   Reworked as *The Last Carnival* (1982).

57   King's *Derek Walcott and West Indian Drama* is a minutely detailed study of the Workshop, to which the present book owes a considerable debt.

58   Robert Hamner provides a detailed partially annotated listing of Walcott's *Trinidad Guardian* journalism in the prose writings section of his Walcott bibliography in Hamner (ed.), *Critical Perspectives*, 411-30.

59   Errol Hill, *The Trinidad Carnival: Mandate for a National Theatre*, Austin: University of Texas Press, 1972.

60   'The Figure of Crusoe', Hamner (ed.), *Critical Perspectives*, 40.

61   The sub-title of *The Prelude*. This aspect of the poem is discussed

in M. Travis Lane, 'A Different "Growth of a Poet's Mind": Derek Walcott's *Another Life*', *ARIEL*, 9:4, 1978, 65–78.

62   Walcott's use of Homeric analogues is discussed in Chapter 6.

63   For example, the myth of El Dorado.

64   See R. W. B. Lewis, *The American Adam: Innocence, Tragedy and Tradition in the Nineteenth Century*, Chicago: University of Chicago Press, 1955.

65   Section headings used in *The Fortunate Traveller*, London: Jonathan Cape, 1982. Subsequent references cite *FT*. Cf. the use of 'Here' and 'Elsewhere' in *The Arkansas Testament*.

66   Originally published in *Is Massa Day Dead?*, ed. Orde Coombs, Garden City, New York: Anchor/Doubleday, 1976, 1–28. Subsequent references are to this version and cite 'Muse'. Sections of the essay are reprinted in John Hearne (ed.), *Caribbean Forum*, Kingston: Carifesta, 1976; Edward Baugh (ed.), *Critics on Caribbean Literature*, London: Allen and Unwin, 1978; and John Thieme (ed.), *The Arnold Anthology of Post-Colonial Literatures in English*, London and New York: Arnold, 1996.

67   The final words of Brathwaite's *Arrivants* trilogy, *The Arrivants*, London: Oxford University Press, 1973, 270.

68   'Meanings', Hamner (ed.), *Critical Perspectives*, 48.

69   *Remembrance and Pantomime*, New York: Farrar, Straus and Giroux, 1980, 131. Subsequent references cite *RP*.

70   Braj Kachru distinguishes between code-switching and code-mixing by seeing the sentence as the basic unit of the former and the morpheme as the basic unit of the latter, *The Alchemy of English*, Urbana: University of Illinois Press, 1986, 63–5. Caribbean literary critics have tended to use the term code-switching to refer to changes of register in both units.

71   *FT*, 53.

72   Earl Lovelace, *The Dragon Can't Dance*, London: André Deutsch, 1979.

73   The Mighty Spoiler (Theophilus Phillip) flourished between 1946 and 1960, the year in which he died, Gordon Rohlehr, *Calypso and Society in Pre-Independence Trinidad*, Port of Spain: privately published, 1990, 522 and 597.

74   Keith Warner, The *Trinidad Calypso*, London: Heinemann, 1982, 112–15.

75   *The Complete Poems of John Wilmot, Earl of Rochester*, ed. David

M. Vieth, New Haven and London: Yale University Press, 1968, 94. As Vieth points out, 'A Satyr against Reason and Mankind' is itself a poem that belongs to a particular satirical tradition: it is based on Boileau's eighth satire and is indebted to Hobbes, Montaigne and the tradition of libertinism.

76   'Bed Bug' or Reincarnation', the calypso for which he is best known, was one of Spoiler's compositions for the 1953 season, Rohlehr, *Calypso and Society*, 428. A recording of the calypso by Lord Invader (Rupert Grant) is available on the CD, Kings of Calypso, Castle Communications, PLS CD 229, 1997.

77   I am grateful to James Booth for discussing this with me.

78   Quoted by Warner, *Calypso*, 112.

79   Hill, *Carnival*, 67. Spoiler was a member of the Young Brigade, less noted for their concern with 'political or moral documentary' and more for 'humour, innovation, energy and imagination', Rohlehr, *Calypso and Society*, 332.

80   Terminology borrowed from the title of the first chapter of Edward Said's *Culture and Imperialism*, London: Chatto and Windus, 1993: 'Overlapping Territories, Intertwined Histories'.

81   The reference to Quevedo in this passage is particularly interesting, since it can be taken to refer both to the seventeenth-century Spanish picaresque novelist and satirist, best known as the author of *El Buscón*, and to the calypsonian Atilla [sic] the Hun, whose real name was Raymond Quevedo. Raymond Quevedo (1892–1962) was a prominent calypsonian for more than half a century, served as Deputy Mayor of Port of Spain and became a member of Trinidad's Legislative Council in the post-war period. He is also notable as the author of *Atilla's Kaiso: A Short History of Trinidad Calypso*, St. Augustine, Trinidad: Extra-Mural Department of the University of the West Indies, 1983.

82   Warner, *Calypso*, 113.

83   Hill, *Carnival*, 35.

84   At a Welsh Arts Council Conference held at Gregynog in October 1980 to mark the occasion of Walcott's being awarded the Council's International Writer's Prize.

85   Edward Kamau Brathwaite, *A History of the Voice: The Development of Nation Language in Anglophone Caribbean Poetry*, London and Port of Spain: New Beacon, 1984, 17 ff.

Chapter 2

1 Edward Hirsch, 'An Interview with Derek Walcott', *Contemporary Literature*, 20:3, 1980, 282.

2 The first six poems in *IGN* are reprinted, in all but one case with minor changes, from 25 Poems'; 'A Country Club Romance' is a reworked version of 'Margaret Verlieu Dies', which originally appeared in *Poems*.

3 Reprinted as 'Elegy' in *IGN* (13).

4 'The Yellow Cemetery', *25 Poems*, 2nd edition, Bridgetown: Advocate Co., 1949, 20–1. Subsequent references are to this edition and cite *25P*.

5 'Notebooks of Ruin', *Poems*, Kingston: Kingston City Printery, n.d. [1951], 16.

6 For examples of Walcott's treatment of this subject in various genres, see *The Joker of Seville, Sea Grapes* and 'The Muse of History'.

7 Robert D. Hamner, 'Conversation with Derek Walcott', *World Literature Written in English*, 16:2, 1977, 411. While generally considered to be an epic, *Omeros* is also heavily autobiographical in parts and could be seen to form a trilogy with *Epitaph for the Young* and *Another Life*.

8 Keith Alleyne, review of *Epitaph for the Young, Bim*, 3:11, 1949, 267–72; repr. in Robert D. Hamner (ed.), *Critical Perspectives on Derek Walcott*, Washington: Three Continents Press, 1993, 99.

9 *Ibid.*, Hamner (ed.), *Critical Perspectives*, 98.

10 Robert D. Hamner, *Derek Walcott*, Boston: Twayne, 1981, 39.

11 Stewart Brown, 'The Apprentice: *25 Poems, Epitaph for the Young, Poems* and *In a Green Night*', Brown (ed.), *The Art of Derek Walcott*, Bridgend, MidGlamorgan: Seren Books, 1991, 13–33.

12 Ned Thomas, *Derek Walcott: Poet of the Islands / Derek Walcott: Bardd yr Ynysoedd*, Cardiff: Welsh Arts Council, 1980, 12.

13 Bill Ashcroft, Gareth Griffiths and Helen Tiffin, *The Empire Writes Back: Theory and Practice in Post-Colonial Literatures*, London and New York: Routledge, 1989, 2.

14 *Ibid.*, 2.

15 Brown, 'The Apprentice: *25 Poems, Epitaph for the Young, Poems* and *In a Green Night*', Brown (ed.), *The Art of Derek Walcott*, 15–16.

16 See Brown's discussion, *ibid.*, 22–3.

17   *The Waste Land*, 1922, I. 22; T. S. Eliot, *Selected Poems*, London: Faber, 1954, 51.

18   Alleyne, in Hamner (ed.), *Critical Perspectives*, 98.

19   See Sections II and V of *Ash-Wednesday*, 1930; *Selected Poems*, 86 and 90.

20   See *The Waste Land*, II. 60-76, *Selected Poems*, 53.

21   Michel Foucault, 'The Discourse on Language' in *The Archaeology of Knowledge and The Discourse on Language*, trans. Rupert Sawyer, New York: Harper and Row, n.d., 229.

22   *AL*, 52.

23   *Ibid.*, 53.

24   With the title 'I with Legs Crossed along the Daylight Watch'.

25   The phrase 'in a green night' is taken from Marvell's poem 'Bermudas'.

26   George Lamming's phrase, *In the Castle of My Skin*, London: Michael Joseph, 1953, 73.

27   Cf. Walcott's response to Watteau's vision of Cythera, discussed in Chapter 5 below; and poems about Gauguin and Watteau in *Midsummer*, New York: Farrar, Straus and Giroux, 1984: XIX: Gauguin and XX: Watteau.

28   Walcott chose to reprint exactly half of them in his *Collected Poems, 1948–84*, New York: Farrar Straus and Giroux, 1985; London: Faber, 1986.

29   Interestingly 'A Far Cry from Africa' is *not* reprinted in *Collected Poems*, but it has been widely quoted and anthologized.

30   See particularly Abdul R. JanMohamed's *Manichean Aesthetics: The Politics of Literature in Colonial Africa*, Amherst: University of Massachusetts Press, 1983. See too the discussion of Walcott's early plays in Chapter 3.

31   Cf. particularly '"And this also," said Marlow suddenly, "has been one of the dark places on the earth"' and the passage which follows, Joseph Conrad, *Heart of Darkness*, 1902; Englewood Cliffs, New Jersey: Prentice Hall, 1960, 3ff.

32   John Donne, *Devotions*, 17.

33   Cf. 'The Muse of History' and Walcott's plays which focus on the fate of former colonial figures in the post-independence world, viz. *Franklin* and *The Last Carnival*.

Chapter 3

1   See Errol Hill, *The Jamaican Stage, 1655–1900: Profile of a Colonial Theatre*, Amherst: University of Massachusetts Press, 1992.

2   'What the Twilight Says', *DMM*, 4.

3   *Ibid.*, 13.

4   *Harry Dernier*, Bridgtown: Advocate Co., n.d. [1952?], front cover. Subsequent references cite *HD*.

5   *Harry Dernier* was broadcast on BBC radio in 1952. Judy Stone records that a stage version was performed in Jamaica in 1952 (Judy J. Stone, *Theatre: Studies in West Indian Literature*, London and Basingstoke: Macmillan, 1994, 195).

6   Errol Hill provides an account of the play in 'The Emergence of a National Drama in the West Indies', *Caribbean Quarterly*, 18:4, 1972, 9–24, from which details included here are taken.

7   Stone suggests that the character 'might have emerged from a Graham Greene novel', Stone, *Theatre*, 93.

8   *Ibid.*

9   See the discussion of *The Castaway* in Chapter 4.

10   'Meanings', Robert D. Hamner (ed.), *Critical Perspectives on Derek Walcott*, Washington: Three Continents Press, 1993, 45.

11   'What the Twilight Says', *DMM*, 6.

12   *The Middle Passage* (1962); Harmondsworth: Penguin, 1969, 43.

13   'What the Twilight Says', *DMM*, 17.

14   *Ibid.*, 17.

15   Anonymous review of *Henri Christophe* in *The West India Committee Circular*, February 1952, 38; quoted by Rhonda Cobham, 'The Background' in Bruce King, ed., *West Indian Literature*, London: Macmillan, 1979, 21.

16   'Meanings', Hamner (ed.), *Critical Perspectives*, 45; and Walcott's prefatory note, *Henri Christophe: A Chronicle in Seven Scenes*, Bridgetown: Advocate Co., 1950, [iii]. Subsequent references cite *HC*.

17   'What the Twilight Says', *DMM*, 11–12. Cf. 'The tongues above our prayers utter the pain of entire races to a Manichean God', 'Muse', 4.

18   In a remark which makes little allowance for the extent to which historiography constructs representations of historical figures, but is none the less interesting, Robert D. Hamner sees Christophe as more suitable than Toussaint for Walcott's purposes because he

'possessed *harmartia* – an essential element for classical tragedy', Robert D. Hamner, *Derek Walcott*, Boston: Twayne, 1981, 52–3.

19 *The Black Jacobins: Toussaint L'Ouverture and the San Domingo Revolution*, 1938; revised 2nd edition, New York: Vintage, 1963.

20 Revised as *The Black Jacobins* in *A Time … and a Season: 8 Caribbean Plays*, ed. Errol Hill, St. Augustine: University of the West Indies Extramural Studies Unit, 1976, 355–420. Subsequent Caribbean plays on the Haitian Revolution include Aimé Césaire's *La Tragedie du Roi Christophe* (1963) and Denis Martin Benn's *Toussaint L'Ouverture* (1968).

21 Stone, *Theatre*, 95.

22 Bruce King, *Derek Walcott and West Indian Drama: 'Not Only a Playwright But a Company': The Trinidad Theatre Workshop 1953–1993*, Oxford: Clarendon Press, 1995, 95.

23 'What the Twilight Says', *DMM*, 11.

24 The stress on 'blood' having committed the protagonist to a course of crime echoes Macbeth's 'I am in blood / Stepp'd in so far that, Should I wade no more, / Returning were as tedious as go o'er' (*Macbeth*, III, iv, 173–4) and Richard III's similar 'I am in / So far in blood that sin will pluck on sin' (*Richard III*, IV, ii, 81–2); and *Henri Christophe* also employs candle imagery reminiscent of Macbeth's use of the candle image in the 'tomorrow and tomorrow and tomorrow' speech (*Macbeth*, V, v, 29). A passage in Scene Six (*HC*, 52) brings these two images together in Walcott's play. The epigraph for the second part of the play is taken from *Richard III* (I, iv, 52–5) and a prose murderers' scene (Scene Four) is strongly redolent of later parts of the same *Richard III* scene (I, iv).

25 Cf. Walcott's poem on the Othello–Desdemona relationship, 'Goats and Monkeys', *The Castaway*, London: Jonathan Cape, 1965, 27–8.

26 Abdul R. JanMohamed, 'The Economy of Manichean Allegory: The Function of Racial Difference in Colonial Literature', *Critical Inquiry* 12:1, 1985, 59–87.

27 In Plato's *Phaedrus*, for example, the soul is likened to a chariot drawn by two horses – the one white, the other black. The charioteer, who stands for the rational element in the soul, has the problem of getting the two horses to pull together, since while the white horse is compliant, the black horse tends to follow its sensual instincts and can only be made to co-operate through the use of the whip.

28 For a complex discussion of Walcott's 'mimicry', which makes a distinction between 'mimicry' and 'mimesis', see Rei Terada, *Derek*

Walcott's Poetry: American Mimesis, Boston: Northeastern University Press, 1992. Terada views 'mimesis' as 'the representation of reality' and 'mimicry' as 'the representauon of a representation' (1).

29   'What the Twilight Says', *DMM*, 9.

30   The earlier play was entitled *Soso's Wake*, Stone, *Theatre*, 97.

31   Robert D. Hamner comments on this debt, Hamner, *Derek Walcott*, 55–6.

32   See 'What the Twilight Says', *DMM*, 16.

33   See Chapter 2.

34   'The Sea is History', *The Star-Apple Kingdom*, London: Jonathan Cape, 1980, 25–8. Subsequent references cite *SAK*.

35   'What the Twilight Says', *DMM*, 21.

36   The play was premiered at the University of the West Indies campus at Mona and subsequently moved to the Ward Theatre in Kingston, King, *Walcott and Drama*, 14.

37   Stone, *Theatre*, 107.

38   King, *Walcott and Drama*, 70

39   *The Wine of the Country*, mimeographed typescript, University of the West Indies library, Mona, n.d., 2. Subsequent references are to this typescript and cite *Wine*.

40   Cf. Walcott's account of travelling this road across the spine of the island, 'Leaving School', Hamner (ed.), *Critical Perspectives*, 26. (Quoted above.)

41   Names which Walcott would later use for major characters in *Omeros*.

42   See Stone, *Theatre*, 101; and Hamner (ed.), *Critical Perspectives*, 113–17.

43   Stone, *Theatre*, 101.

44   *Ione*, Mona: University of the West Indies Extramural Department, n.d. [1957?], 4. Subsequent references are to this edition.

45   A term used to describe a woman of loose morality; said to be derived from the French *sans diamètre*.

46   'What the Twilight Says', *DMM*, 10; *Wine*, 5.

47   Such a stance offers interesting parallels with Homi K. Bhabha's comments on 'Third Space' enunciation; see *The Location of Culture*, London and New York: Routledge, 1994, 36–9.

48   For example, 'What the Twilight Says', *DMM*, 8–10; and in the play *Dream on Monkey Mountain* itself.

49   See Stone, *Theatre*, 102.

50   'Derek's "Most West Indian Play"', *Sunday Guardian Magazine* [Trinidad], 21 June 1970; quoted Stone, *Theatre*, 102.

51   'What the Twilight Says', *DMM*, 23–4.

52   Albert Olu Ashaolu finds no less than six levels of allegory in *Ti-Jean*, 'Allegory in *Ti-Jean and His Brothers*', *World Literature Written in English*, 16:1, 1977, 203–11.

53   Walcott's working script for the 1972 Joseph Papp New York Shakespeare Festival production of the play in Central Park includes illustrations (of Walcott's own) which suggest an indebtedness to Afro-Caribbean folk traditions that goes well beyond his drawing on the Ti-Jean cycle. It includes sketches of a kumina celebrant and a soucouyante. Kumina is an ancestor worship cult of Bantu (Zairean) origin. Commenting on its importance in Jamaica, Olive Senior describes it as 'the most "African" of Jamaican cults', *A–Z of Jamaican Heritage*, Kingston: Heinemann/Gleaner Co. (1983); 2nd edition, 1987, 91. In St. Lucian (and other Caribbean) folklore, a soucouyante is a sorceress who flies by night, leaving her human skin behind, and sucks the blood of babies.

54   Cf. the figure of the half-child in Wole Soyinka's play *A* Dance *of the Forests* (1960).

55   Held in Trinidad. The production of the play, *Drums and Colours*, was performed in the open air on an Elizabethan apron stage in the Royal Botanical Gardens, Port of Spain.

56   From the Extramural Department of the University of the West Indies.

57   *Drums and Colours, Caribbean Quarterly*, 7:1 and 2, 1961, 1. Subsequent references are to this edition and cite *DC*.

58   Stone, *Theatre*, 10.

59   *The Middle Passage*, London: André Deutsch, 1962, 29. The reference to 'West Indian historians who … tell the story of the slave trade as if it were just another aspect of mercantilism' suggests the work of the Trinidadian historian and prime minister, Eric Williams, particularly *Capitalism and Slavery*, Chapel Hill: University of North Carolina Press, 1944.

60   'The Art of Poetry', Walcott interviewed by Edward Hirsch, Hamner (ed.), *Critical Perspectives*, 73.

61   See particularly Hayden White, *Metahistory: The Historical Imagination in Nineteenth-Century Europe*, Baltimore: Johns Hopkins University Press, 1973.

62   'Muse', 2.

63   *Ibid.*, 2.

64   *Ibid*, 2.

65   *Ibid.*, 1.

66   V. S. Reid, *New Day*, New York: Knopf, 1949; Roger Mais, *George William Gordon* in *A Time ... and a Season: 8 Caribbean Plays*, ed. Errol Hill, St. Augustine: University of the West Indies, Extramural Unit, 1976, 1–92. Mais's play was written at least twenty years before its publication in this collection.

67   For example, Stone, *Theatre*, 104 and King, *Walcott and Drama*, 22.

68   See the discussion of *The Last Carnival* in Chapter 5.

69   Stone, *Theatre*, 100.

70   Also published as *Malcauchon: Malcauchon, or The Six in the Rain*, St. Augustine, Trinidad: University of the West Indies Extramural Department, 1966.

71   Theodore Colson, 'Derek Walcott's Plays: Outrage and Compassion', Hamner (ed.), *Critical Perspectives*, 129; originally published in *World Literature Written in English*, 12, 1, 1973, 80–96.

72   Hamner, *Derek Walcott*, 74.

73   Cf. the final poem of *The Bounty*, where Walcott focuses on the figure of Oedipus at Colonus, *The Bounty*, London: Faber, 1997, 78. Subsequent references are to this edition.

74   Cf. Walcott's comment on the play's being 'derivative' of *Rashomon*, quoted in Chapter 1.

75   See particularly the following *Trinidad Guardian* articles by Walcott: 'Future of Art Promising', 31 August 1963, Independence Progress Supplement, 26–7; 'The New British Theatre', 10 November 1963, 5; 'National Theatre is the Answer', 12 August 1964, 5; 'The Outlook for a National Theatre', 22 March 1965, 17; 'The Prospect for a National Theatre', 6 March 1966, 6; 'Writer's Cramp on a Stage', 8 June 1966, 5; and 'Maybe Some Small Voice is Buried under Confusion', 4 August 1966, 7.

76   A masquerade of Venezuelan and Indo-Caribbean origins, also used in *The Joker of Seville*, where it is referred to as a *burroquette*. See too Walcott's comments on his use of the form in Therese Mills, 'Don Juan Was a Stickman!', *Trinidad Guardian*, 18 November 1973, 4.

77 Cf. its representation in *Masks* (1968), the second part of Edward Kamau Brathwaite's Arrivants trilogy.

78 JanMohamed, 'The Economy of Manichaen Allegory: The Function of Racial Difference in Colonial Literature', *Critical Inquiry* 12:1, 1985, 59–87.

79 Cf. V. S. Naipaul, *The Mimic Men*, London: André Deutsch, 1967, where the protagonist, Ralph Singh, identifies himself with huge trees, washed across the ocean and 'shipwrecked' on Caribbean beaches.

80 The most significant New World transportee from the Akan pantheon of gods, Anansi (or Anancy) appears to have undergone a transformation during the period of slavery and, according to Arthur Kemoli, his cunning can he seen as an allegorical representation of the slaves using their wits to survive in a hostile environment, dominated by figures such as Lion (the white plantation owner or manager) and Tiger (the overseer), *Caribbean Anansi Stories*, London: Commonwealth Institute, n.d., 1.

81 Cf. the reference to a 'Lestrade sallow and humped like a provincial Sherlock Holmes' in a catalogue of St. Lucian 'derelicts' who performed monodramas in the street in Walcott's youth, 'What the Twilight Says', *DMM*, 23.

Chapter 4

1 *The Castaway and Other Poems*, London: Jonathan Cape, 1965, 45. Subsequent references are to this edition and cite *Castaway*.

2 The poems 'Laventville' and 'The Voyage Up River' (*Castaway*, 32–5 and 50) are dedicated to V. S. Naipaul and Wilson Harris respectively. The whole collection is dedicated to John Hearne ([7]).

3 'The Figure of Crusoe', an edited version of Walcott's 1965 paper edited by Robert D. Hamner, *Critical Perspectives on Derek Walcott*, Washington: Three Continents Press, 1993, 35–6.

4 Ibid., 38

5 *AL*, 152.

6 'The Art of Poetry', Walcott interviewed by Edward Hirsch, in Hamner (ed.), *Critical Perspectives*, 70.

7 *Ibid.*, 74.

8 V. S. Naipaul, *The Middle Passage*, London: André Deutsch, 1962, 29.

9   The area is actually called Laventille.

10 Cf. the use of the same vantage point in the opening words *of Another Life*, 'Verandahs, where the pages of the sea / are a book left open by an absent master ... ', *AL*, 3.

11 'Walcott on Walcott', Walcott interviewed by Dennis Scott, *Caribbean Quarterly*, 14:1 and 2, 1968, 141.

12 *The Gulf and Other Poems*, London: Jonathan Cape, 1969, 29. Subsequent references are to this edition and cite *Gulf*. The poem draws on rhetoric popular among Afro-American liberation writers of the period, for example, Cf. Eldridge Cleaver, *Soul on Ice*, London: Panther, 1970.

13 Cf. 'Orient and Immortal Wheat', *IGN*, 48. The phrase 'orient and immortal wheat' is taken from Traherne's *Centuries of Meditation*.

14 Cf. *The Fortunate Traveller* (1982), where Walcott uses 'North' and 'South' as titles for the sections of the volume.

15 See Chapter 6.

16 'Walcott on Walcott', Walcott interviewed by Dennis Scott, *Caribbean Quarterly*, 14:1 and 2, 1968, 137.

17 The title of the first section of the poem.

18 The title of Barbadian-born novelist Austin Clarke's autobiographical memoir of his early years, Toronto: McClelland and Stewart, 1980.

19 *Desire in Language: A Semiotic Approach to Literature and Art*, ed. Leon S. Roudiez, trans. Thomas Gora, Alice Jardine and Leon S. Roudiez, New York: Columbia University Press, 1980, 66.

20 Dante's *Inferno* begins '*Nel mezzo del cammin di nostra vita ...*'.

21 Kenneth Ramchand's phrase, *The West Indian Novel and Its Background*, London: Faber, 1970. See particularly, 32–8.

22 See Chapter 2 for a discussion of poems in *IGN* which pursue this project.

23 'Thematics' in *Russian Formalist Criticism: Four Essays*, trans. Lee T. Lemon and Marion J. Reis, Lincoln, Nebraska: University of Nebraska Press, 1965, 64; quoted in Shirely Neuman and Robert Wilson, *Labyrinths of Voice: Conversations with Robert Kroetsch*, Edmonton: NeWest Press, 1982, 3.

24 Cf. *AL*, 89 and 133.

25 NB the poet's abandonment of his attempts to become a painter when he realizes, 'I lived in a different gift, / its element metaphor' (*AL*, 59). Cf. also the emphasis on metaphorical transformation in

The Gulf, discussed above.

26 Probably an allusion to the title of Charles Kingsley's *At Last: A Christmas in the West Indies* (1871).

27 'Muse', 4–5.

28 See Chapter 1, notes 25 and 39.

29 See Edward Baugh, *West Indian Poetry, 1900–1970: A Study in Cultural Decolonisation*, Kingston: Savacou Publications, n.d. (1971?).

30 Walcott links the two in his 'Figure of Crusoe' essay, Hamner (ed.), *Critical Perspectives*, 35.

31 'Muse', 2.

32 *Ibid.*, 5.

33 For example, 'Nearing Forty', *Gulf*, 67–8 and the opening line of *AL*.

34 Both 'Nearing Forty' and 'To Return to the Trees' are dedicated to John Figueroa.

35 I am grateful to John Figueroa for confirming this.

36 'Any Revolution Based on Race is Suicidal', *Caribbean Contact*, 1:8, August 1973, 14. Cf. the treatment of Trinidad's 1970 Black Power rebellion in *The Last Carnival*.

Chapter 5

1 Bruce King's summary, Bruce King, *Derek Walcott and West Indian Drama: 'Not Only a Playwright But a Company': The Trinidad Theatre Workshop 1953–1993*, Oxford: Clarendon Press, 1995, 181.

2 *IGN*, 29.

3 There are five versions in all, if one takes Judy Stone's view that *The Wine of the Country* is an early version of *Franklin*. For details, see Stone, *Theatre: Studies in West Indian Literature*, London and Basingstoke: Macmillan, 1994, 107–8.

4 See King, *Walcott and Drama*, 181–2.

5 *Franklin*, mimeographed typescript of the third version of the play (the first full-length [three-act] version), premiered in Guyana in 1969, Georgetown, n.d. [1969]. Subsequent references are to this typescript.

6   One of the two epigraphs to this version of the play is also taken from 'Recessional': Walcott quotes the famous lines: 'The tumult and the shouting skies / The Captains and the Kings depart', *Franklin*, 1.

7   Cf. a primarily naturalistic play such as Arthur Miller's *Death of a Salesman* (1958), which Miller originally entitled 'The Inside of His Head'.

8   The 1969 Guyanese production used here and a 1990 Barbados production.

9   Quoted in King, *Walcott and Drama*, 338.

10 See Chapter 2 .

11 Therese Mills, 'Don Juan Was a Stickman!', *Trinidad Guardian*, 18 November 1973, 4. The play was never staged by the RSC, apparently because the success of the Company's 'Hollow Crown' sequence (of Shakespeare's tetralogy of History Plays, *Richard II*, *1 and 2 Henry IV* and *Henry V*) led them to extend its run at the expense of other commissioned work. I am indebted to Diana Fairfax and Terry Hands for this information.

12 Mills, *Ibid.*, 4.

13 Walcott mentions these associations in 'Soul Brother to *The Joker of Seville*', *Trinidad Guardian*, 4 November 1974, 4. This article is a rather fuller version of his introductory note to the play *The Joker of Seville and O Babylon!* New York: Farrar Straus and Giroux, 1978; London: Jonathan Cape, 1979, 3. Subsequent references cite *Joker*.

14 'Soul Brother', p. 4.

15 Walcott refers to his use of the *burroquette* and *parang* in 'Don Juan was a Stickman!', *'Soul Brother'*. *Parang* songs were traditionally sung by Trinidadian Spaniards at Christmas time, C. R. Ottley, *The Trinidad Callaloo: Life in Trinidad and Tobago from 1851– 1900*, Diego Martin, Trinidad: Crusoe Publishing House, 1978, 68.

16 On Caribbean mummers' plays, see Errol Hill, *The Trinidad Carnival: Mandate for a National Theatre*, Austin: University of Texas, 1972, 11–13; and Judith Bettelheim 'Jonkonnu and Other Christmas Masquerades' in John W. Nunley and Judith Bettelheim, *Caribbean Festival Arts*, Seattle and London: University of Washington Press, 1988, 39–84.

17 Roy Campbell's translation of the play, which Walcott acknowledges as his main source (*Joker*, 4), employs the title *The Trickster of Seville and His Guest of Stone*. Campbell's translation is included in Eric Bentley (ed.), *Six Spanish Plays*, New York:

Doubleday/Anchor, 1959.

18 Anansi has been variously identified: as a figure who represents the slaves' descent to subterfuge as a survival strategy, for example, by Arthur Kemoli, *Caribbean Anansi Stories*, London: Common-wealth Institute, n.d., 1; as an artist figure, for example, in Edward Kamau Brathwaite's poem 'Ananse', *The Arrivants*, London: Oxford University Press, 1973, 165–7; and as a shaman capable of effecting psychic transformations, for example, in Wilson Harris's depictions of the trickster figure in the character of da Silva in *Heartland*, London; Faber, 1964, and the eponymous hero *of Black Marsden*, London: Faber, 1972. See too Michael Gilkes's discussion of Harris's use of the trickster figure, *Wilson Harris and the Caribbean Novel*, London: Longman, 1975, particularly 41. See too, Chapter 3, note 78.

19 D. L. Macdonald, 'Derek Walcott's Don Juans', *Connotations*, 4:1/2, 1994/95, 98–118, has very reasonably attacked the view that I expressed in an earlier version of this discussion, in which I simply refer to Juan as 'a folk hero' ('A Caribbean Don Juan: Derek Walcott's *Joker of Seville*', *World Literature Written in English*, 23:1, 1984, 62–75). My intention was, and is, not, of course, to suggest that Juan's behaviour as a sexual trickster is in *any* sense commendable, simply to draw attention to the way in which Walcott draws on the usually comic mythologization of such a figure in Caribbean storytelling, particularly post-war calypsoes. For a cognate discussion of the exposure of macho pretence in Trinidadian society, see my earlier article, 'Calypso Allusions in Naipaul's *Miguel Street*', *Kunapipi*, 3:2, 1981, 18–31.

20 Walcott notes that 'C. L. R. James has pointed out … the similarity between Sparrow's "The Village Ram" and Mozart's "Don Giovanni"', 'Soul Brother to The *Joker of Seville*', *Trinidad Guardian*, 4 November 1974, 4.

21 The original Trinidad Theatre Workshop cast recorded an album, containing a dozen of the songs from the musical, *The Joker of Seville*, Port of Spain: Semp Productions, unnumbered, n.d.

22 C. G. Jung, 'On the Psychology of the Trickster-Figure', *Collected Works*, 9:1, trans. R. F. C. Hull, London: Routledge and Kegan Paul, 1959, 256.

23 See the comments on Wilson Harris in note 18 above.

24 The play was unique in the Workshop's repertory in being given three runs, each of about ten nights, within a year: the first was in November–December 1974; the second in March 1975; and the third in October 1975.

25 Walcott, 'The Joker: Closer to Continuous Theatre', *Trinidad Guardian*, 22 March 1975, 6.

26 Hill, *Carnival*, 35. See also Gordon Rohlehr, *Calypso and Society in Pre-Independence Trinidad*, Port of Spain: privately published, 1990, 11–15, for a broader-based account of the *kalinda* (or *calinda*) in the Antilles and Louisiana.

27 Cf. Catalinion's remark 'He's found the New World' (*Joker*, 46) with Donne's 'O my America! my new-found-land!', 'To His Mistris Going to Bed', line 27.

28 Bentley (ed.), *Six Spanish Plays*, 261–2.

29 Quoted in anon., 'Calypso', *Living in Britain*, London: Virtue and Co., 1970, 515.

30 See Hill, *Carnival*, 62–3.

31 On the Middle Passage origins of the limbo and its symbolic significance, see Edward Kamau Brathwaite, *The Arrivants*, London: Oxford University Press, 1973, 274; and Gordon Rohlehr, *Pathfinder: Black Awakening in The Arrivants of Edward Kamau Brathwaite*, Port of Spain: privately pbld., 1981, 225. Wilson Harris suggests parallels between the limbo and the transformations of Anansi, *History, Fable and Myth in the Caribbean and Guianas*, Edgar Mittelholzer Memorial Lectures, Georgetown: National History and Arts Council, 1970, 9.

32 See Hill on masquerade band coronations, *Carnival*, 34–7, Carnival Kings and Queens, *ibid.*, 100–5, and the *belair* dance as a parody of the minuet, *ibid.*, 63.

33 On Carnival Devil Bands, see Hill, *Carnival*, 88-90.

34 D. L. Macdonald, 'Derek Walcott's Don Juans', *Connotations*, 4:1/2, 1994/95, 105.

35 'Derek Walcott Talks about *The Joker of Seville*', edited transcript of a seminar conducted by Walcott at the College of the Virgin Islands, St. Thomas in 1979, *Carib*, 4, 1986, 1.

36 *Ibid.*, 2.

37 See Chapter 4.

38 'Derek Walcott Talks about *The Joker of Seville*', 4. Here Walcott's use of 'Manichean' seems to be closer to the orthodox Christian view than in his earlier usages of the term.

39 Ezra Pound, *Pisan Cantos*, London: Faber, 1949, 19.

40 Alan Brody, *The English Mummers and their Plays*, London: Routledge and Kegan Paul, London: n.d. [1971?], 3.

41   See note 16 above.

42   Cf. the ending of Dream *on Monkey Mountain.*

43   Music from *O Babylon!* was issued on an album by Kilmarnock Records, Kil 72030, 1980.

44   Walcott and MacDermot were encouraged to develop a script for possible Broadway production by Michael Butler, the producer of *Hair*, for which MacDermot had composed the score, see King, *Walcott and Drama*, 245–6.

45   The play was premiered in Trinidad by the Workshop in March 1976; they subsequently performed it in Jamaica at the regional arts festival, Carifesta, in July 1976.

46   Stone, *Theatre*, 122.

47   Sule Mombara (Horace Campbell), 'O Babylon! – Where It Went Wrong', *Caribbean Contact*, 4:2, 1976, 15; repr. in Hamner (ed.), *Critical Perspectives*, 270.

48   *Ibid.*, 271.

49   Set in 1966, the play could hardly be expected to represent Jamaican society in the 1970s.

50   Victor Questel, 'Interlude for Rest or Prelude to Disaster?', *Tapia*, 6:13, 28 March 1976, 4 and 11; repr. in Hamner (ed.), *Critical Perspectives*, 266.

51   Reprinted in the programme for the Talawa Theatre Company production of the play at the Riverside Studios, London, 1988.

52   King, *Walcott and Drama*, 254.

53   Mombara, 'O Babylon!', Hamner (ed.), *Critical Perspectives*, 270.

54   Robert D. Hamner, *Derek Walcott*, Boston: Twayne, 1981, 116 and 121.

55   *IGN*, 12. First published in *25 Poems.*

56   Rewritten from an earlier version, which had been premiered in Jamaica in 1954 and which drew in turn on the earlier uncompleted *Robin and Andrea*, Stone, *Theatre*, 94 and 97–9.

57   A view expressed by Walcott in the notes for the 1974 Los Angeles production of *The Charlatan* and quoted by King, *Walcott and Drama*, 200.

58   Stone, *Theatre*, 130.

59   *Ibid.*, 128.

60   For example, four pans had to represent a full steelband, *ibid.*, 139.

61   Martin Kettle, 'Simon's Show Suffers Sound of Silence', *The Guardian*, 7 March 1998, 1.

62   See King, *Walcott and Drama*, 259–64 for an account of the circumstances surrounding Walcott's resignation.

63   Lowel Fiet, 'Mapping a New Nile: Derek Walcott's Later Plays', in Stewart Brown (ed.), *The Art of Derek Walcott*, Bridgend, MidGlamorgan: Seren Books, 1991, 140.

64   Walcott's programme note for the 1979 New York production of *Remembrance;* quoted Stone, *Theatre*, 124.

65   *Ibid.,* 124.

66   'Mapping a New Nile: Derek Walcott's Later Plays', Brown (ed.), *The Art of Derek Walcott*, 142.

67   *Remembrance* has proved very successful as a radio play; for example, in the version broadcast by BBC Radio 4 in 1981.

68   *RP*, 29.

69   Thomas Gray, 'Elegy Written in a Country Churchyard', line 55. Quoted *RP*, 7.

70   For a particularly illuminating discussion of the 'body' in Caribbean literature, see Michael Dash, 'In Search of the Lost Body: Redefining the Subject in Caribbean Literature', *Kunapipi*, 11:1, 1989, 17–26.

71   By the Guyanese actors Wilbert Holder (in St. Croix in 1977), Norman Beaton (for the 1981 BBC Radio 4 production) and Michael Gilkes (in Barbados in 1982); and by Roscoe Lee Browne (in New York in 1979).

72   'Elegy Written in a Country Churchyard', line 59. Quoted *RP*, 7.

73   And had played the part of Jordan in the first production of *Remembrance*, see note 65.

74   See my essay, 'Passages to England', Theo d'Haen and Hans Bertens (eds), *Liminal Postmodernisms. The Postmodern, the (Post-)Colonial and the (Post-)Feminist* (*Postmodern Studies* 8), Amsterdam and Atlanta: Rodopi, 1994, 55–78.

75   Cf. Homi K. Bhabha, 'Of Mimicry and Man: The Ambivalence of Colonial Discourse', *The Location of Culture*, London and New York: Routledge, 1994, 85–92.

76   Walcott's footnote explains, 'A Judas effigy beaten at Easter in Trinidad and Tobago' (*RP*, 117).

77   Mikhail Bakhtin, *Rabelais and His World,* trans. Helene Iswolsky, Cambridge, Mass. and London: MIT Press, 1965, 10.

78   Earl Lovelace's novel *The Dragon Can't Dance,* London: André Deut-
     sch, 1979, offers a particularly probing fictional exploration of this
     debate. Cf. also my discussion of Walcott's play *The Last Carnival.*

79   Biodun Jeyifo, 'On Eurocentric Critical Theory: Some Paradigms
     from the Texts and Sub-Texts of Post-Colonial Writing', *Kunapipi*,
     11:1, 1989, 118.

80   *SG*, 40–2.

81   Homi K. Bhabha, 'How Newness Enters the World: Postmodern
     Space, Postcolonial Times and the Trials of Cultural Transition', *The
     Location of Culture*, London and New York: Routledge, 1994, 231.

82   Quoted Stone, *Theatre*, 126.

83   As *Three Plays*, New York: Farrar, Straus and Giroux, 1986, 132.
     Subsequent references cite *TP*.

84   King, *Walcott and Drama*, 82.

85   *In a Fine Castle,* premiered in Jamaica in October 1970 and staged
     in Trinidad in the following year.

86   See those quoted in Stone, *Theatre*, 131–2 and King, *Walcott and
     Drama*, 282–3, 344 and 347. Judy Stone's own review of the 1985
     Stage One production in Barbados is included in Hamner (ed.),
     Critical Perspectives, 369–71.

87   Lines 1–2 and 51–2 of 'The Deserted Village' are recited by school-
     children, with 'Couva' being substituted for Goldsmith's 'Auburn',
     TP, 166 and 201.

88   Stone, *Theatre*, 116.

89   See Stone, *Theatre*, 116–17; and King, *Walcott and Drama*, 314–16.

90   Cf. the character of Rose, the 'Cockney memsahib' in Nayantara
     Sahgal's *Rich Like Us* (1985), a novel which also contains another
     striking correspondence with *The Last Carnival* in its use of the
     image of Cythera as an index of European responses to an 'other'
     world.

91   Watteau painted at least five versions of this subject, but the play
     does not distinguish between them, Programme notes to the 1992
     Birmingham Rep production of *The Last Carnival.*

92   Historically there have been various attempts to ban Carnival,
     particularly in the nineteenth century, because of its association
     with rioting. See Hill, *Carnival*, 20–1.

93   Hill, *Carnival*, 7-11.

94   *Ibid.*, 23–31.

95   *Ibid.*, 21.

96   On the Pierrot Grenade figure, see John W. Nunley, 'Masquerade Mix-Up in Trinidad Carnival: Live Once, Die Forever' in John W. Nunley and Judith Bettelheim, *Caribbean Festival Arts*, Seattle and London: University of Washington Press, 1988, 91–2; and Hill, *Carnival*, 29 and 91–2.

97   He reads the first line of the second stanza, *TP*, 42.

98   *The Oxford Dictionary of Art*, ed. Ian Chilvers, Harold Osborne and Dennis Farr, Oxford and New York: Oxford University Press, revised edn, 1994, 531.

99   Watteau's reputation owes much to nineteenth-century commentary by the Goncourt Brothers whose 'image of the eighteenth century … was one of easy, light-hearted dalliance and pleasure, an era untroubled by the realities of life, by moral concerns or doubts', *The Art of the Western World*, ed. Denise Hooker, London: Boxtree, 1989, 287.

100   Programme notes to the 1992 Birmingham Rep production of *The Last Carnival*.

101   *Midsummer*, New York: Farrar Straus and Giroux, 1984, Poem XX [n.p.].

102   To the de Chirico painting that gives the novel its title. See particularly *The Enigma of Arrival*, London: André Deutsch, 1987, 91–3.

103   Mikhail Bakhtin, *Rabelais and His World*, 10.

104   The two parts have been played by the same actor in certain productions.

105   Cf. 'What the Twilight Says', *DMM*, 10; *Wine*, 5 and 15–16.

106   Earl Lovelace, review of *The Last Carnival*, *Trinidad Express*, 25 July 1982; repr. in Hamner (ed.), *Critical Perspectives*, 374.

107   Stephen P. Breslow, who uses a Bakhtinian approach to discuss the polyphonic mode of the play finds passages from *three* plays by Chris within the text, 'Trinidadian Heteroglossia: A Bakhtinian View of *A Branch of the Blue Nile*', Hamner (ed.), *Critical Perspectives*, 388. I prefer to see the references as coming from two plays.

108   See King, *Walcott and Drama*, 334.

109   'Meanings', Hamner (ed.), *Critical Perspectives*, 48; this essay was originally published in *Savacou*, 2, 1970, 45–51.

110   *Antony and Cleopatra*, V, ii, 321–60.

111   *Ibid.*, V, ii, 361 ff.

112 Cf. Walcott's construction of 'Greece', particularly in *Omeros*.

113 To *King Lear* and *Richard III*, as well as *Antony and Cleopatra*.

114 For example, Marilyn's likening Sheila's moment of acting greatness to the rise and fall of a meteor (*TP*, 275).

115 His 1992 play *The Odyssey*, published the follwing year, is discussed in Chapter 6.

116 Stone, *Theatre*, 138.

117 See particularly Derek Walcott, *Omeros*, London: Faber, 1990, 174–82 and 212–19.

118 Two Walcott screenplays *were* filmed in the 1980s: *The Rig*, a script which examined the effects of Trinidad's oil wealth on a local community was made by Banyan Productions, Trinidad in 1982 and shown on Trinidad and Tobago Television in 1984; *Hart Crane*, a documentary-drama about the American poet, was filmed in St. Lucia and the USA between 1983 and 1986 and premiered on America's Public Broadcasting System in 1986.

119 For example, Creole songs in the second and seventh scenes *Haytian Earth*, mimeographed typescript, n.d., 1, 7 and 1, 20 (Subsequent references cite *HE* and act and page number); and the peasants' engaging in harvest-time Lawoz (La Rose) celebrations (*HE*, 2, 22). The Lawoz, which had already achieved dramatic prominence in Walcott's brother Roderick's play, *The Banjo Man*, is one of the most important of St. Lucian folk festivals. For an account of it, see the 'Author's Note' to the printed edition of *The Banjo Man* in *A Time … and a Season: 8 Caribbean Plays*, ed. Errol Hill, St. Augustine: University of the West Indies Extramural Studies Unit, 1976, 215–16. In *The Haytian Earth*, the French Archbishop Brelle contrasts the mock-war of the festival with the deadliness of the national conflict, wishing that as in the festival "our corpses / were slain for flowers. What a perfume / would saturate the *Haytian Earth* instead" (*HE*, 2, 22).

120 *Voyage à Saint-Dominque pendant les années 1788, 1789 et 1790* (1790).

121 Cf. Chapter 3, note 27 on the representation of the two chariot-horses in Plato's *Phaedrus*.

122 This, of course, raises the issue of whether *racial* stereotyping overrides possible gender stereotyping and, if so, whether such a practice occludes gender differentiation.

123 *The Black Jacobins: Toussaint L'Ouverture and the San Domingo Revolution*, 1938; revised 2nd edition, New York: Vintage, 1963.

124 For example, in *AL*, Chapter 22.

125 Mimeographed typescript of *To Die for Grenada*, n.d., 1, 11. Subsequent references cite *TDG* and act and page number.

Chapter 6

1   'What the Twilight Says', *DMM*, 16.

2   'Homecoming: Anse La Raye', *Gulf*, 50.

3   Paula Burnett, 'Hegemony or Pluralism? The Literary Prize and the Post-Colonial Project in the Caribbean', *Commonwealth Essays and Studies*, 16:1, 1993, 14

4   The island was fought over by the British and French and changed hands more than a dozen times before eventually becoming a British colony in 1802. See Chapter 1.

5   Luigi Sampietro, 'On *Omeros*: An Interview with Derek Walcott', *Caribana*, 3, 1992/93, 38.

6   *Omeros,* London: Faber, 1990, 323. Subsequent references are to this edition.

7   Cf. *Omeros*, 283, where the poet tells the figure of Omeros, '"I never read it, … Not all the way through"'.

8   I am grateful to Victor Ramraj for this suggestion.

9   Cf. Harold Bloom, *A Map of Misreading*, New York: Oxford University Press, 1975, 33: '[E]veryone who now reads and writes in the West, of whatever racial background, sex or ideological camp, is still a son or daughter of Homer'.

10 Several post-colonial writers have used *The Odyssey* as an intertext as part of revisionist projects, for example, three Canadian versions: Hugh MacLennan's *Barometer Rising* (1941), Robert Kroetsch's *The Studhorse Man* (1969) and Michael Ondaatje's *The English Patient* (1992). For a discussion of this aspect of *The English Patient*, see Annick Hillger, '"And this is the world of nomads in any case": *The Odyssey* as Intertext in Michael Ondaatje's *The English Patient*', *Journal of Commonwealth Literature*, 33:1, 1998, 23–33. Along with Walcott, the Caribbean writer who has used Homeric intertexts most extensively is Wilson Harris. See particularly his early collection of poems, *From Eternity to Season* (1954) and his 'Carnival Trilogy': *Carnival* (1985), *The Infinite Rehearsal* (1987) and *The Four Banks of the River of Space* (1990). Hena Maes-Jelinek discusses the Odyssean parallels in 'Ulyssean

Carnival: Epic Metamorphoses in Wilson Harris's Trilogy', *Callalloo*, 18:1, 1995, 46–58.

11   See Edward Said's discussion of *The Persians* and *The Bacchae in Orientalism: Western Conceptions of the Orient*, 1978; Harmondsworth: Penguin, 1991, 21 and 56–7. The contemporary Greek assertion of difference from Turkey offers an obvious parallel. I am indebted to Smaro Kamboureli for alerting me to some of the issues surrounding the construction of Greek identity.

12   Cf. the figure of Billy Blue, the blind singer who tells the tale and clearly functions as a Caribbean Homer in *The Odyssey: A Stage Version*.

13   Edward Baugh, *Derek Walcott: Memory as Vision: Another Life*, London: Longman, 1978, 28.

14   Cf. 'when he ulysseed, she bloomed again' (*AL*, 31).

15   In *London Magazine*, August 1960, 15.

16   As in Donne's 'A Valediction: Forbidding Mourning'.

17   See particularly *AL*, Chapter 22.

18   Cf. his reference to having been nicknamed 'Shabine, the patois for / any red nigger' (*SAK*, 4).

19   Cf. Walcott's break with the Trinidad Theatre Workshop in 1976.

20   Cf. Walcott's account of this episode in a passage in *Another Life* (*AL*, 71–2), in which there is a very similar, first-person identification. See also Edward Baugh's discussion of the passage in *Another Life, Derek Walcott: Memory as Vision: Another Life*, London: Longman, 1978, 44–7. Baugh links the Sauteurs' suicide with that of Harry Simmons, seeing both as containing 'the paradoxical quality of defeat and victory, pride and humiliation' (47).

21   Cf. Walcott's response to 'the stuffed dark nightingale of Keats' as so much 'romantic taxidermy' (*AL*, 41).

22   Lévi-Strauss's 'culinary triangle' predicates a second binary opposition, between the raw and the *rotten* and he draws a distinction between the *transformation* of food through *cultural* means (cooking) and *natural* means (rotting). The emphasis is on the processes that *change* the raw, rather than the raw itself and this can be related to the ways in which cultures are inscribed: 'raw' experience, according to this model, lies beyond language. See Claude Lévi-Strauss, *Mythologiques I, Le cru et le cuit*, Paris: Plon, 1964; and Edmund Leach's discussion, *Lévi-Strauss*, London: Fontana, 1970, 29–30.

23   See particularly his photographs of the lives of sharecroppers in the American South in James Agee and Walker Evans, *Let Us Now Praise Famous Men*, 1941, London: Panther, 1969.

24   Cf. also *FT*, 81.

25   A popular reference-point for the exploration of themes of exile among post-colonial writers: see particularly David Malouf's *An Imaginary Life*, Sydney: Picador, 1978.

26   See the end of Chapter 1 for an extended discussion of this poem.

27   Jorge Luis Borges, *Labyrinths*, 1964; Harmondsworth: Penguin, 1970, 62–71.

28   *Midsummer*, New York; Farrar Straus and Giroux, 1984, VI. Subsequent references are to this edition and in all cases cite the number of the poem (with sub-section if appropriate), since the collection is unpaginated. Each poem or sub-section occupies a single page.

29   See particularly a group of poems which appears towards the end of the first of the volume's two parts: XVII–XX.

30   Robert Bensen, 'The Painter as Poet: Derek Walcott's *Midsummer*', Robert D. Hamner (ed.), *Critical Perspectives on Derek Walcott*, Washington: Three Continents Press, 1993, 336–47; originally published in *The Literary Review*, 29:3, 1986, 257–68.

31   See the discussion in Chapter 3 and 'What the Twilight Says', *DMM*, 6.

32   Homeric and other Greek parallels are less prominent in *Midsummer*, but they do occur in certain poems, for example, XXV and XXXIII.

33   'The Art of Poetry', Walcott interviewed by Edward Hirsch, Hamner (ed.), *Critical Perspectives*, 72.

34   Peter Balakian refers to *Midsummer* as Walcott's 'most American book' and notes that there are poems set in Rome, New York, Boston, Warwickshire and Chicago, 'The Poetry of Derek Walcott', Hamner (ed.), *Critical Perspectives*, 354. This ignores the fact that far more poems have Caribbean, particularly St. Lucian, settings and reference-points and that a sense of the Caribbean frequently pervades the American poems, while the reverse is seldom the case.

35   In this case the landscape evoked appears to be rural Trinidad rather than St. Lucia.

36   Cf. 'Crusoe's Journal', *Castaway*, 51.

37 The forced march westwards of a group of Cherokees in 1838.

38 Cf. 'Ruins of a Great House', *IGN*, 19, discussed in Chapter 2.

39 'Of Peleus' son, Achilles, sing, O muse, / the vengeance deep and deadly', *Homer's Iliad*, trans. Lord Derby, London: Dent, 1910, 1.

40 Quoted from W. B. Stanford, *The Ulysses Theme*, programme notes, *The Odyssey: A Stage Version*, The Other Place, Stratford-upon-Avon, 1992.

41 Programme notes, *The Odyssey: A Stage Ver*sion. This comment is exemplified by quotations from C. P. Cavafy, George Seferis, Jorge Luis Borges, Lawrence Durrell, Joachim du Bellay and Louis MacNeice.

42 Unlike *The Odyssey*, *The Joker of Seville* was never performed by the Company. See Chapter 5, note 11.

43 Cf. Walcott's having repeatedly been referred to as a Caribbean Homer. See note 3 above.

44 *The Odyssey: A Stage Version*, London: Faber, 1993, 8. Subsequent references are to this edition.

45 See Harold Bloom's comment, quoted above, note 9.

46 The use of black actors, such as Rudolph Walker who played Billy Blue and Bella Enahoro who played Circe, in the Homeric context can be seen as a further expression of this reversal.

47 Cf. Robert Kroetsch's *The Studhorse Man*, New York: Simon and Schuster, 1969, another post-colonial response to *The Odyssey*, in which male and female stereotypes are reworked in a complex range of ways, with the exploits of the eponymous hero, Hazard Lepage, ultimately being subverted by an androgynous vision of gender relations on the Canadian Prairies.

48 Cf. 'The Schooner *Flight*', *SAK*, 4; and *Joker*, 14 and 18.

49 Cf. his elegy for his father 'In My Eighteenth Year', *25 Poems*, 18, a poem which is referred to here, *Bounty*, 8. Cf. also *AL*, 11–12; and Walcott's nostalgic representation of his mother's generation of colonial schoolteachers in *Remembrance*, which is partly dedicated to her.

50 See particularly 'Homecoming', *Bounty*, 31–3.

51 Alluding to the plague that struck Thebes, supposedly as a consequence of Oedipus's patricide and incestuous marriage to his mother.

52 Cf. Walcott's plays *The Sea at Dauphin* and *To Die for Grenada*. Also *AL*, Chapter 22 and 'The Sea is History', *SAK*, 25–8.

53   See particularly Rei Terada's excellent study of Walcott as a postmodemist writer, *Derek Walcott's Poetry: American Mimicry*, Boston: Northeastern University Press, 1992.

54   This could be seen as equally true of Naipaul, particularly in the work he has published since *The Enigma of Arrival* (1987).

Chapter 7

1   An Internet search undertaken shortly before the completion of this book yielded nearly a quarter of a million references to Walcott!

2   See Chapter 1.

3   Bruce King, *Derek Walcott and West Indian Drama: 'Not Only a Playwright But a Company': The Trinidad Theatre Workshop 1953–1993*, Oxford: Clarendon Press, 1995.

4   Judy J. Stone, *Theatre: Studies In West Indian Literature*, London and Basingstoke: Macmillan, 1994, 91–142.

5   See, for example, his poem 'The Man Who Loved Islands', where he writes, 'that tired artifice called history / which in its motion is as false as fiction, / requires an outline, a summary. I can think of none' (*FT*, 38); and my discussion of this poem in 'Alternative Histories: Narrative Modes in West Indian Literature (with particular reference to Derek Walcott and V. S. Reid)', Britta Olinder (ed.), *A Sense of Place: Essays in Post-Colonial Literatures*, Gothenburg; Gothenburg University Commonwealth Studies, 1984, 142–50.

6   Originally published in *Caribbean Quarterly*, 17:3/4, 1971, 54–71; repr. in Robert D. Hamner (ed.), *Critical Perspectives on Derek Walcott*, Washington: Three Continents Press, 1993, 220–36. Ismond attributes the origin of the imperative to choose between the two poets to Edward Lucie-Smith, Hamner (ed.), *Critical Perspectives*, 220.

7   *Ibid.*, 230.

8   *Ibid.*, 236.

9   Michel Fabre, '"Adam's Task of Giving Things Their Names": The Poetry of Derek Walcott', *New Letters*, 14:1, 1974, 91–107.

10   For example, two reviews of *Ione* included in Hamner (ed.), *Critical Perspectives*, 113–17.

11   See Robert D. Hamner's bibliography in *Critical Perspectives*, 411–30, for details of Walcott's *Guardian* journalism; and Chapter 3, note 73 above for details of articles relating to the future direction of Caribbean theatre.

12   Edward Baugh, *Derek Walcott: Memory as Vision: Another Life*, London: Longman, 1978.

13   Ned Thomas, *Derek Walcott: Poet of the Islands / Derek Walcott: Bardd yr Ynysoedd*, Cardiff: Welsh Arts Council, 1980.

14   Robert D. Hamner, *Derek Walcott*, Boston: Twayne, 1981.

15   Stewart Brown's, 'The Apprentice: *25 Poems, Epitaph for the Young, Poems* and In a *Green Night*' in Brown (ed.), *The Art of Derek Walcott*, Bridgend, MidGlamorgan: Seren Books, 1991, 13–33 is the other notable discussion of this early poetry to have appeared to date.

16   Kenneth Ramchand, *An Introduction to the Study of West Indian Literature*, Sunbury-on-Thames, Middlesex: Nelson, 1976, 108–26.

17   Mervyn Morris, 'Derek Walcott', Bruce King (ed.), *West Indian Literature*, London: Macmillan, 1979, 144–60.

18   David Dabydeen (ed.), *A Handbook for Teaching Caribbean Literature*, London: Heinemann, 1988, 86–95 and 96–103.

19   Cameron King and Louis James, 'In Solitude for Company: The Poetry of Derek Walcott', Louis James (ed.), *The Islands in Between*, London: Oxford University Press, 1968, 86–99.

20   Hamner (ed.), *Critical Perspectives*.

21   Irma E. Goldstraw's *Derek Walcott: A Bibliography of Published Poems with Dates of Publication and Variant Versions 1944–1979*, St. Augustine, Trinidad: University of the West Indies Research and Publications Committee, 1979; and *Derek Walcott: An Annotated Bibliography of His Works*, New York; Garland, 1984.

22   Rei Terada, *Derek Walcott's Poetry: American Mimicry*, Boston: Northeastern University Press, 1992.

23   *Ibid.*, 2.

24   For example, in *Pantomime*, but throughout his work. See particularly Chapter 5.

25   Having abandoned the idea of being an artist when quite young, he has also continued to paint water-colours throughout his life and has produced a considerable body of non-dramatic prose writing.

Select bibliography

The primary bibliography lists Walcott's collections of verse, his published plays and a selection of his essays and interviews. See the Chronology for dates of first performance of his unpublished plays.

The secondary bibliography is highly selective. Robert Hamner, ed., *Critical Perspectives on Derek Walcott* provides an excellent primary and secondary bibliography up to the early 1990s. Irma E. Goldstraw's *Derek Walcott: A Bibliography of Published Poems with Dates of Publication and Variant Versions 1944–1979*, St. Augustine, Trinidad: University of the West Indies Research and Publications Committee, 1979 and *Derek Walcott: An Annotated Bibliography of His Works*, New York: Garland, 1984 are very full bibliographies of Walcott's primary works up to the date of their appearance. Judy J. Stone's *Theatre: Studies In West Indian Literature*, London and Basingstoke: Macmillan, 1994 contains an excellent bibliography of Walcott's plays; Bruce King's *Derek Walcott and West Indian Drama: 'Not Only a Playwright But a Company': The Trinidad Theatre Workshop 1953–1993*, Oxford: Clarendon Press, 1995, provides a theatre calendar of the Workshop's productions.

Works by Derek Walcott

COLLECTIONS OF POETRY

25 Poems, Bridgetown: Advocate Co., 1949.

Epitaph for the Young, Bridgetown: Advocate Co., 1949.

Poems, Kingston: Kingston City Printery, n.d. [1951].

In a Green Night, London: Jonathan Cape, 1962.

The Castaway and Other Poems, London: Jonathan Cape, 1965.

The Gulf and Other Poems, London: Jonathan Cape, 1969; *The Gulf: Poems*, New York: Farrar Straus and Giroux, 1970.

Another Life, London: Jonathan Cape, 1973; New York: Farrar Straus and Giroux, 1973.

Sea Grapes, London: Jonathan Cape, 1976; New York: Farrar Straus and Giroux, 1976.

The Star-Apple Kingdom, New York: Farrar Straus and Giroux, 1979; London: Jonathan Cape, 1980.

Selected Poetry, ed. Wayne Brown, London: Heinemann, 1981 .

The Fortunate Traveller, New York: Farrar Straus and Giroux, 1981; London: Jonathan Cape, 1982.

Midsummer, New York: Farrar Straus and Giroux, 1984; London: Faber, 1984.

Collected Poems, 1948–84, New York: Farrar Straus and Giroux, 1985; London: Faber, 1986.

The Arkansas Testament, New York: Farrar Straus and Giroux, 1987; London: Faber, 1987.

Omeros, New York: Farrar Straus and Giroux, 1990; London: Faber, 1990.

Poems, 1965–1980, London: Jonathan Cape, 1992.

The Bounty, New York: Farrar Straus and Giroux, 1997; London: Faber, 1997.

PUBLISHED PLAYS

Henri Christophe: A Chronicle in Seven Scenes, Bridgetown: Advocate Co., 1950.

Harry Dernier, Bridgetown: Advocate Co., n.d. [1952?].

Ione, Mona, Jamaica: University of the West Indies Extramural Department, n.d. [1957?].

Drums and Colours, Caribbean Quarterly, 7:1 and 2, 1961.

Malcauchon, or The Six in the Rain, St. Augustine, Trinidad: University of the West Indies Extramural Department, 1966.

The Sea at Dauphin, St. Augustine, Trinidad: University of the West Indies Extramural Department, 1966.

Dream on Monkey Mountain and Other Plays, New York: Farrar Straus and Giroux, 1970; London: Jonathan Cape, 1972.

The Joker of Seville and O Babylon!, New York: Farrar, Straus and Giroux, 1978; London: Jonathan Cape, 1979.

Remembrance and Pantomime, New York: Farrar, Straus and Giroux, 1980.

Three Plays, New York: Farrar, Straus and Giroux, 1986.

Ti-Jean and His Brothers in *Plays for Today*, ed. Errol Hill, Harlow: Longman, 1985, 21–71.

The Odyssey: A Stage Version, London: Faber, 1993.

ESSAYS AND MISCELLANEOUS OTHER WORKS

'The Antilles: Fragments of Epic Memory', Nobel Lecture, Stockholm: Nobel Foundation, 1992.

'Café Martinique' [short story], *House and Garden*, March 1985, 140, 222, 224, 226 and 228.

'Caligula's Horse', *Kunapipi*, 11:1, 1989, 138–42.

'A Colonial's-Eye View of the Empire', *Tri-quarterly*, 65, 1986, 73–84.

'Derek Walcott Talks about *The Joker of Seville*', *Carib*, 4, 1986, 1–15 [edited transcript of a seminar Walcott gave at the College of the Virgin Islands, St. Thomas in the autumn of 1979 by Jeannette B. Ellis and Gilbert A. Sprauve, with further editing by Edward Baugh].

'The Figure of Crusoe', Hamner (ed.), *Critical Perspectives*, 33–40.

'Leaving School', *The London Magazine*, 5:6, 1965, 4–14; repr. in Hamner (ed.), *Critical Perspectives*, 24–32.

'Meanings', *Savacou*, 2, 1970, 45–51; repr. in Hamner (ed.), *Critical Perspectives*, 45–50.

'The Muse of History', *Is Massa Day Dead?*, ed. Orde Coombs, Garden City, New York: Anchor/Doubleday, 1976, 1–28.

'On Choosing Port of Spain', *David Frost Introduces Trinidad and Tobago*, eds. Michael Anthony and Andrew Carr, London: André Deutsch, 1975, 45–51.

'The Poet in the Theatre', *Poetry Review*, 80:4, 1990/91, 4–8.

'What the Twilight Says: An Overture', *Dream on Monkey Mountain and Other Plays*, 3–40.

PUBLISHED INTERVIEWS

'Any Revolution Based on Race is Suicidal', Walcott interviewed by Raoul Pantin, *Caribbean Contact*, 1:8, August 1973, 14 and 16.

Baer, William, ed., *Conversations with Derek Walcott*, Jackson, Mississippi; University of Mississippi Press, 1996.

Dance, Daryl Cumber, 'Conversation with Derek Walcott', *New World Adams: Conversations with Contemporary West Indian Writers*, Leeds: Peepal Tree Press, 1992, 256–73

Hamner, Robert D., 'Conversation with Derek Walcott', *World Literature Written in English*, 16:2, 1977, 409–20.

Hirsch, Edward, 'An Interview with Derek Walcott', *Contemporary Literature*, 20:3, 1980, 279–92,

— 'The Art of Poetry', *Paris Review*, 28, Winter 1986, 197–230.

Rowell, Charles H., 'An Interview with Derek Walcott', *Callalloo*, 34, 1988, 80–9.

Sampietro, Luigi, '"An Object Beyond One's Own Life": An Interview with Derek Walcott [Part 1]', *Caribana*, 2, 1991, 25–36.

— 'On *Omeros*: An Interview with Derek Walcott' [Part 2], *Caribana*, 3, 1992/93, 31–44.

'Walcott on Walcott', Walcott interviewed by Dennis Scott, *Caribbean Quarterly*, 14:1 and 2, 1968, 77–82.

Selected criticism

Ashaolu, Albert Olu, 'Allegory in *Ti-Jean and His Brothers*', *World Literature Written in English*, 16:1, 1977, 203–11.

Baugh, Edward, 'Derek Walcott', *Fifty Caribbean Writers*, ed. Daryl Cumber Dance, New York: Greenwood Press, 1986, 462–73.

— *Derek Walcott: Memory as Vision: Another Life*, London: Longman, 1978.

— ed., *Critics on Caribbean Literature*, London: Allen and Unwin, 1978.

Brown, Lloyd W., *West Indian Poetry*, Boston: Twayne, 1978.

Brown, Stewart, ed., *The Art of Derek Walcott*, Bridgend, Mid-Glamorgan: Seren Books, 1991.

Burnett, Paula, 'Hegemony or Pluralism? The Literary Prize and the Post-Colonial Project in the Caribbean', *Commonwealth Essays and Studies*, 16:1, 1993, 1–20.

Chamberlin, J. Edward, *Come Back to Me My Language: Poetry and the West Indies*, Toronto: McClelland and Stewart, 1993.

Dabydeen, David, ed., *A Handbook for Teaching Caribbean Literature*, London: Heinemann, 1988.

Fabre, Michel, '"Adam's Task of Giving Things Their Names": The Poetry of Derek Walcott', *New Letters*, 14:1, 1974, 91–107.

Hamner, Robert D., *Derek Walcott*, Boston: Twayne, 1981.

— 'Mythological Aspects of Derek Walcott's Drama', *ARIEL*, 8:3, 1977, 35–58.

— ed., *Critical Perspectives on Derek Walcott*, Washington: Three Continents Press, 1993.

Hanford, H. Robin, 'Derek Walcott's "Forest of Europe"', *Commonwealth Essays and Studies*, 20:2, 1998, 1–8.

Hill, Errol, 'The Emergence of a National Drama in the West Indies', *Caribbean Quarterly*, 18:4, 1972, 9–24.

Hirsch, Edward, 'Derek Walcott: Either Nobody – or a Nation', *Georgian Review*, 49, 1995, 303–13.

Ismond, Patricia, 'Derek Walcott's Later Drama: From *Joker* to *Remembrance*', *ARIEL*, 16:3, 1985, 89–101.

— 'Walcott versus Brathwaite', *Caribbean Quarterly*, 17:3/4, 1971, 54–71; repr. in Hamner (ed.), *Critical Perspectives*, 220–36.

James, Louis, ed., *The Islands in Between*, London: Oxford University Press, 1968.

Jeyifo, Biodun, 'On Eurocentric Critical Theory: Some Paradigms from the Texts and Sub-Texts of Post-Colonial Writing', *Kunapipi*, 11:1, 1989, 107–18.

King, Bruce, *Derek Walcott and West Indian Drama: 'Not Only a Playwright But a Company': The Trinidad Theatre Workshop 1959–1993*, Oxford: Clarendon Press, 1995.

Lane, M. Travis, 'A Different "Growth of a Poet's Mind": Derek Walcott's *Another Life*', *ARIEL*, 9:4, 1978, 65–78.

Macdonald, D. L., 'Derek Walcott's Don Juans', *Connotations*, 4:1/2, 1994/95, 98–118.

Morris, Mervyn, 'Derek Walcott', *West Indian Literature*, ed. Bruce King, London: Macmillan, 1979, 144–60.

Omotoso, Kole, *The Theatrical into Theatre*, London and Port of Spain: New Beacon, 1982.

Ramchand, Kenneth, *An Introduction to the Study of West Indian Literature*, Sunbury-on-Thames, Middlesex: Nelson, 1976.

Rohlehr, Gordon, *My Strangled City and Other Essays*, Port of Spain: Longman Trinidad, 1992.

Stone, Judy J., *Theatre: Studies In West Indian Literature*, London and Basingstoke: Macmillan, 1994.

Terada, Rei, *Derek Walcott's Poetry: American Mimicry*, Boston: Northeastern University Press, 1992.

Thieme, John, 'A Caribbean Don Juan: Derek Walcott's *Joker of Seville*', *World Literature Written in English*, 23:1, 1984, 62–75.

— 'Alternative Histories: Narrative Modes in West Indian Literature (with particular reference to Derek Walcott and V. S. Reid)', *A Sense of Place: Essays in Post-Colonial Literatures*, ed. Britta Olinder, Gothenburg; Gothenburg University Commonwealth Studies, 1984, 142–50.

Thomas, Ned, *Derek Walcott: Poet of the Islands/Derek Walcott: Barrd yr Ynysoedd*, Cardiff: Welsh Arts Council, 1980.

Wieland, James, *The Ensphering Mind: History, Myth and Fictions in the Poetry of Allen Curnow, Nissim Ezekiel, A. D. Hope, A. M. Klein, Christopher Okigbo and Derek Walcott*, Washington: Three Continents Press, 1988.

Wilson-Tagoe, Nana, *Historical Thought and Literary Representation in West Indian Literature*, Gainesville: University Press of Florida; Barbados, Jamaica, Trinidad and Tobago: The Press, University of the West Indies; Oxford: James Currey, 1998.

General works

Ashcroft, Bill, Gareth Griffiths and Helen Tiffin, *The Empire Writes Back: Theory and Practice in Post-Colonial Literatures*, London and New York: Routledge, 1989.

Baugh, Edward, *West Indian Poetry, 1900–1970: A Study in Cultural Decolonisation*, Kingston: Savacou Publications, n.d. [1971?].

Bakhtin, Mikhail, *Rabelais and His World*, trans. Helene Iswolsky, Cambridge, Mass. and London: MIT Press, 1965.

Bhabha, Homi K., *The Location of Culture*, London and New York: Routledge, 1994.

Bloom, Harold, *A Map of Misreading*, New York: Oxford University Press, 1975.

Brathwaite, Edward Kamau, *The Arrivants*, London: Oxford University Press, 1973.

— *A History of the Voice: The Development of Nation Language in Anglophone Caribbean Poetry*, London and Port of Spain: New Beacon, 1984.

Cobham, Rhonda, 'The Background', Bruce King, ed., *West Indian Literature*, London: Macmillan, 1979, 9–29.

Dash, Michael, 'In Search of the Lost Body: Redefining the Subject in Caribbean Literature', *Kunapipi*, 11:1, 1989, 17–26.

Foucault, Michel, *The Archaeology of Knowledge* and *The Discourse on Language*, trans. Rupert Sawyer, New York: Harper and Row, n.d.

Gilkes, Michael, *Wilson Harris and the Caribbean Novel*, London: Longman, 1975.

Harris, Wilson, *Black Marsden*, London: Faber, 1972.

— *The Carnival Trilogy*, London: Faber, 1993.

— *From Eternity to Season*, 1954; London and Port of Spain: New Beacon, 1978.

— *Heartland*, London; Faber, 1964.

— *History, Fable and Myth in the Caribbean and Guianas*, Edgar Mittelholzer Memorial Lectures, Georgetown: National History and Arts Council, 1970.

Hill, Errol, *The Jamaican Stage, 1655–1900: Profile of a Colonial Theatre*, Amherst: University of Massachusetts Press, 1992

— *The Trinidad Carnival: Mandate for a National Theatre*, Austin: University of Texas Press, 1972.

James, C. L. R., *The Black Jacobins* in *A Time ... and a Season: 8 Caribbean Plays*, ed. Errol Hill, St. Augustine: University of the West Indies Extramural Studies Unit, 1976, 355–420.

— *The Black Jacobins: Toussaint L'Ouverture and the San Domingo Revolution*, 1938; revised 2nd edition, New York: Vintage, 1963.

JanMohamed, Abdul R., *Manichean Aesthetics: The Politics of Literature in Colonial Africa*, Amherst: University of Massachusetts Press, 1983.

— 'The Economy of Manichean Allegory: The Function of Racial Difference in Colonial Literature', *Critical Inquiry* 12:1, 1985, 59–87.

Kemoli, Arthur, *Caribbean Anansi Stories*, London: Commonwealth Institute, n.d.

Kristeva, Julia, *Desire in Language: A Semiotic Approach to Literature and Art*, ed. Leon S. Roudiez; trans. Thomas Gora, Alice Jardine and Leon S. Roudiez, New York: Columbia University Press, 1980.

Lamming, George, *In the Castle of My Skin*, London: Michael Joseph, 1953.

Lévi-Strauss, Claude, *Mythologiques I, Le cru et le cuit*, Paris: Plon, 1964

Lewis, Gordon, *The Growth of the Modern West Indies*, London: MacGibbon and Kee, 1968.

Lewis, R. W. B., *The American Adam: Innocence, Tragedy and Tradition in the Nineteenth Century*, Chicago: University of Chicago Press, 1955.

Lovelace, Earl, *The Dragon Can't Dance*, London: André Deutsch, 1979.

Mais, Roger, *George William Gordon* in *A Time … and a Season: 8 Caribbean Plays*, ed. Errol Hill, St. Augustine: University of the West Indies, Extramural Studies Unit, 1976, 1–92.

Naipaul, V. S., *The Enigma of Arrival*, London: André Deutsch, 1987.

— *The Middle Passage*, London: André Deutsch, 1962.

— *The Mimic Men*, London: André Deutsch, 1967.

Nunley, John W. and Judith Bettelheim, *Caribbean Festival Arts*, Seattle and London: University of Washington Press, 1988.

Ramchand, Kenneth, *The West Indian Novel and Its Background*, London: Faber, 1970.

Reid, V. S., *New Day*, New York: Knopf, 1949.

Rochester, Earl of, *The Complete Poems of John Wilmot, Earl of Rochester*, ed. David M. Vieth, New Haven and London: Yale University Press, 1968.

Rohlehr, Gordon, *Calypso and Society in Pre-Independence Trinidad*, Port of Spain: privately published, 1990.

— *Pathfinder: Black Awakening in The Arrivants of Edward Kamau Brathwaite*, Port of Spain: privately published, 1981.

Rushdie, Salman, *Imaginary Homelands: Essays and Criticism, 1981–1991*, London: Granta, 1991.

Said, Edward, *Culture and Imperialism*, London: Chatto and Windus, 1993.

— *Orientalism: Western Conceptions of the Orient*, London: Routledge and Kegan Paul, 1978.

Senior, Olive, *A-Z of Jamaican Heritage*, Kingston: Heinemann/ Gleaner Co., 1983; 2nd edition, 1987.

Tirso de Molina, *The Trickster of Seville and His Guest of Stone*, trans. Roy Campbell, in Eric Bentley, ed., *Six Spanish Plays*, New York: Doubleday/Anchor, 1959.

Tomashevsky, Boris, 'Thematics' in *Russian Formalist Criticism: Four Essays*, trans. Lee T. Lemon and Marion J. Reis, Lincoln, Nebraska: University of Nebraska Press, 1965.

Walcott, Roderick, *The Banjo Man* in *A Time … and a Season: 8 Caribbean Plays*, ed. Errol Hill, St. Augustine: University of the West Indies Extramural Studies Unit, 1976, 213–56.

Warner, Keith, *The Trinidad Calypso*, London: Heinemann, 1982.

White, Hayden, *Metahistory: The Historical Imagination in Nineteenth-Century Europe*, Baltimore: Johns Hopkins University Press, 1973.

Index

M8202-TX
50